1 & 2 KINGS

J. Vernon McGee

THOMAS NELSON PUBLISHERS

Nashville • Atlanta • London • Vancouver

Published in Nashville, Tennessee, by Thomas Nelson, Inc.

Scripture quotations are from the KING JAMES VERSION of the Bible.

Library of Congress Cataloging-in-Publication Data

McGee, J. Vernon (John Vernon), 1904–1988
   [Thru the Bible with J. Vernon McGee]
   Thru the Bible commentary series / J. Vernon McGee.
      p.   cm.
   Reprint. Originally published: Thru the Bible with J. Vernon McGee. 1975.
   Includes bibliographical references.
   ISBN 0-7852-1014-8 (TR)
   ISBN 0-7852-1080-6 (NRM)
   1. Bible—Commentaries. I. Title.
BS491.2.M37 1991
220.7′7—dc20
                                       90–41340
                                          CIP

Printed in the United States of America

6 7 8 9 10 – 03 02 01 00

CONTENTS

1 KINGS

Preface v
Introduction vii
Outline ix
Chapter 1 11
Chapter 2 20
Chapters 3 and 4 32
Chapters 5 and 6 43
Chapter 7 51
Chapter 8 56
Chapters 9 and 10 61
Chapter 11 72
Chapters 12—14 77
Chapters 15 and 16 91
Chapter 17 104
Chapter 18 111
Chapter 19 124
Chapter 20 132
Chapter 21 135
Chapter 22 140

2 KINGS

Chapter 1 155
Chapter 2 159
Chapters 3 and 4 169
Chapter 5 176
Chapter 6 186
Chapter 7 197
Chapters 8—10 201
Chapters 11 and 12 217
Chapter 13 228
Chapters 14—16 235
Chapter 17 242
Chapter 18 249
Chapter 19 258
Chapter 20 268
Chapter 21 276
Chapters 22 and 23 282
Chapters 24 and 25 295
Bibliography 305

PREFACE

The radio broadcasts of the Thru the Bible Radio five-year program were transcribed, edited, and published first in single-volume paperbacks to accommodate the radio audience.

There has been a minimal amount of further editing for this publication. Therefore, these messages are not the word-for-word recording of the taped messages which went out over the air. The changes were necessary to accommodate a reading audience rather than a listening audience.

These are popular messages, prepared originally for a radio audience. They should not be considered a commentary on the entire Bible in any sense of that term. These messages are devoid of any attempt to present a theological or technical commentary on the Bible. Behind these messages is a great deal of research and study in order to interpret the Bible from a popular rather than from a scholarly (and too-often boring) viewpoint.

We have definitely and deliberately attempted "to put the cookies on the bottom shelf so that the kiddies could get them."

The fact that these messages have been translated into many languages for radio broadcasting and have been received with enthusiasm reveals the need for a simple teaching of the whole Bible for the masses of the world.

I am indebted to many people and to many sources for bringing this volume into existence. I should express my especial thanks to my secretary, Gertrude Cutler, who supervised the editorial work; to Dr. Elliott R. Cole, my associate, who handled all the detailed work with the publishers; and finally, to my wife Ruth for tenaciously encouraging me from the beginning to put my notes and messages into printed form.

Solomon wrote, ". . . of making many books there is no end; and much study is a weariness of the flesh" (Eccl. 12:12). On a sea of books that flood the marketplace, we launch this series of THRU THE BIBLE with the hope that it might draw many to the one Book, *The Bible.*

J. Vernon McGee

The Book of
1 KINGS

INTRODUCTION

First and Second Kings is the second in a series of three double books: 1 and 2 Samuel, 1 and 2 Kings, and 1 and 2 Chronicles. Originally, the double books were single books—one book of Samuel, one of Kings, and one of Chronicles. The Septuagint translators were the ones who made the divisions, and they did so more or less for the convenience of the reader. I think that it probably was a very wise decision.

Although the writer is unknown, 1 and 2 Kings were written while the first temple was still standing (1 Kings 8:8). Jeremiah is considered to be the traditional writer, while modern scholarship assigns the authorship to "the prophets."

The theme of these two Books of Kings is found in this expression that occurs nine times in 1 Kings: "as David his father." In other words, we are following the line of David, and each king was measured by the standard set by David. Very frankly, it was a human standard, and it was not the highest standard in the world. But we find that king after king failed to attain even to it. Thank God there were those who did measure up to it. However, we will find that this section of Scripture is a sorry and sordid section. It is history, and it reveals the decline and fall of the kingdom: first the kingdom was divided, and then each kingdom fell.

There are key verses that summarize the thrust of these two books. The first key verses describe the decline and fall of the northern kingdom: "For the children of Israel walked in all the sins of Jeroboam which he did; they departed not from them; Until the LORD removed

Israel out of his sight, as he had said by all his servants the prophets. So was Israel carried away out of their own land to Assyria unto this day" (2 Kings 17:22–23).

The second key verse describes the fall of the southern kingdom: "And the king of Babylon smote them, and slew them at Riblah in the land of Hamath. So Judah was carried away out of their land" (2 Kings 25:21).

In 1 Kings we have the record of the *division* of the kingdom, and 2 Kings records the *collapse* of the kingdom. Considering the two books as a unit, they open with King David, and they close with the king of Babylon. They are the book of man's rule over God's kingdom—and the results are not good, of course. The throne on earth must be in tune with the throne in heaven if blessings are to come and benefits are to accrue to God's people. Yet man's plan cannot overthrow God's purposes, as we shall see.

First and Second Kings are actually a continuation of the narrative that was begun in First and Second Samuel. These four books can be considered as a whole since they trace the history of the nation from the time of its greatest extension, influence, and prosperity under David and Solomon to the division, then captivity and exile of both kingdoms.

The moral teaching of these books is to show man his inability to rule himself and the world. In these four historical books we get a very graphic view of the rise and fall of the kingdom of Israel.

OUTLINE FOR 1 AND 2 KINGS

I. **Death of David, 1 Kings 1—2**

II. **Glory of Solomon's Reign, 1 Kings 3—11**
   A. Solomon's Prayer for Wisdom, Chapters 3—4
   B. Building of Temple, Chapters 5—8
   C. Fame of Solomon, Chapters 9—10
   D. Shame and Death of Solomon, Chapter 11

III. **Division of the Kingdom (See Chronological Table of the Kings of the Divided Kingdom, p. 227), 1 Kings 12—2 Kings 16**

IV. **Captivity of Israel by Assyria, 2 Kings 17**

V. **Decline and Captivity of Judah by Babylon, 2 Kings 18—25**

CHAPTER 1

THEME: Adonijah's abortive coup; Solomon anointed king

The Books of Kings continue the narrative that was begun in the Books of Samuel. In this first chapter David is a senile old man. One of his sons, Adonijah, attempts to seize the throne. David, aroused by Nathan and Bathsheba, orders another son, Solomon, anointed as king of Israel. This is a tremendous chapter that opens 1 Kings.

DAVID'S DECLINING STRENGTH AND ADONIJAH'S PLOT

We begin on a sad note.

> Now king David was old and stricken in years; and they covered him with clothes, but he gat no heat [1 Kings 1:1].

David is now an old man. It is difficult to conceive of him as an old man. We always think of David as a shepherd boy. It is hard to picture him as an old, senile man who needs nursing care.

His son Adonijah takes advantage of him in this condition. He attempts to put himself on the throne and make himself king. Of course, that is not going to fit in with God's plan. A great deal of intrigue goes on—intrigue is one of the things that characterize the reign of David.

Let us find out who Adonijah is. First Kings is the first time that he is mentioned in any prominent connection.

> Then Adonijah the son of Haggith exalted himself, saying, I will be king: and he prepared him chariots and horsemen, and fifty men to run before him.

And his father had not displeased him at any time in saying, Why hast thou done so? and he also was a very goodly man; and his mother bare him after Absalom [1 Kings 1:5–6].

Adonijah was David's fourth son, born to him in Hebron (2 Sam. 3:4). His mother was Haggith, one of David's wives, of whom we know nothing except that her name means "festive."

"Adonijah the son of Haggith exalted himself." That word *exalted* is interesting because there is a verse of Scripture that you can put right down over it: "For whosoever exalteth himself shall be abased; and he that humbleth himself shall be exalted" (Luke 14:11). "He that exalteth himself shall be abased" is going to be true of Adonijah. He certainly exalted himself.

The Scriptures tell us many things about Adonijah. He was a very proud young man with a high regard for himself. He was conceited, and you can detect in him some of the traits of his half brother Absalom who had led a rebellion against David. Adonijah, had something not been done, would also have led a rebellion against his father. David never had a reputation of disciplining his family. He had a disorganized family life; organized chaos reigned in David's palace, and Adonijah took full advantage of the situation. David never rebuked him. When he did wrong, I think David just smiled over his boy as an old indulgent man would do.

And he conferred with Joab the son of Zeruiah, and with Abiathar the priest: and they following Adonijah helped him [1 Kings 1:7].

Joab, who had been loyal to David for many years, now gives his allegiance to Adonijah. You can see his position; he is feathering his nest and preparing for the future. David is old, and in a short time he will be gone. Joab wants to be on the winning side. The only one on the scene who is making any move toward the throne is Adonijah. Joab has had tremendous influence in the palace and court of David. He has been David's right-hand man from the very beginning, and I am confident that he was loyal to David. I do not believe he would have permitted Adonijah to touch a hair of David's head, but he does want someone to come to the throne at this time. No other son of David seems to be a likely candidate. That is interesting because it implies that Joab would not have chosen Solomon to be king. In my judgment, David's choice was Absalom, not Solomon, and now he will probably smile when Adonijah makes his move for the throne, because he was very much like Absalom.

Now we find that Adonijah made a banquet. That is always a good way to get some support for any project. If you want to do something, have a church banquet, and you will receive a lot of support.

And Adonijah slew sheep and oxen and fat cattle by the stone of Zoheleth, which is by En-rogel, and called all his brethren the king's sons, and all the men of Judah the king's servants [1 Kings 1:9].

Adonijah's intention was to announce at the banquet that he was king. By right of primogeniture he probably had a claim upon the throne. We are told that he was older than Solomon; according to the rules and regulations of the day, the oldest son was always the crown prince and was the successor. Absalom, of course, was dead, which put Adonijah next in line.

It was a bold move to send invitations to the king's sons, especially in light of the fact that Solomon did not receive an invitation; he was left out.

But Nathan the prophet, and Benaiah, and the mighty men, and Solomon his brother, he called not [1 Kings 1:10].

Adonijah knew that Nathan would be on Bathsheba's side. Nathan was the one who guided David during that awful period of David's great sin. Bathsheba, of course, was Solomon's mother. Now Nathan goes to her.

THE PLAN OF NATHAN AND BATHSHEBA

Wherefore Nathan spake unto Bath-sheba the mother of Solomon, saying, Hast thou not heard that Adonijah the son of Haggith doth reign, and David our lord knoweth it not? [1 Kings 1:11].

Adonijah was beginning to move behind David's back—he was not consulting the king at all. Now Nathan begins to move.

Go and get thee in unto king David, and say unto him, Didst not thou, my lord, O king, swear unto thine handmaid, saying, Assuredly Solomon thy son shall reign after me, and he shall sit upon my throne? why then doth Adonijah reign? [1 Kings 1:13].

David had made a promise to Bathsheba. When their second son was born (their first son had died), David promised her that he would be the next king. That son is Solomon. Now David was making no move to put him on the throne. I do not think David was enthusiastic about making him the king.

Behold, while thou yet talkest there with the king, I also will come in after thee, and confirm thy words [1 Kings 1:14].

Nathan is saying, "We had better alert David to what is taking place. You tell David what is happening, and I will enforce your words." Nathan wanted to wake up this senile king to what was going on right under his nose.

And Bath-sheba went in unto the king into the chamber: and the king was very old; and Abishag the Shunammite ministered unto the king.

And Bath-sheba bowed, and did obeisance unto the king. And the king said, What wouldest thou? [1 Kings 1:15–16].

It seems as though David had not seen Bathsheba for a long time.

> And she said unto him, My lord, thou swarest by the
> LORD thy God unto thine handmaid, saying, Assuredly
> Solomon thy son shall reign after me, and he shall sit
> upon my throne.

> And now, behold, Adonijah reigneth; and now, my lord
> the king, thou knowest it not:

> And he hath slain oxen and fat cattle and sheep in abun-
> dance, and hath called all the sons of the king, and
> Abiathar the priest, and Joab the captain of the host: but
> Solomon thy servant hath he not called.

> And thou, my lord, O king, the eyes of all Israel are
> upon thee, that thou shouldest tell them who shall sit
> on the throne of my lord the king after him [1 Kings
> 1:17–20].

David had made no move to pick a successor from his several sons.
Probably Adonijah was a very attractive, handsome, capable boy, and
there were many people who wanted him for their next king.

> Otherwise it shall come to pass, when my lord the king
> shall sleep with his fathers, that I and my son Solomon
> shall be counted offenders.

> And, lo, while she yet talked with the king, Nathan the
> prophet also came in.

> And they told the king, saying, Behold Nathan the
> prophet. And when he was come in before the king, he
> bowed himself before the king with his face to the
> ground.

> And Nathan said, My lord, O king, hast thou said,
> Adonijah shall reign after me, and he shall sit upon my
> throne? [1 Kings 1:21–24].

Nathan and Bathsheba wanted to know if David had chosen Adonijah to reign after him. David, of course, knew nothing about it.

> **Then king David answered and said, Call me Bathsheba. And she came into the king's presence, and stood before the king.**
>
> **And the king sware, and said, As the LORD liveth, that hath redeemed my soul out of all distress,**
>
> **Even as I sware unto thee by the LORD God of Israel, saying, Assuredly Solomon thy son shall reign after me, and he shall sit upon my throne in my stead; even so will I certainly do this day [1 Kings 1:28–30].**

When David spoke to Bathsheba about Solomon, notice that he said, "your son," and not "our son." David was not too enthusiastic about this boy. I don't think they had too much in common, as we shall soon see.

> **Then Bath-sheba bowed with her face to the earth, and did reverence to the king, and said, Let my lord king David live for ever.**
>
> **And king David said, Call me Zadok the priest, and Nathan the prophet, and Benaiah the son of Jehoiada. And they came before the king.**
>
> **The king also said unto them, Take with you the servants of your lord, and cause Solomon my son to ride upon mine own mule, and bring him down to Gihon [1 Kings 1:31–33].**

The mule was the animal kings rode upon, while the horse was the animal of warfare. You will find in the Book of Revelation that the riding of the four horses speaks of turmoil and warfare. Also the Lord Jesus Christ will come again to this earth riding on a white horse, which speaks of warfare. He will come to put down rebellion on the earth; and before Him every knee shall bow. When the Lord came to earth the first time, He did not come to make war; He came to offer Himself as Israel's Messiah, and as such He rode a little donkey into Jerusalem. That is the animal upon which kings ride. Now David's own royal mount, a mule, is to be brought out, and Solomon is to be put upon it.

SOLOMON IS ANOINTED AS KING

So Zadok the priest, and Nathan the prophet, and Benaiah the son of Jehoiada, and the Cherethites, and the Pelethites, went down, and caused Solomon to ride upon king David's mule, and brought him to Gihon.

And Zadok the priest took an horn of oil out of the tabernacle, and anointed Solomon. And they blew the trumpet; and all the people said, God save king Solomon [1 Kings 1:38–39].

Now there is no question as to whom David has chosen to be his successor. Solomon is to be the next king.

And all the people came up after him, and the people piped with pipes, and rejoiced with great joy, so that the earth rent with the sound of them.

And Adonijah and all the guests that were with him heard it as they had made an end of eating. And when Joab heard the sound of the trumpet, he said, Wherefore is this noise of the city being in an uproar? [1 Kings 1:40–41].

The messenger who brought the details to Adonijah concluded with this:

And moreover the king's servants came to bless our lord king David, saying, God make the name of Solomon bet-

> ter than thy name, and make his throne greater than thy throne. And the king bowed himself upon the bed.
>
> And also thus said the king, Blessed be the LORD God of Israel, which hath given one to sit on my throne this day, mine eyes even seeing it [1 Kings 1:47–48].

David put his seal of approval upon Solomon as king. David was an old man, and soon he would sleep with his fathers.

> And all the guests that were with Adonijah were afraid, and rose up, and went every man his way.
>
> And Adonijah feared because of Solomon, and arose, and went, and caught hold on the horns of the altar [1 Kings 1:49–50].

Adonijah's supporters were afraid and got out of there in a hurry. They knew they would be regarded as traitors. Adonijah, fearing for his life, ran to the tabernacle and caught hold of the horns of the altar for sanctuary.

> And it was told Solomon, saying, Behold, Adonijah feareth king Solomon: for, lo, he hath caught hold on the horns of the altar, saying, Let king Solomon swear unto me today that he will not slay his servant with the sword.
>
> And Solomon said, If he will shew himself a worthy man, there shall not an hair of him fall to the earth: but if wickedness shall be found in him, he shall die [1 Kings 1:51–52].

Solomon is being very fair with Adonijah. If Adonijah shows himself to be a loyal subject, then nothing will happen to him.

So king Solomon sent, and they brought him down from the altar. And he came and bowed himself to king Solomon: and Solomon said unto him, Go to thine house [1 Kings 1:53].

Adonijah, brought into the king's presence, submitted himself to the new king. Then Solomon dismissed him in peace.

CHAPTER 2

THEME: *David's deathbed charge to Solomon and the beginning of Solomon's reign*

This chapter records David's final instructions to Solomon before his death and Solomon's wise execution of David's wishes.

DAVID'S CHARGE TO SOLOMON

Now the days of David drew nigh that he should die; and he charged Solomon his son, saying,

I go the way of all the earth: be thou strong therefore, and shew thyself a man [1 Kings 2:1–2].

First of all David said, "I go the way of all the earth." This is the way of man. In Romans 5:12 the apostle Paul says, "Wherefore, as by one man sin entered into the world, and death by sin; and so death passed upon all men, for that all have sinned." By man came death, and death is passed on to all men because all have sinned. The sin of Adam has been passed down to you and me; if the Lord tarries, we will go through the doorway of death. Why? Because this is the way of all the earth, the conclusion of this life's journey. It is not a very attractive subject. We don't like to think about death today because it is something a little too depressing for the human race.

In Psalm 23:4 David says, "Yea, though I walk through the valley of the shadow of death, I will fear no evil: for thou art with me; thy rod and thy staff they comfort me." David is not speaking about the fact that he has come to his deathbed. As someone has said, "The moment that gives you life begins also to take it away from you." David is likening life to a walk through a valley. At birth you start down through the valley, and the farther you walk the narrower it gets. At the end of the valley is death. All of us are walking through that valley today. You may be in robust health today, but you can be dead before the sun goes down.

Next David says to Solomon, "Be thou strong therefore, and shew thyself a man." The Lord Jesus Christ put it like this to the crowd who had come to see John the Baptist: "But what went ye out for to see? A man clothed in soft raiment? behold, they that wear soft clothing are in kings' houses" (Matt. 11:8). John the Baptist had been brought up in the wilderness. He was rugged. Our Lord was a rugged man also. I don't like the paintings I see of Him because they make Him almost effeminate, although some of the more recent pictures have tried to make Him look more masculine. May I say to you that if you could have seen Him when He walked upon this earth, you would have seen a rugged man. He had calluses on His hands—He was a carpenter. He was God, but He was a real man. He was very man of very man and very God of very God.

Solomon was not quite like his father. David was a man. Solomon was not much of a man. David was rugged. Solomon had been brought up in the palaces—in fact, he had been brought up in the women's palaces. Why did Solomon have a thousand women around him? My friend, the answer is quite obvious. All Solomon knew about was women. He was a sissy if there ever was one. I don't think he and David had much in common. So David says to him, "I have made you king. I want you to play the man. I don't think you are one, but do the best that you can." This is the injunction David gave to this boy who had been brought up with soft clothing. Solomon was not like David. He was not like John the Baptist. He was not like our Lord, either. But now he is the king of Israel.

And keep the charge of the LORD thy God, to walk in his ways, to keep his statutes, and his commandments, and his judgments, and his testimonies, as it is written in the law of Moses, that thou mayest prosper in all that thou doest, and whithersoever thou turnest thyself:

That the LORD may continue his word which he spake concerning me, saying, If thy children take heed to their

way, to walk before me in truth with all their heart and with all their soul, there shall not fail thee (said he) a man on the throne of Israel [1 Kings 2:3–4].

David urges Solomon to stay close to the Lord and to the Word of God. His advice to this young man is very important.

There is very little attention ever given to David's legacy to Solomon, but I believe that what David left to him enabled him to become one of the great kings of the earth. In fact, Solomon is probably one of the best known kings who has ever lived.

Eason, in his *New Bible Survey* (Zondervan), enumerates David's legacy to Solomon:

1. *He transferred the leadership of the nation from the house of Saul and the tribe of Benjamin to Judah and established the royal house of David.* This becomes all-important as we shall see when we get to the New Testament. The Gospel of Matthew opens with the statement, "The book of the generation of Jesus Christ, the son of David, the son of Abraham" (Matt. 1:1). Then in Luke 1:31–32 the angel Gabriel said to Mary, "And, behold, thou shalt conceive in thy womb, and bring forth a son, and shalt call his name JESUS. He shall be great, and shall be called the Son of the Highest: and the Lord God shall give unto him the throne of his father David." Only a descendant of David is to occupy the throne of Israel.

2. *He established Jerusalem as the Holy City and as the religious center and national capital for all Jews.* This has continued down to this day. When Israel took the city of Jerusalem from the Arabs in the Six Day War of 1967, they declared that they had no intention of giving it up because it is a legacy that goes back to David. Jerusalem was David's favorite city, and he made it the capital for the nation of Israel. Solomon beautified the city by building the temple and making it the religious center of Israel. We should note, however, that it was David who made the preparations for the temple.

3. *He stamped out idolatry, practically speaking, and made the worship of Jehovah universal in the land.* This was his most important contribution.

4. He made conquests of many nations which paid tribute to Israel

and its king. *He extended the borders of the country to Egypt on the south, and to the River Euphrates on the north and east.* David is actually the one who extended Israel's borders farther than they had ever been extended before or since. The peace during the reign of Solomon was possible because David had subdued Israel's enemies.

5. Although an Oriental monarch with a sizable harem, *David's foreign marriages were largely political and relatively free from religious and moral corruption.* Having a harem was the custom of that day, but God did not approve of David's many wives, and it was largely due to them that he was in hot water all of the time. The many sons that were born to him by these women caused constant dissension inside the palace. It was something that caused David woe and sorrow all of his life. It was Solomon, and not David, who was influenced by a foreign wife. It is true that David committed an awful sin, but it occurred *before* his marriage to Bathsheba. There was not even a breath of scandal after that.

6. David was a poet and musician who endeared himself to the people as the *"sweet psalmist of Israel"* and gave to us at least seventy-three psalms.

7. *David planned the temple,* which was to exalt the religious life of the nation and the worship of Jehovah, although he was not permitted to build the Lord's house.

8. Although there was still rivalry of a sort between the ten tribes of the north and Judah and Benjamin in the south—and had been since the death of Saul and his son—David had no serious difficulty in *uniting all tribes under his rule* and making Jerusalem the national capital.

9. At the time of David's death, Israel was second to none in *power and military prowess,* and the people had a large measure of peace and freedom, as every man "sat under his own vine and fig tree." The peace that Solomon enjoyed during his reign was a peace that had been made by David during his reign.

And, behold, thou hast with thee Shimei the son of Gera, a Benjamite of Bahurim, which cursed me with a grievous curse in the day when I went to Mahanaim: but

he came down to meet me at Jordan, and I sware to him by the LORD, saying, I will not put thee to death with the sword.

Now therefore hold him not guiltless: for thou art a wise man, and knowest what thou oughtest to do unto him; but his hoar head bring thou down to the grave with blood [1 Kings 2:8–9].

David is revealing here what seems like a vengeful spirit, but it actually is not. Although Shimei had demonstrated that he was a traitor, because David had made an oath not to touch him, Shimei was still alive. David was a man of his word. Now, however, he tells Solomon to keep his watchful eye on him, and if he reveals any of his treachery, Solomon is to deal with him accordingly. The time does come, by the way, when Solomon deals with Shimei, but only after he disobeys and reveals that he is indeed a traitor.

DAVID'S DEATH

So David slept with his fathers, and was buried in the city of David.

And the days that David reigned over Israel were forty years: seven years reigned he in Hebron, and thirty and three years reigned he in Jerusalem.

Then sat Solomon upon the throne of David his father; and his kingdom was established greatly [1 Kings 2:10–12].

There is a note of sadness in the death of David. He had been a great man of God. Do you recall the first son of David and Bathsheba? He died when he was just a few days old. David said of him, "He will never come to me, but I will go to him." Now David has gone to be with that child.

Solomon, now that his father is gone, comes to the throne. At the change of any dynasty or ruler there is always a time of turmoil and great change.

SOLOMON'S ACCESSION TO THE THRONE

And Adonijah the son of Haggith came to Bath-sheba the mother of Solomon. And she said, Comest thou peaceably? And he said, Peaceably.

He said moreover, I have somewhat to say unto thee. And she said, Say on [1 Kings 2:13–14].

Even though Solomon is now on the throne, Adonijah has not given up the idea about wanting to be king. He comes to Bathsheba still harboring this thought. She does not have much confidence in him and inquires about his mission. He says that it is a peaceful one. She says, "Say on"—in other words, "I'm listening."

And he said, Thou knowest that the kingdom was mine, and that all Israel set their faces on me, that I should reign: howbeit the kingdom is turned about, and is become my brother's: for it was his from the LORD [1 Kings 2:15].

He is saying that he was more popular than Solomon and the people wanted him as king.

And now I ask one petition of thee, deny me not. And she said unto him, Say on.

And he said, Speak, I pray thee, unto Solomon the king, (for he will not say thee nay,) that he give me Abishag the Shunammite to wife [1 Kings 2:16–17].

He is saying, "Since the kingdom has been taken away from me, I have only one small request. I would like Abishag for my wife." Abishag, you recall, nursed David during his last days.

> **And Bath-sheba said, Well; I will speak for thee unto the king.**
>
> **Bath-sheba therefore went unto king Solomon, to speak unto him for Adonijah. And the king rose up to meet her, and bowed himself unto her, and sat down on his throne, and caused a seat to be set for the king's mother; and she sat on his right hand.**
>
> **Then she said, I desire one small petition of thee; I pray thee, say me not nay. And the king said unto her, Ask on, my mother: for I will not say thee nay.**
>
> **And she said, Let Abishag the Shunammite be given to Adonijah thy brother to wife [1 Kings 2:18–21].**

This was an audacious request, but Adonijah knew that Solomon would not deny his mother anything. That is the reason he went to Bathsheba instead of going directly to Solomon.

> **And king Solomon answered and said unto his mother, And why dost thou ask Abishag the Shunammite for Adonijah? ask for him the kingdom also; for he is mine elder brother; even for him, and for Abiathar the priest, and for Joab the son of Zeruiah.**
>
> **Then king Solomon sware by the LORD, saying, God do so to me, and more also, if Adonijah have not spoken this word against his own life [1 Kings 2:22–23].**

What Adonijah was actually doing was making a move toward the throne. He was doing a dangerous thing, but he was being very clever about it all. Adonijah was Solomon's elder brother, and Solomon, of course, had been aware of his brother's move to seize the throne before David named a successor. Although Bathsheba, in her simplicity, felt that Adonijah's request for Abishag was reasonable, Solomon's keen mind instantly penetrated the plot.

> Now therefore, as the LORD liveth, which hath established me, and set me on the throne of David my father, and who hath made me an house, as he promised, Adonijah shall be put to death this day.

> And king Solomon sent by the hand of Benaiah the son of Jehoiada; and he fell upon him that he died [1 Kings 2:24–25].

Adonijah's death was a brutal thing, of course, but his death eliminated a contender for the throne. It was necessary to execute him in order to establish Solomon on the throne. As long as Adonijah lived, he would continue to connive and plot in an attempt to seize the throne.

Now, having removed Adonijah, Solomon realized it would be necessary to remove from positions of influence those who had supported him.

> And unto Abiathar the priest said the king, Get thee to Anathoth, unto thine own fields; for thou art worthy of death: but I will not at this time put thee to death, because thou barest the ark of the Lord GOD before David my father, and because thou hast been afflicted in all wherein my father was afflicted.

> So Solomon thrust out Abiathar from being priest unto the LORD; that he might fulfil the word of the LORD, which he spake concerning the house of Eli in Shiloh [1 Kings 2:26–27].

Abiathar, a descendent of Aaron, was removed from his priestly office and sent home in disgrace because he had participated in Adonijah's rebellion. The only reason he was not executed was because of his faithfulness to David during Absalom's rebellion. This ended the line of Eli.

> **Then tidings came to Joab: for Joab had turned after Adonijah, through he turned not after Absalom, And Joab fled unto the tabernacle of the LORD, and caught hold on the horns of the altar.**

> **And it was told king Solomon that Joab was fled unto the tabernacle of the LORD; and, behold, he is by the altar. Then Solomon sent Benaiah the son of Jehoiada, saying, Go, fall upon him.**

> **And Benaiah came to the tabernacle of the LORD, and said unto him, Thus saith the king, Come forth. And he said, Nay; but I will die here. And Benaiah brought the king word again, saying, Thus said Joab, and thus he answered me [1 Kings 2:28–30].**

When Joab heard what happened to Abiathar and Adonijah, he took off for the tall timber. He ran to the tabernacle of the Lord and caught hold of the horns of the altar for sanctuary. Solomon chose Benaiah, the son of Jehoiada, to be Joab's executioner. He went after Joab and asked him to come outside the tabernacle. Joab refused, saying, "I'll die here if I have to die."

> **And the king said unto him, Do as he hath said, and fall upon him, and bury him; that thou mayest take away the innocent blood, which Joab shed, from me, and from the house of my father.**

> **And the LORD shall return his blood upon his own head, who fell upon two men more righteous and better than**

> he, and slew them with the sword, my father David not knowing thereof, to wit, Abner the son of Ner, captain of the host of Israel, and Amasa the son of Jether, captain of the host of Judah [1 Kings 2:31–32].

Joab had been a bloody man.

> Their blood shall therefore return upon the head of Joab, and upon the head of his seed for ever: but upon David, and upon his seed, and upon his house, and upon his throne, shall there be peace for ever from the LORD.

> So Benaiah the son of Jehoiada went up, and fell upon him, and slew him: and he was buried in his own house in the wilderness [1 Kings 2:33–34].

He was executed because of his part in a rebellion against Solomon.
    Shimei was another traitor. David would not touch him because he had given his word that he would not. Solomon now puts restrictions on him.

> And the king sent and called for Shimei, and said unto him, Build thee an house in Jerusalem, and dwell there, and go not forth thence any whither [1 Kings 2:36].

Solomon wanted Shimei to be where he could keep his eye on him. Wherever Shimei went, he sowed seeds of rebellion. Solomon wanted to watch his every move.

> For it shall be, that on the day thou goest out, and passest over the brook Kidron, thou shalt know for certain that thou shalt surely die: thy blood shall be upon thine own head.

> And Shimei said unto the king, The saying is good:
> as my lord the king hath said, so will thy servant do.
> And Shimei dwelt in Jerusalem many days [1 Kings
> 2:37–38].

Solomon commanded Shimei to build a home in Jerusalem and to remain within the city limits. He was forbidden to return and live with his own tribe. Shimei promised to be obedient to Solomon's terms.

> And it came to pass at the end of three years, that two of
> the servants of Shimei ran away unto Achish son of
> Maachah king of Gath. And they told Shimei, saying,
> Behold, thy servants be in Gath.
>
> And Shimei arose, and saddled his ass, and went to
> Gath to Achish to seek his servants: and Shimei went,
> and brought his servants from Gath [1 Kings 2:39–40].

Shimei went outside the city limits. He did this in direct disobedience to Solomon's orders. Solomon was told what Shimei had done; so the king sent for him.

> Why then hast thou not kept the oath of the Lord, and
> the commandment that I have charged thee with?
>
> The king said moreover to Shimei, Thou knowest all the
> wickedness which thine heart is privy to, that thou
> didst to David my father: therefore the Lord shall return
> thy wickedness upon thine own head;
>
> And king Solomon shall be blessed, and the throne of
> David shall be established before the Lord for ever.
>
> So the king commanded Benaiah the son of Jehoiada;
> which went out, and fell upon him, that he died. And

**the kingdom was established in the hand of Solomon
[1 Kings 2:43–46].**

With Shimei's death Solomon had completed the charge made to him
by David his father. Solomon had removed most of the contenders to
the throne. Now he could reign in peace.

CHAPTERS 3 AND 4

THEME: Solomon's prayer for wisdom and God's answer

In the chapters before us God appears to Solomon in a dream saying, "Ask what I shall give thee." Solomon asks for wisdom to govern Israel. His unselfish request so pleases God that He promises him much more than he asked for. In addition to wisdom, He gives him riches and honor. Solomon's decision in the cases of two mothers claiming one child demonstrates that God had truly given him a wise and understanding heart.

And Solomon made affinity with Pharaoh king of Egypt, and took Pharaoh's daughter, and brought her into the city of David, until he had made an end of building his own house, and the house of the LORD, and the wall of Jerusalem round about.

Only the people sacrificed in high places, because there was no house built unto the name of the LORD, until those days [1 Kings 3:1–2].

One of the first things Solomon did after he became king was to marry a daughter of Pharaoh, king of Egypt. His marriage formed an alliance with Egypt. Solomon's marriages with heathen women were terrible mistakes and finally became his undoing. Remember that Solomon was brought up in a court of women. He was not acquainted with life as was David, his father. I do not believe that Solomon ever had the spiritual capacity for God that David had nor the longing for God in his life. Solomon did, however, recognize his shortcomings. After he married Pharaoh's daughter (and we only wish he had done this before), he went to the Lord and asked for wisdom.

After David's reign there was a period of relaxation. The people began to offer sacrifices in high places which was actually heathen, pagan worship. It was a return to idolatry.

SOLOMON'S SACRIFICE AND
PRAYER FOR WISDOM

And Solomon loved the LORD, walking in the statutes of David his father: only he sacrificed and burnt incense in high places.

And the king went to Gibeon to sacrifice there; for that was the great high place: a thousand burnt offerings did Solomon offer upon that altar [1 Kings 3:3–4].

Solomon was perfectly willing to offer sacrifices on heathen altars—something that David never would have done. Although Solomon loved the Lord, he was not the kind of a man David was. Solomon was walking in the statutes of David, but he had that little flaw that we have already seen makes second-rate material.

In Gibeon the LORD appeared to Solomon in a dream by night: and God said, Ask what I shall give thee [1 Kings 3:5].

The Lord appeared to Solomon in a dream by night. Again, I must repeat that God today is not appearing to men in dreams. If you have had a dream, do not try to say that the Lord appeared to you. Just remember what you had for supper, and you will find out why you had the dream. God speaks to us today in His Word. Solomon did not have all of God's Word in his day, so God appeared to him in a dream and said, "Ask what you will. I will grant it to you." What is Solomon going to ask for? He has the choice of asking for anything he wants. The fact that he is going to make a wise choice indicates that he had a certain amount of human wisdom before God gave him His wisdom.

When the Lord told Solomon He would grant any wish, I think He recognized that Solomon had many deficiencies and was wholly and totally inadequate. But, my friend, who is adequate for these things? Who is adequate for living the Christian life? Not one of us. The fact of the matter is that we cannot live the Christian life, and God has never asked us to live it. He has asked that *He* might live that life through us. Now He is wanting to do something through Solomon. This king could have asked for riches or power. Instead, recognizing his deficiency, notice what he asks for.

And Solomon said, Thou hast shewed unto thy servant David my father great mercy, according as he walked before thee in truth, and in righteousness, and in uprightness of heart with thee; and thou hast kept for him this great kindness, that thou hast given him a son to sit on his throne, as it is this day [1 Kings 3:6].

Solomon realized that he was attempting to fill not the shoes but the throne of David. He recognized that he was totally inadequate for the job.

And now, O Lord my God, thou hast made thy servant king instead of David my father: and I am but a little child: I know not how to go out or come in.

And thy servant is in the midst of thy people which thou hast chosen, a great people, that cannot be numbered nor counted for multitude [1 Kings 3:7–8].

He considered himself "a little child" in experience. He felt incapable of governing this great nation. There are so many folk today attempting to serve God who do not seem to recognize their inadequacies. All of us are wholly inadequate to serve God. We should recognize that fact so that we are in a position where God can help us.

> Give therefore thy servant an understanding heart to
> judge thy people, that I may discern between good and
> bad: for who is able to judge this thy so great a people?
> [1 Kings 3:9].

Solomon asked for an understanding heart to judge God's people. I want to consider this for just a moment. We always say that Solomon prayed for wisdom. That is certainly true, but what kind of wisdom did he pray for? He prayed for political wisdom. He wanted the ability to be a statesman. He wanted to know how to judge and rule over these people and make great national decisions. He did not pray for spiritual discernment. This is something that needs to be made very clear. In the books Solomon wrote, Proverbs and Ecclesiastes, we will find wisdom that will guide us in this world—Proverbs is a fine book to give to young men starting out on their own. Although in the Song of Solomon he does reveal spiritual discernment, in his old age his heathen wives turned away his heart from the Lord. Solomon did not pray for spiritual discernment. Solomon prayed for political wisdom, and this God gave him throughout his life.

SOLOMON'S PRAYER IS ANSWERED

> And the speech pleased the LORD, that Solomon had
> asked this thing.

> And God said unto him, Because thou hast asked this
> thing, and hast not asked for thyself long life; neither
> hast asked riches for thyself, nor hast asked the life of
> thine enemies; but hast asked for thyself understanding
> to discern judgment [1 Kings 3:10–11].

Solomon wanted to make wise decisions. In the sickening scene in every government today we see a group of men clamoring for positions. They want to be elected to an office. All of them are telling us how great they are and what marvelous abilities they have. They assure us that they are able to solve the problems. By now, friend, some of us have come to the conclusion that these boys are just kidding us. They don't have the solution and they don't have the wisdom. If only some men would come on the scene and say, "I don't have the wisdom; I recognize my inadequacies. But I am going to depend on God to lead and guide me." Something like that would be so startling it would probably rock the world. That is what Solomon said, and God commended him for it. It was a great step.

> **Behold, I have done according to thy words: lo, I have given thee a wise and an understanding heart; so that there was none like thee before thee, neither after thee shall any arise like unto thee [1 Kings 3:12].**

Solomon does stand out as being a wise ruler. When you read the Books of Proverbs and Ecclesiastes, you will find human wisdom on the highest plane. I do not mean that these books are not inspired of God. It is obvious that God through Solomon is giving the highest of human wisdom, making it clear in both books that mere human wisdom is totally inadequate to meet the issues of life.

> **And I have also given thee that which thou hast not asked, both riches, and honour: so that there shall not be any among the kings like unto thee all thy days.**
>
> **And if thou wilt walk in my ways, to keep my statutes and my commandments, as thy father David did walk, then I will lengthen thy days [1 Kings 3:13–14].**

The standard, as we have indicated before, is David. That is a human standard and is not very high. But, frankly, few of the kings even came up to that standard.

> And Solomon awoke; and, behold, it was a dream. And
> he came to Jerusalem, and stood before the ark of the
> covenant of the LORD, and offered up burnt offerings,
> and offered peace offerings, and made a feast to all his
> servants [1 Kings 3:15].

The burnt offerings and peace offerings point to the Lord Jesus Christ.
The burnt offering speaks of who He is. The peace offering speaks of
the fact that He made peace by shedding His blood on the cross. Because of who He is, He is able to bring us into a right relationship with
God. The shedding of His blood makes it possible to remove the guilt
of our sins.

In the last part of this chapter we have a demonstration of Solomon's wisdom. He gives a clever solution to a real problem. There
were two women. They were harlots, and they had one child between
them. Each woman claimed the child as her own. They brought the
matter to Solomon. How would you solve the problem? How would
you find out who the real mother was? I suppose today some scientific
method of determining the mother would be pursued, but Solomon
had no such recourse. Solomon said to the women, "Since both of you
claim the child, we will cut the baby in half, and each of you may have
half of the child." The one who was not the mother, who had no love
for the child and apparently had it in for the real mother, replied,
"Sure, go ahead and cut the child in half." The real mother, however,
said, "Oh, no, no. Don't do that. Give her the child." Solomon knew
that the woman who was willing to give up the child in order to save
its life was the real mother.

> And all Israel heard of the judgment which the king had
> judged; and they feared the king: for they saw that the
> wisdom of God was in him, to do judgment [1 Kings
> 3:28].

This is only one example of the many wise decisions Solomon was
able to make during his reign.

SOLOMON'S ELEVEN PRINCES

In chapter 4 Solomon brings the kingdom to its zenith. The things that marked his kingdom were peace and prosperity. Peace is what we would like to have, is it not? I think we could call Solomon the prince of peace while David was a man of war. But the peace that Solomon and those in his kingdom enjoyed was made possible by David, the man of war.

This has a spiritual application for us. We like to feel that God forgives sin because He is sentimental. God does not forgive sin on a low plane like that. A battle has been fought, my friend, and a great sacrifice has been made. Blood has been shed that we might have forgiveness of sin. The Lord Jesus Christ made peace by the blood of His cross. It is only through His blood that we can enter into peace.

So king Solomon was king over all Israel.

And these were the princes which he had; Azariah the son of Zadok the priest,

Elihoreph and Ahiah, the sons of Shisha, scribes; Jehoshaphat the son of Ahilud, the recorder.

And Benaiah the son of Jehoiada was over the host: and Zadok and Abiathar were the priests:

And Azariah the son of Nathan was over the officers; and Zabud the son of Nathan was principal officer, and the king's friend:

And Ahishar was over the household: and Adoniram the son of Abda was over the tribute [1 Kings 4:1–6].

In the first few verses of this chapter a list of Solomon's princes is given. Some of them apparently were the sons of the sons of David, which would mean that they were Solomon's nephews. Azariah is mentioned in verse 5. This man was either a son of Nathan, David's son, or a son of Nathan, the prophet.

SOLOMON'S TWELVE OFFICERS

And Solomon had twelve officers over all Israel, which provided victuals for the king and his household: each man his month in a year made provision [1 Kings 4:7].

Solomon had twelve officers. Each officer came from a tribe of Israel. They were in charge of providing the needs of the king and his household. This was Solomon's method of taxation.

THE GREATNESS OF THE KINGDOM

Judah and Israel were many, as the sand which is by the sea in multitude, eating and drinking, and making merry.

And Solomon reigned over all kingdoms from the river unto the land of the Philistines, and unto the border of Egypt: they brought presents, and served Solomon all the days of his life [1 Kings 4:20–21].

This was a time of great prosperity and peace. The wars were over. There was plenty for everyone. And this, my friend, is just a little adumbration, a little preview, of the kingdom that is coming on this earth—the millennial kingdom.

And Judah and Israel dwelt safely, every man under his vine and under his fig tree, from Dan even to Beersheba, all the days of Solomon [1 Kings 4:25].

There are several things we need to note here. This was a time of security and safety, something which we do not have in this world today. "There is no peace, saith my God, to the wicked" (Isa. 57:21). But peace is coming on the earth when the Prince of Peace comes. In Solomon's day every man dwelt under his own vine and fig tree. That tells us that one man was not living in a mansion and another in a hovel. Each man had his vine and fig tree; he was living comfortably on his own property. It was so from Dan to Beer-sheba—that is, from the northern border to the southern border—all the days of Solomon.

And Solomon had forty thousand stalls of horses for his chariots, and twelve thousand horsemen [1 Kings 4:26].

I want to call attention to this verse. The horse was the animal of war, and God had forbidden the multiplication of horses. God gave a specific law that a king was not to multiply horses or wives: "But he shall not multiply horses to himself, nor cause the people to return to Egypt, to the end that he should multiply horses: forasmuch as the Lord hath said unto you, Ye shall henceforth return no more that way" (Deut. 17:16). Solomon multiplied both horses and wives. He had stables all over the land of Israel. I visited the ruins of Megiddo; that is, the mound that overlooks the Valley of Esdraelon where we believe that the great issue will be finally settled in the last days at the battle, or war, of Armageddon. It is a tremendous view, by the way. But the thing that impressed me was the ruins there of Solomon's stables, stalls, and the troughs where his horses ate. These stables would accommodate at least 450 horses. Second Chronicles 9:25 says he had 4,000 stalls for horses! Solomon certainly multiplied horses, contrary to the wisdom of God.

SOLOMON'S GREAT WISDOM AND RENOWN

Now we are told something of the wisdom of Solomon.

And God gave Solomon wisdom and understanding exceeding much, and largeness of heart, even as the sand that is on the sea shore.

And Solomon's wisdom excelled the wisdom of all the children of the east country, and all the wisdom of Egypt [1 Kings 4:29-30].

The east is where the wise men came from.

> **For he was wiser than all men; than Ethan the Ezrahite, and Heman, and Chalcol, and Darda, the sons of Mahol: and his fame was in all nations round about [1 Kings 4:31].**

Four outstanding wise men are mentioned in this verse.

> **And he spake three thousand proverbs: and his songs were a thousand and five.**

> **And he spake of trees, from the cedar tree that is in Lebanon even unto the hyssop that springeth out of the wall: he spake also of beasts, and of fowl, and of creeping things, and of fishes [1 Kings 4:32–33].**

We are told that Solomon spoke three thousand proverbs. We have only a few hundred recorded in the Bible. His songs were a thousand and five. Believe me, he was a song writer. We have only one of his songs, The Song of Solomon. Solomon was a dendrologist—"He spake of trees, from the cedar tree that is in Lebanon even unto the hyssop that springeth out of the wall." The hyssop is a humble little plant that grows on rocks. Solomon was also a zoologist—"he spake also of beasts"—and an ornithologist since he spoke of birds. He was an entomologist: he spoke of creeping things, or insects. He was an ichthyologist: he spoke of fishes. He spoke of these things because he had studied them and was an authority in these particular realms. This, apparently, is the beginning of the sciences. Solomon was interested in these things.

> **And there came of all people to hear the wisdom of Solomon, from all kings of the earth, which had heard of his wisdom [1 Kings 4:34].**

Solomon gained a worldwide reputation for his wisdom, and many came to hear him. We have a few of the proverbs that he wrote recorded in the Book of Proverbs. As I have said before, these proverbs are extremely helpful to any young person entering adult life. There are certain proverbs that can guide a young man in life and business. You see, God is very practical with us. He gets right down to the nitty-gritty, where you and I walk in and out of the marts of trade, where we enter into the courts of the land and into social gatherings. Certain guiding principles of life are given to us in Proverbs. I am not saying that a young man can become a Christian by following the proverbs of Solomon, but he certainly will have a marvelous guide for his life.

CHAPTERS 5 AND 6

THEME: Preparation and construction of the temple

In chapter 5 Solomon works out a business deal with King Hiram of Tyre for cedar and workmen. Also out of Israel he raises a levy of thirty thousand workmen.

Chapter 6 details the construction of this costly and ornate temple which took seven years to complete.

> **And Hiram king of Tyre sent his servants unto Solomon; for he had heard that they had anointed him king in the room of his father: for Hiram was ever a lover of David [1 Kings 5:1].**

Whatever King Hiram of Tyre is going to do will not be because of Solomon but because of his love, esteem, and respect for King David.

> **And Solomon sent to Hiram, saying,**

> **Thou knowest how that David my father could not build an house unto the name of the Lord his God for the wars which were about him on every side, until the Lord put them under the soles of his feet.**

> **But now the Lord my God hath given me rest on every side, so that there is neither adversary nor evil occurrent [1 Kings 5:2–4].**

Friend, only God can give peace, whether it is world peace or peace in the human heart. God alone can give the rest today that the human heart needs. That is why our Lord, when they rejected Him as king, could send out His personal, private, individual invitation, "Come unto me, all ye that labour and are heavy laden"—that is, burdened with sin—"and I will give you rest" (Matt. 11:28). Only Christ can give that kind of rest. Now God had given Solomon rest from warfare. There was peace on every side.

And, behold, I purpose to build an house unto the name of the LORD my God, as the LORD spake unto David my father, saying, Thy son, whom I will set upon thy throne in thy room, he shall build an house unto my name [1 Kings 5:5].

Although the building of the temple all stems from David, he was not permitted to build it because he was a man of war.

Perhaps we should consider some of the background relative to the building of the temple. Man has been a builder from the beginning. In Genesis 4:17 we are told that Cain ". . . builded a city, and called the name of the city, after the name of his son, Enoch." The face of the earth is scarred by great mounds that hide the ruins of great cities and splendid buildings of the past. The spade of the archaeologist has penetrated into the depths, and you can judge each civilization by the height of the buildings. There are those who say that the cave men of the Stone Age (if they ever existed) were barbarians and uncivilized. They were not builders but sought refuge in caves. The Egyptians, the Assyrians, the Babylonians, the Greeks, and the Romans are all counted as civilized, and it is evidenced in their architecture. Modern man claims a high degree of culture because he has built subdivisions, shopping centers, apartment buildings, and tall office buildings. Today man is building his own cave in which to live and work—like a gopher. The rest of the time he crawls on the freeway like a worm. As long as he can push a button and turn a switch, he says he is living. That is modern man.

The first buildings of impressive design were the temples. All pagan peoples had temples. Some temples were crude; others, such as the Parthenon in Greece, were the highest expression of beauty. All of this building stems from the Tower of Babel, which was a monument to man's gargantuan resistance to God. Pagan temples have always been the highest architectural expression, but the pagans who have attended, both civilized and uncivilized, have been on the lowest spiritual level. These temples have been elaborate, large, ornate, rich, and impressive. The temples of the kings on the River Nile, Asshur of Nineveh, Marduk of Babylon, the ziggurats in the Tigris-Euphrates Valley, Baal of the Phonenicians, Athena of the Greeks and in Athens the Parthenon, Jupiter of the Romans, the Aztec temples of Mexico— all of them are manifestations of rebellion against God. ". . . When they knew God, they glorified him not as God, neither were thankful; but became vain in their imaginations. . . ." What did they do? They built temples, changing ". . . the glory of the uncorruptible God into an image made like to corruptible man, and to birds, and fourfooted beasts, and creeping things" (Rom. 1:21, 23). Each made a house for his god to live in. They put their gods in a box like a jack-in-the-box.

The temple Solomon built, however, was never considered in Scripture as a house in which God would live. In the Book of 2 Chronicles at the dedication of the temple, Solomon made it quite clear that God did not dwell in that place. "But will God in very deed dwell with men on the earth? behold, heaven and the heaven of heavens cannot contain thee; how much less this house which I have built!" (2 Chron. 6:18). If you think that the temple was built as a house in which God would dwell, you have missed the entire point. It was an approach for man to God and an access to God through sacrifices.

Notice now the conception of the temple, then its construction and character. It is rather important.

The building of the temple was first in David's mind, although God would not let him build it. First Chronicles 28:1–3 tells us part of the story: "And David assembled all the princes of Israel, the princes of the tribes, and the captains of the companies that ministered to the king by course, and the captains over the thousands, and captains over the hundreds, and the stewards over all the substance and possession of the king, and of his sons, with the officers, and with the mighty men, and with all the valiant men, unto Jerusalem. Then David the king stood up upon his feet, and said, Hear me, my brethren, and my people: As for me, I had in mine heart to build an house of rest for the ark of the covenant of the LORD, and for the footstool of our God, and had made ready for the building: But God said unto me,

Thou shalt not build an house for my name, because thou hast been a man of war, and hast shed blood." The temple was not a dwelling place for God; it was to be His footstool.

It was in David's heart to build the temple. The pattern for the building was given to David, not Solomon. First Chronicles 28:19 tells us, "All this, said David, the LORD made me understand in writing by his hand upon me, even all the works of this pattern." In other words, David was given the blueprint of the temple even though God did not permit him to build it. David gave this pattern or blueprint to Solomon. "Take heed now; for the LORD hath chosen thee to build an house for the sanctuary: be strong, and do it. Then David gave to Solomon his son the pattern of the porch, and of the houses thereof, and of the treasuries thereof, and of the upper chambers thereof, and of the inner parlours thereof, and of the place of the mercy seat, and the pattern of all that he had by the spirit, of the courts of the house of the LORD, and of all the chambers round about, of the treasuries of the house of God, and of the treasuries of the dedicated things" (1 Chron. 28:10–12). David also gathered the material: "Now I have prepared with all my might for the house of my God the gold for things to be made of gold, and the silver for things of silver, and the brass for things of brass, the iron for things of iron, and wood for things of wood; onyx stones, and stones to be set, glistering stones, and of divers colours, and all manner of precious stones, and marble stones in abundance" (1 Chron. 29:2). The conception of the temple, you see, was in the heart of David. Solomon merely executed the construction of it.

Now with all David's accumulation of material at hand, Solomon contracts with Hiram king of Tyre for cedar and fir timber for the actual construction of the edifice.

And Hiram sent to Solomon, saying, I have considered the things which thou sentest to me for: and I will do all thy desire concerning timber of cedar, and concerning timber of fir.

My servants shall bring them down from Lebanon unto the sea: and I will convey them by sea in floats unto the

> place that thou shalt appoint me, and will cause them to
> be discharged there, and thou shalt receive them: and
> thou shalt accomplish my desire, in giving food for my
> household [1 Kings 5:8–9].

In addition to the workmen from Tyre, Solomon employed a large work force of Israelites.

> And king Solomon raised a levy out of all Israel; and the
> levy was thirty thousand men.
>
> And he sent them to Lebanon, ten thousand a month by
> courses: a month they were in Lebanon, and two months
> at home: and Adoniram was over the levy [1 Kings
> 5:13–14].

This was a tremendous enterprise. After Solomon had built the temple, he went on to build other things. He had a building project that was too big, and he overtaxed his people.

Chapter 6 brings us to the actual construction of the temple. You will notice that the temple is twice as large as the tabernacle was. It is more ornate, elaborate, and costly. The simplicity of the tabernacle was lost, and there appears to be a spiritual deterioration, as we shall see.

> And the house which king Solomon built for the LORD,
> the length thereof was threescore cubits, and the
> breadth thereof twenty cubits, and the height thereof
> thirty cubits [1 Kings 6:2].

Although the temple was twice as large as the tabernacle, it may have been smaller than we realize. The tabernacle was 30 x 10 cubits "and the height thereof 30 cubits." The temple was three times higher than the tabernacle, which had been nothing in the world but a tent.

Even though the temple was small, it was like a jewel. Now a diamond is not as big as a straw stack, but it is much more valuable. That was true of the temple Solomon built.

> And the porch before the temple of the house, twenty cubits was the length thereof, according to the breadth of the house; and ten cubits was the breadth thereof before the house.
>
> And for the house he made windows of narrow lights.
>
> And against the wall of the house he built chambers round about, against the walls of the house round about, both of the temple and of the oracle: and he made chambers round about:
>
> The nethermost chamber was five cubits broad, and the middle was six cubits broad, and the third was seven cubits broad: for without in the wall of the house he made narrowed rests round about, that the beams should not be fastened in the walls of the house.
>
> And the house, when it was in building, was built of stone made ready before it was brought thither: so that there was neither hammer nor axe nor any tool of iron heard in the house, while it was in building [1 Kings 6:3–7].

Let me say a word about the construction of the temple. As we have seen, it was only twice as large as the tabernacle. It was surrounded on three sides by a three-story building. This was the place where the priests lived during their course of service. In the front there was a portico that was 10 x 20 x 120 cubits—half as long as a football field. The brazen altar was 20 x 20 x 10 cubits, while the altar of the tabernacle was 5 x 5 x 3 cubits. There were ten lampstands to replace the one of the tabernacle. There were ten tables of showbread rather than one. There was a multiplication of some of the articles of furniture.

There were 30,000 Israelites used in the construction; they were drafted for the work. There were 150,000 extra workers and 3,300 overseers used in the construction of the building. Hiram, king of Tyre, furnished the material and the artifices. The temple was completed in seven years and six months. The temple was made of stone, and the sound of a hammer was not heard during the building. The cost of the building is estimated around five million dollars. It was like a jewel box. There were two pillars in it which were very impressive. Later on we will see what they mean.

I have mentioned these details by way of comparison. The temple was inferior to the tabernacle, not only in innate quality, but in that which the temple characterizes.

First of all, it was complicated. The simplicity of the tabernacle was lost. In the New Testament the temple is bypassed and the tabernacle is used for the typology. Why? Well, the temple had become very complicated. This has an application for us. We are living in a day when the emphasis is put on methods rather than on the Word of God. The church is filled with new programs and new methods.

When I first began my ministry I pastored in a little white church on a red clay hill in Georgia, surrounded by a cotton patch. We just had a back room that served as Sunday school. We didn't have very good facilities. We did have central heating, however, as a great big old potbellied stove sat right in the middle of the church. I went by that church a short time ago. The city of Atlanta has grown all around it now. The church now has a big Christian education department and all of the latest equipment. I asked a member of the church, one who had been saved during my ministry, "Does anybody ever get saved here today?" He said, "No. Nobody has been saved." May I say to you that there is a girl out on the mission field who was saved when it was a little old simple church. Although it was very simple, people got saved. I don't like all of the methods employed today. I think we need to get back to the Word of God.

The second thing I want you to notice is that Solomon made windows of narrow lights. There had been no windows in the tabernacle. Now Solomon's windows did not let in much light, but they did let in a little. The people no longer depended upon divine light as they had in the tabernacle. They depended on the natural light which came from outside.

The third indication of inferiority is that the cherubim were made of olive wood. They were ten cubits high—very impressive—but they were no longer made of solid gold. The fourth thing is that the temple was more ornate and gaudy than the tabernacle, and there was more ceremony and ritual connected with it.

This is the temple that was destroyed by Nebuchadnezzar. The temple put up by Zerubbabel was destroyed in turn and then supplanted by Herod's temple in Christ's day. The temple actually pointed to the Lord Jesus Christ. In John 2:19 Jesus said, "Destroy this temple, and in three days I will raise it up." He wasn't talking about Herod's temple; He was talking about His body: "Then said the Jews, Forty and six years was this temple in building, and wilt thou rear it up in three days? But he spake of the temple of his body" (John 2:20–21). The temple is equated with the body of Christ.

Because this chapter is largely a record of building detail, I have not quoted much of it. However, you will find it very interesting to read. As you read of the magnificence of the temple, keep in mind that it was conceived in the mind and heart of David, as he wanted a suitable place to house the ark of the covenant. (He had no idea, of course, of building a dwelling place for God; he said it was only a footstool for Him.) Its purpose was to provide access to God by sacrifice. Also notice how complicated it is in comparison to the tabernacle. After I had written a book on the tabernacle, I was going to follow it with a book on the temple. After a great deal of study, I threw up my hands in despair. It is much too complicated to illustrate or set before us the wonderful person of the Lord Jesus Christ. However, God honored it with His presence, and the place was filled with the Shekinah glory, as we shall see in the following chapter.

CHAPTER 7

THEME: Solomon's building projects

In chapter 7 we learn that not only did Solomon build the temple, but he built his own palace, the house of the forest of Lebanon, and a palace for the daughter of Pharaoh. Also in this chapter we have details concerning the construction of the porch of the temple, the molten sea for the temple, the ten lavers of brass, and the ten golden lampstands for the temple.

But Solomon was building his own house thirteen years, and he finished all his house [1 Kings 7:1].

It took seven years to build the temple, but it took almost twice that long to build his own house. It must have been a very elaborate palace.

He built also the house of the forest of Lebanon; the length thereof was an hundred cubits, and the breadth thereof fifty cubits, and the height thereof thirty cubits, upon four rows of cedar pillars, with cedar beams upon the pillars [1 Kings 7:2].

Solomon also built the house of the forest of Lebanon. That was his lodge, his second house. Perhaps that is where he went on vacation. We are told that the "length thereof was an hundred cubits," which is half the length of a football field. The breadth was fifty cubits, which is seventy-five feet. The height of it was thirty cubits; that is forty-five feet. It was built "upon four rows of cedar pillars, with cedar beams upon the pillars." Hiram, king of Tyre, furnished the stone and the cedars, which were the cedars of Lebanon. There are very few of those tall, graceful cedars left today. All of that country, including Palestine, has been denuded. Apparently at one time it was heavily timbered.

> And his house where he dwelt had another court within
> the porch, which was of the like work. Solomon made
> also an house for Pharaoh's daughter, whom he had
> taken to wife, like unto this porch [1 Kings 7:8].

"Of the like work" indicates it was also very ornate and elaborate. He built a house for Pharaoh's daughter—he seems to have put her in a favored position. He could not build each wife such a palace. If he had, he would have built a thousand palaces! That would have been a staggering building program, like a government housing development.

HIRAM, THE ARTISAN

> And king Solomon sent and fetched Hiram out of Tyre.
>
> He was a widow's son of the tribe of Naphtali, and his
> father was a man of Tyre, a worker in brass: and he was
> filled with wisdom, and understanding, and cunning to
> work all works in brass. And he came to king Solomon,
> and wrought all his work [1 Kings 7:13–14].

This man is Hiram, the artisan, and not Hiram, the king. He was a skilled worker in brass. He was the one who made all of the delicate pieces of statuary and the items that were made out of iron, brass, and gold. His work was highly ornamented, which is what Solomon wanted. Elaborate ornamentation is evidence of the affluent period and time of peace in which he lived. It is during an era of peace and prosperity that the arts develop. During Solomon's reign there was peace and plenty.

Now we are given more detail relative to the temple.

> And he set up the pillars in the porch of the temple: and
> he set up the right pillar, and called the name thereof
> Jachin: and he set up the left pillar, and called the name
> thereof Boaz [1 Kings 7:21].

Jachin means "God shall establish," *Boaz* means "in it is strength." You will find that there are psalms which include these two concepts of strength and beauty. For example, Psalm 96:6 says, "Honour and majesty are before him: strength and beauty are in his sanctuary." Strength speaks of salvation—God is able to deliver those who are His. Beauty speaks of the beauty of worship. We are to worship God in the beauty of holiness. These two pillars were prominent in the temple. Spiritually, these two pillars should be in the life of anyone who is going to worship God. If you are going to worship God, you must have experienced the power of God in delivering you from sin. Then you can worship Him in the beauty of holiness. I see nothing wrong in having a beautiful sanctuary; I think it is quite proper. A beautiful sanctuary may be conducive to worship, but it does not always inspire worship and certainly is no substitute for worship. We worship Him in the beauty of holiness. That is, when we come into the presence of God, sense His presence, and realize our inadequacies, then we can see *Him* in all of His beauty and glory. This was Isaiah's experience when he went into the temple and saw a vision of God seated upon a throne, high, and holy, and lifted up. When Isaiah saw himself in the light of the presence of God, he saw his own uncleanness. "Then said I, Woe is me! for I am undone; because I am a man of unclean lips, and I dwell in the midst of a people of unclean lips: for mine eyes have seen the King, the LORD of hosts" (Isa. 6:5). The pillars Jachin and Boaz speak of that which worship really is—a redeemed soul who comes into the presence of a holy God.

Realizing that I am no authority in the realm of music, I still insist that music which does not lift you into the presence of God is not music for the church. There is a great deal of music in the church which definitely does not prepare anyone for worship. I have discovered in my ministry and conference work that many times a musical number given by the choir or a soloist before the message is absolutely devastating and destructive to the giving out of the Word of God. We need to recognize that the worship of God is based on the fact that He is high, holy, and lifted up.

Solomon also greatly enlarged the laver in the temple.

> **And he made a molten sea, ten cubits from the one brim
> to the other: it was round all about, and his height was
> five cubits: and a line of thirty cubits did compass it
> round about [1 Kings 7:23].**

This huge laver was supported on twelve oxen cast in brass, three oxen looking in each direction. The brim of it was ornate with lilies. The laver was for the priests to wash in. While there was only one simple laver in the tabernacle, here we have multiplication and beautification in Solomon's temple.

> **Then made he ten lavers of brass: one laver contained
> forty baths: and every laver was four cubits: and upon
> every one of the ten bases one laver [1 Kings 7:38].**

The purpose of these ten lavers was to cleanse such things as they offered for the burnt offering.

It takes more than size and beauty to bring cleansing to the heart. There are many churches today that conduct beautiful services, yet they do not cleanse the congregation nor bring them into the presence of God. They do not refresh the soul nor bring peace and joy to the heart. All the lavers in the world cannot cleanse one from sin. It is the water in the laver that cleanses. The water represents the Word of God. To wash in the Word of God is to apply the Word to the life.

> **And Solomon made all the vessels that pertained unto
> the house of the LORD: the altar of gold, and the table of
> gold, whereupon the shewbread was.**
>
> **And the candlesticks of pure gold, five on the right side,
> and five on the left, before the oracle, with the flowers,
> and the lamps, and the tongs of gold [1 Kings 7:48–49].**

In the tabernacle there was one lampstand which spoke of Christ. In the temple there were ten. Again there is multiplication that has an application for us. In our contemporary society there is danger in becoming overly familiar with the Lord Jesus Christ. For example, the other day I listened to a message given on the radio in which the speaker mentioned the name of Jesus over fifty times before he was halfway through his message. To keep mentioning His name over and over is like multiplying lampstands. Also I heard a man say the other day that he was going to come into the presence of Jesus and sit down and talk with Him. Maybe he will; I don't know. But the Bible does not suggest such familiarity with the glorified Christ. A man who was very familiar with Him when He was here on earth—who rebuked Him and made suggestions to Him, and reclined on His bosom in the upper room—was John. He was very familiar with Him in the days of His flesh. But John writes of his reaction when he sees the glorified Christ in these terms: "And when I saw him, I fell at his feet as dead . . ." (Rev. 1:17). I think that is where you and I are going to be when we come into Christ's presence. My friend, let's not keep multiplying lampstands, becoming overly familiar with Him. He is the One whom we *worship* and adore. He is the One before whom we fall down upon our faces.

So was ended all the work that king Solomon made for the house of the LORD. And Solomon brought in the things which David his father had dedicated; even the silver, and the gold, and the vessels, did he put among the treasures of the house of the LORD [1 Kings 7:51].

CHAPTER 8

THEME: Dedication of the finished temple

In the chapter before us the ark of the covenant is brought into the completed temple, the Shekinah glory fills the house of the Lord, and Solomon gives his message and prayer of dedication.

> **Then Solomon assembled the elders of Israel, and all the heads of the tribes, the chief of the fathers of the children of Israel, unto king Solomon in Jerusalem, that they might bring up the ark of the covenant of the LORD out of the city of David, which is Zion [1 Kings 8:1].**

When the ark is brought from the tabernacle and installed in the place prepared for it in the holy of holies, the glory of the Lord fills the temple.

> **And it came to pass, when the priests were come out of the holy place, that the cloud filled the house of the LORD.**
>
> **So that the priests could not stand to minister because of the cloud: for the glory of the LORD had filled the house of the LORD [1 Kings 8:10–11].**

In Solomon's message of dedication he gives proper credit to David.

> **And it was in the heart of David my father to build an house for the name of the LORD God of Israel.**
>
> **And the LORD said unto David my father, Whereas it was in thine heart to build an house unto my name, thou didst well that it was in thine heart.**

Nevertheless thou shalt not build the house; but thy son that shall come forth out of thy loins, he shall build the house unto my name.

And the Lord hath performed his word that he spake, and I am risen up in the room of David my father, and sit on the throne of Israel, as the Lord promised, and have built an house for the name of the Lord God of Israel [1 Kings 8:17–20].

The desire for a permanent structure to house the ark of God originated in the heart of David, as we have seen in 2 Samuel 7. Solomon merely executed David's plans. I think it should be called David's temple rather than Solomon's temple.

In Solomon's prayer of dedication he says that this temple is to be a place for the name of God, and a place where God's people are to approach Him. It is not a pagan temple in which there is an idol—nor in which God lives. Solomon understands that the temple is, as David had said, the footstool of God.

But will God indeed dwell on the earth? behold, the heaven and heaven of heavens cannot contain thee; how much less this house that I have builded? [1 Kings 8:27].

It was merely a place for man to come and bow before Him and offer his sacrifices before Him. It served as an approach to God. It is a pagan notion to think that God can dwell in a house down here. Solomon said, "The heaven and heaven of heavens cannot contain thee." God is omnipresent—He is everywhere. He is also transcendent, above His creation.

Now here is a section that is quite interesting. It looks forward to the day when Israel would sin against God and be sent into captivity.

If they sin against thee, (for there is no man that sinneth not,) and thou be angry with them, and deliver them to

the enemy, so that they carry them away captives unto
the land of the enemy, far or near [1 Kings 8:46].

This, by the way, is God's estimate of you and me—"there is no man
that sinneth not." Don't tell me that you don't sin. God says you do.

Yet if they shall bethink themselves in the land whither
they were carried captives, and repent, and make supplication unto thee in the land of them that carried them
captives, saying, We have sinned, and have done per-
versely, we have committed wickedness.

And so return unto thee with all their heart, and with
all their soul, in the land of their enemies, which led
them away captive, and pray unto thee toward their
land, which thou gavest unto their fathers, the city
which thou hast chosen, and the house which I have
built for thy name [1 Kings 8:47-48].

This is what they are to do when their temple is destroyed and they are
captives in a strange land. This is exactly what Daniel will do over in
Babylon. He will open his window toward Jerusalem and pray toward
that temple, confessing the sins of his people and his own sins.

Then hear thou their prayer and their supplication in
heaven thy dwelling place, and maintain their cause.

And forgive thy people that have sinned against thee,
and all their transgressions wherein they have transgressed against thee, and give them compassion before
them who carried them captive, that they may have
compassion on them [1 Kings 8:49-50].

As we shall see, God will answer this prayer.

And it was so, that when Solomon had made an end of
praying all this prayer and supplication unto the LORD,

he arose from before the altar of the LORD, from kneeling
on his knees with his hands spread up to heaven
[1 Kings 8:54].

There has always been a question about the proper posture of prayer.
Should you stand, kneel, get down on all fours, or prostrate yourself
before the Lord on the ground? Solomon knelt when he prayed. Although no particular posture is essential—you can pray in most any
position—this is where the posture of kneeling is mentioned. I think
it was Victor Hugo who said that the soul is on its knees many times
regardless of the posture of the body. It is the posture of the heart that
is important.

And Solomon offered a sacrifice of peace offerings,
which he offered unto the LORD, two and twenty thousand oxen, and an hundred and twenty thousand sheep.
So the king and all the children of Israel dedicated the
house of the LORD.

The same day did the king hallow the middle of the
court that was before the house of the LORD: for there he
offered burnt offerings, and meat offerings, and the fat
of the peace offerings: because the brasen altar that was
before the LORD was too little to receive the burnt offerings, and meat offerings, and the fat of the peace offerings.

And at that time Solomon held a feast, and all Israel
with him, a great congregation, from the entering in of
Hamath unto the river of Egypt, before the LORD our
God, seven days and seven days, even fourteen days
[1 Kings 8:63–65].

Obviously, the altars in the temple could not accommodate all the animal sacrifices mentioned in this passage. Therefore temporary altars
were erected to handle the large number of animals which were sacrificed at this time. I think that these altars reached all the way up north

to Hamath and all the way south to the river of Egypt. After the animals were offered, they were taken off the altars and divided among the people. It was a time of great celebration and picnicking, you might say.

> **On the eighth day he sent the people away: and they blessed the king, and went unto their tents joyful and glad of heart for all the goodness that the LORD had done for David his servant, and for Israel his people [1 Kings 8:66].**

CHAPTERS 9 AND 10

THEME: *The fame of Solomon; the visit of the queen of Sheba*

God appears to Solomon a second time to encourage him, and He sets up David as a standard of measurement for him. The remainder of these two chapters gives proof of Solomon's greatness and of the prosperity of his reign.

GOD APPEARS TO SOLOMON A SECOND TIME

And it came to pass, when Solomon had finished the building of the house of the LORD, and the king's house, and all Solomon's desire which he was pleased to do,

That the LORD appeared to Solomon the second time, as he had appeared unto him at Gibeon.

And the LORD said unto him, I have heard thy prayer and thy supplication, that thou hast made before me: I have hallowed this house, which thou hast built, to put my name there for ever; and mine eyes and mine heart shall be there perpetually [1 Kings 9:1-3].

God is saying to Solomon, "I will meet with you here at the temple. This is the place for you to come, for the people to come, and for the world to come. This is the meeting place."

And if thou wilt walk before me, as David thy father walked, in integrity of heart, and in uprightness, to do according to all that I have commanded thee, and wilt keep my statutes and my judgments [1 Kings 9:4].

Now God charges Solomon, "And if thou wilt walk before me, as David thy father walked . . . then I will establish the throne of thy kingdom upon Israel for ever." David is a human standard, not a high standard according to God's standards. David had a tremendous capacity for God. He loved God but he failed, fumbled, faltered, and fell. But he got up and came to God in confession. He wanted to have fellowship with God. God told Solomon that He wanted him to walk before Him as David his father had done—in integrity of heart.

Integrity of heart is important for us today because there is so much subterfuge and hypocrisy in Christian circles. I spoke at a church banquet some time ago where there were over one thousand people present. One of the politicians of that area got up and said a few words. You would have thought he was the most pious fellow in that crowd. But he managed to leave before the message. Do you know why? He did not want to hear it. He was not interested in God's Word. There is so much of that kind of hypocrisy today. One sees dishonesty and hypocrisy revealed on Sunday morning. Here comes a man out of the business world. He has been careless in his life; he has not been a good example in his home. Yet he walks into church with a Bible under his arm and talks about God and God's will, using all sorts of pious expressions. Whom is he attempting to fool? Does he think he is fooling God?

My friend, we don't fool God. We might as well tell Him the facts because He already knows them. David walked before God in integrity of heart. When he sinned, he confessed it and asked for cleansing. Although his faith failed for a moment, beneath the faith that failed was a faith that never failed. Imperfect though he was, God set him up as a standard: "walk before me, as David thy father walked."

> Then I will establish the throne of thy kingdom upon Israel for ever, as I promised to David thy father, saying, There shall not fail thee a man upon the throne of Israel [1 Kings 9:5].

As long as Israel had a king, he was in the line of David. And there is One today in David's line whose nail-pierced hands hold the scepter of this universe.

> But if ye shall at all turn from following me, ye or your children, and will not keep my commandments and my statutes which I have set before you, but go and serve other gods, and worship them:
>
> Then will I cut off Israel out of the land which I have given them; and this house, which I have hallowed for my name, will I cast out of my sight; and Israel shall be a proverb and a byword among all people [1 Kings 9:6-7].

The Jews are certainly a proverb and a byword today. This has come to pass literally.

> And at this house, which is high, every one that passeth by it shall be astonished, and shall hiss; and they shall say, Why hath the LORD done thus unto this land, and to this house?
>
> And they shall answer, Because they forsook the LORD their God, who brought forth their fathers out of the land of Egypt, and have taken hold upon other gods, and have worshipped them, and served them: therefore hath the LORD brought upon them all this evil [1 Kings 9:8-9].

This also has come to pass literally. If you go to the spot where the temple once stood, you will see that it has been destroyed. The Mosque of Omar now stands there. Why is the land of Israel like it is? Why is the Mosque of Omar there? Israel forsook God, friend. That is the answer.

SOLOMON'S FAME

Next we are told that Solomon and Hiram had a little difficulty.

> And it came to pass at the end of twenty years, when
> Solomon had built the two houses, the house of the LORD,
> and the king's house,
>
> (Now Hiram the king of Tyre had furnished Solomon
> with cedar trees and fir trees, and with gold, according
> to all his desire,) that then king Solomon gave Hiram
> twenty cities in the land of Galilee.
>
> And Hiram came out from Tyre to see the cities which
> Solomon had given him; and they pleased him not
> [1 Kings 9:10–12].

When Hiram saw the twenty cities, he felt that he had not been given
full payment for all that he had done for Solomon in the building of
the temple. Actually there was a misunderstanding, and this is the
thing that caused a breach between these two men.

> And he said, What cities are these which thou hast
> given me, my brother? And he called them the land of
> Cabul unto this day.
>
> And Hiram sent to the king sixscore talents of gold
> [1 Kings 9:13–14].

This last sentence should read "Hiram *had* sent . . ."—explaining that
the cities were in payment for the gold he had furnished (the timber,
stone, and labor had been paid for in corn, wine, and oil).

> And this is the reason of the levy which king Solomon
> raised; for to build the house of the LORD, and his own
> house, and Millo, and the wall of Jerusalem, and Hazor,
> and Megiddo, and Gezer.
>
> And Solomon built Gezer, and Beth-horon the nether,
>
> And Baalath, and Tadmor in the wilderness, in the
> land,

> And all the cities of store that Solomon had, and cities
> for his chariots, and cities for his horsemen, and that
> which Solomon desired to build in Jerusalem, and in
> Lebanon, and in all the land of his dominion [1 Kings
> 9:15, 17–19].

This passage describes the extension of Solomon's kingdom and his tremendous building program.

> And king Solomon made a navy of ships in Ezion-geber,
> which is beside Eloth, on the shore of the Red sea, in the
> land of Edom.
>
> And Hiram sent in the navy his servants, shipmen that
> had knowledge of the sea, with the servants of Solomon.
>
> And they came to Ophir, and fetched from thence gold,
> four hundred and twenty talents, and brought it to king
> Solomon [1 Kings 9:26–28].

Solomon just about cornered the gold market in that day. He also had quite a navy. Ezion-geber was situated on the eastern arm of the Red Sea. This was Solomon's seaport. It was situated near Israeli Eilat. It is thought that his navy extended its navigation as far away as Ophir in southwestern Arabia.

SOLOMON IS VISITED BY THE QUEEN OF SHEBA

The visit of the queen of Sheba reveals that Solomon had succeeded in witnessing for God to the world of that day. Solomon's fame had spread, and obviously multitudes were coming to Jerusalem to worship the living and true God. In the present dispensation, the church is to go to the world, but the commission to go into all the world was not given to the nation Israel. As Israel was true to God, she was a witness to the world, and the world came to Jerusalem to worship.

In chapter 10 we have a great illustration of the influence of Solo-

mon in that day. The visit of this queen shows the effect of the reign of
Solomon, as God's representative, upon the nations of the world.

> **And when the queen of Sheba heard of the fame of Solo-
> mon concerning the name of the LORD, she came to prove
> him with hard questions [1 Kings 10:1].**

The queen of Sheba came to Solomon because of what she had heard.
She had heard of a temple where man could approach God—she
wanted to know about that. She had heard of Solomon's wisdom; so
she came to test him with difficult questions.

> **And she came to Jerusalem with a very great train, with
> camels that bare spices, and very much gold, and pre-
> cious stones: and when she was come to Solomon, she
> communed with him of all that was in her heart.**
>
> **And Solomon told her all her questions: there was not
> any thing hid from the king, which he told her not.**
>
> **And when the queen of Sheba had seen all Solomon's
> wisdom, and the house that he had built,**
>
> **And the meat of his table, and the sitting of his servants,
> and the attendance of his ministers, and their apparel,
> and his cupbearers, and his ascent by which he went up
> unto the house of the LORD; there was no more spirit in
> her [1 Kings 10:2–5].**

Now the phrase, "and his ascent by which he went up unto the house
of the LORD," should be translated, "and his burnt offering by which
he went up unto the house of the LORD." She witnesses that Solomon
approached God by a burnt offering. This is the offering that speaks
more fully of Christ and His substitutionary death than all the others.
Hebrews 9:22 says, "And almost all things are by the law purged with
blood; and without shedding of blood is no remission." The burnt offering was a testimony to the queen of Sheba.

She was also impressed with the wisdom of Solomon and with his building program: the palace, the temple and the other buildings. All around were bounty, luxury, and temporal prosperity. For a brief moment in time, God's people were faithful and true witnesses of Him. And so the queen responds to all that she has seen and heard:

> **And she said to the king, It was a true report that I heard in mine own land of thy acts and of thy wisdom.**

> **Howbeit I believed not the words, until I came, and mine eyes had seen it: and, behold, the half was not told me: thy wisdom and prosperity exceedeth the fame which I heard [1 Kings 10:6–7].**

She had not believed half of what she had been told and came to find that the half had not been told her. And I don't think the half has been told today concerning our Lord.

> **Happy are thy men, happy are these thy servants, which stand continually before thee, and that hear thy wisdom.**

> **Blessed be the LORD thy God, which delighted in thee, to set thee on the throne of Israel: because the LORD loved Israel for ever, therefore made he thee king, to do judgment and justice [1 Kings 10:8–9].**

This now is her testimony, and I think it reveals that she has come to know the living and true God.

> **And she gave the king an hundred and twenty talents of gold, and of spices very great store, and precious stones: there came no more such abundance of spices as these which the queen of Sheba gave to king Solomon [1 Kings 10:10].**

She brought a great amount of wealth and gave it to Solomon.

> And the navy also of Hiram, that brought gold from
> Ophir, brought in from Ophir great plenty of almug
> trees, and precious stones.
>
> And the king made of the almug trees pillars for the
> house of the LORD, and for the king's house, harps also
> and psalteries for singers: there came no such almug
> trees, nor were seen unto this day [1 Kings 10:11–12].

Hiram was king of Tyre—of the Phoenicians who were a seagoing
people. We see here that Solomon continued his building program.
He made pillars for the house of the Lord and for the king's house, also
harps and psalteries for singers.

> And king Solomon gave unto the queen of Sheba all her
> desire, whatsoever she asked, beside that which Solo-
> mon gave her of his royal bounty. So she turned and
> went to her own country, she and her servants [1 Kings
> 10:13].

The story of the queen of Sheba is one example of the many who came
to know God at this time. Similarly, the Book of Acts records only
certain conversations such as those of the Ethiopian eunuch, Saul of
Tarsus and Cornelius. Yet we know that literally thousands came to
know Christ during that period. And there were thousands who came
to know God through the temple in Jerusalem and the witness of the
people of Solomon's day.

Now we are told something of the gold that came to Solomon:

> Now the weight of gold that came to Solomon in one year
> was six hundred threescore and six talents of gold,
>
> Beside that he had of the merchantmen, and of the traf-
> fic of the spice merchants, and of all the kings of Arabia,
> and of the governors of the country.

And king Solomon made two hundred targets of beaten gold: six hundred shekels of gold went to one target [1 Kings 10:14-16].

I cannot comprehend it when it says there were six hundred threescore and six talents of gold that came to him every year—he simply cornered the gold market. The kingdom had reached its zenith. Actually, David brought it to this position, but now Solomon is the one who is able to move in and enjoy the peace, the plenty, and the prosperity.

For the king had at sea a navy of Tharshish with the navy of Hiram: once in three years came the navy of Tharshish, bringing gold, and silver, ivory, and apes, and peacocks [1 Kings 10:22].

All of these are luxury items: apes for entertainment (these were Solomon's zoo); peacocks for beauty; and gold, silver, and ivory for magnificent decorations. There is a frivolous and tragic note here which is symptomatic of the condition of Solomon's kingdom. He is called to give a witness to the world—the world is coming to his door—and what does he do? He spends his time and energy with apes and peacocks simply to satisfy a whim.

So king Solomon exceeded all the kings of the earth for riches and for wisdom.

And all the earth sought to Solomon, to hear his wisdom, which God had put in his heart [1 Kings 10:23-24].

It was during this period that the kingdom reached its zenith and was characterized by very faithful witnessing. We have seen that illustrated in the life of the queen of Sheba, and now we are told that many others came to Jerusalem also. There was a real witness given to the world by Solomon—a witness for God.

> And they brought every man his present, vessels of silver, and vessels of gold, and garments, and armour, and spices, horses, and mules, a rate year by year [1 Kings 10:25].

Frankly, the presents from these visitors enabled Solomon to build up a kingdom that was noted for its riches. Later, of course, that made Israel the subject of spoil by other nations when the kingdom was divided and weakened.

> And Solomon gathered together chariots and horsemen: and he had a thousand and four hundred chariots, and twelve thousand horsemen, whom he bestowed in the cities for chariots, and with the king at Jerusalem [1 Kings 10:26].

Solomon, as he gathered horses and horsemen, expanded in a department in which God had forbidden him to expand. Solomon's stables would make these modern race tracks look like a tenant farmer's barn in Georgia.

> And the king made silver to be in Jerusalem as stones, and cedars made he to be as the sycomore trees that are in the vale, for abundance.
>
> And Solomon had horses brought out of Egypt, and linen yarn: the king's merchants received the linen yarn at a price.
>
> And a chariot came up and went out of Egypt for six hundred shekels of silver, and an horse for an hundred and fifty: and so for all the kings of the Hittites, and for the kings of Syria, did they bring them out by their means [1 Kings 10:27–29].

Solomon really built up tremendous wealth in the kingdom. At that time he actually cornered the market on gold, silver, and precious stones.

My friend, what are you busy doing today? Are you getting out the Word of God or are you in the business of gathering a bunch of apes? Do you pay more for entertainment than you do for the Word of God? How about the peacocks for beauty? More money is spent today on beauty preparations than is given to the Lord's work. What about gold, silver, and precious stones? Are you so busy making money that you have no time left for the Lord? Oh, my friend, we are called to witness to the world. God have mercy on us for going into the business of apes and peacocks. How frivolous!

CHAPTER 11

THEME: The shame and death of Solomon

Solomon is the most colossal failure in the pages of Scripture. ". . . For unto whomsoever much is given, of him shall be much required . . ." (Luke 12:48). He had the greatest opportunity of any man who ever lived. He began by failing to remove false religion (1 Kings 3:3). What was at first only a spot became a plague of leprosy. He had a harem of one thousand wives, pagan women, who turned his heart away from the Lord. For this reason God stirred up enemies against Solomon and allowed Jeroboam to rise to prominence and finally split the kingdom.

SOLOMON FORSAKES GOD

But king Solomon loved many strange women, together with the daughter of Pharaoh, women of the Moabites, Ammonites, Edomites, Zidonians, and Hittites [1 Kings 11:1].

As far as women were concerned, Solomon was patterning his life after his father David. It is too bad he did not pattern his life after other areas of David's life, but he did not. Remember that Solomon had been brought up in the king's palace. He was sort of an effeminate fellow, unaccustomed to the rough and rugged life that David had known. Solomon began to gather women, just as someone else might have a hobby of gathering antique automobiles. He collected women of all nationalities.

Now these women turned the head of Solomon, causing him to go into idolatry and to permit it in the land. He violated God's prescribed law at this particular point.

Of the nations concerning which the LORD said unto the children of Israel, Ye shall not go in to them, neither shall they come in unto you: for surely they will turn away your heart after their gods: Solomon clave unto these in love [1 Kings 11:2].

I think this is the one place in Scripture where the word *love* can be changed to *sex*. That was Solomon's motive. He had been raised in the women's palace and had never known anything rough or manly. When he became an adult, Solomon spent his time gathering women. He was accustomed to their company. He was a dandy. He was like many men we have in our society today. God is going to deal with him in this connection. The Lord did not approve of what Solomon did, for the Scripture says:

And the LORD was angry with Solomon, because his heart was turned from the LORD God of Israel, which had appeared unto him twice,

And had commanded him concerning this thing, that he should not go after other gods: but he kept not that which the LORD commanded.

Wherefore the LORD said unto Solomon, Forasmuch as this is done of thee, and thou hast not kept my covenant and my statutes, which I have commanded thee, I will surely rend the kingdom from thee, and will give it to thy servant.

Notwithstanding in thy days I will not do it for David thy father's sake: but I will rend it out of the hand of thy son.

Howbeit I will not rend away all the kingdom; but will give one tribe to thy son for David my servant's sake, and for Jerusalem's sake which I have chosen [1 Kings 11:9–13].

"The LORD was angry with Solomon." Let's be fair with the Word of God. There are those who say, "Oh, look, God permitted Solomon to have a thousand wives." The record gives us the number accurately; that is history. But God's attitude toward it is also revealed: "the LORD was angry with Solomon."

The Lord said that he would not rend away all of the kingdom from Solomon. One tribe would be left for Solomon's son. That one tribe, I would say, was Benjamin. Solomon was a member of the tribe of Judah; naturally that tribe would also stand with him. So Benjamin and Judah were in the division that will go with the family of David. The other ten tribes in the north will follow Jeroboam.

SOLOMON IS CHASTENED

Now we come to the time at the end of Solomon's reign. God begins to stir up trouble for this man. "There is no peace, saith my God, to the wicked" (Isa. 57:21). Solomon had enjoyed peace. Now for the first time during his reign there was to be warfare.

And the LORD stirred up an adversary unto Solomon, Hadad the Edomite: he was of the king's seed in Edom [1 Kings 11:14].

Next we are introduced to Jeroboam.

And Jeroboam the son of Nebat, an Ephrathite of Zereda, Solomon's servant, whose mother's name was Zeruah, a widow woman, even he lifted up his hand against the king.

And this was the cause that he lifted up his hand against the king: Solomon built Millo, and repaired the breaches of the city of David his father.

And the man Jeroboam was a mighty man of valour: and Solomon seeing the young man that he was indus-

trious, he made him ruler over all the charge of the
house of Joseph [1 Kings 11:26-28].

Although Jeroboam was the son of a servant, Solomon recognized that
he was a young man of considerable ability and talent. Solomon,
therefore, elevated him to a high position and made him overseer of
his public works.

And it came to pass at that time when Jeroboam went out
of Jerusalem, that the prophet Ahijah the Shilonite
found him in the way; and he had clad himself with a
new garment; and they two were alone in the field:

And Ahijah caught the new garment that was on him,
and rent it in twelve pieces:

And he said to Jeroboam, Take thee ten pieces: for thus
saith the LORD, the God of Israel, Behold, I will rend the
kingdom out of the hand of Solomon, and will give ten
tribes to thee:

(But he shall have one tribe for my servant David's sake,
and for Jerusalem's sake, the city which I have chosen
out of all the tribes of Israel:) [1 Kings 11:29-32].

Ahijah the prophet took Jeroboam's new garment and tore it into
twelve pieces. He gave ten pieces to Jeroboam and said to him, "God
is going to give you ten tribes. The kingdom is going to be divided."
Why would God divide Israel into two kingdoms?

Because that they have forsaken me, and have worshipped Ashtoreth the goddess of the Zidonians, Chemosh the god of the Moabites, and Milcom the god of the
children of Ammon, and have not walked in my ways, to
do that which is right in mine eyes, and to keep my statutes and my judgments, as did David his father [1 Kings
11:33].

The prophet continues with his message. For David's sake, God will not take the kingdom out of the hand of Solomon, but He will take it out of the hand of Solomon's son and give ten tribes to Jeroboam.

After these things, Jeroboam is forced to flee for his life.

Solomon sought therefore to kill Jeroboam. And Jeroboam arose, and fled into Egypt, unto Shishak king of Egypt, and was in Egypt until the death of Solomon [1 Kings 11:40].

SOLOMON'S DEATH

And the rest of the acts of Solomon, and all that he did, and his wisdom, are they not written in the book of the acts of Solomon?

And the time that Solomon reigned in Jerusalem over all Israel was forty years.

And Solomon slept with his fathers, and was buried in the city of David his father: and Rehoboam his son reigned in his stead [1 Kings 11:41–43].

We will see more of the acts of Solomon and his wisdom in 1 and 2 Chronicles. He was a colorful ruler in the sense that he accumulated so much of this world's goods. Everything in the kingdom denoted wealth, affluence, and prosperity. In the New Testament our Lord refers to the glory that was Solomon's. There was indeed an earthly glory in his kingdom.

CHAPTERS 12—14

THEME: Division of the kingdom under Rehoboam and Jeroboam

In chapter 12 Rehoboam, son of Solomon, succeeds to the throne. Jeroboam returns from Egypt and leads ten tribes in demanding a reduction in taxes. Rehoboam, under the influence of the young men of his kingdom, having rejected the counsel of the old men who were Solomon's advisors, turns down the request of the ten northern tribes. Instead of reducing taxes, he threatens to raise them. Therefore, Jeroboam leads the ten tribes in revolt.

Jeroboam divides the nation religiously as well as politically by setting up a golden calf in Bethel and one in the tribe of Dan. The northern tribes go into idolatry.

REHOBOAM'S ACCESSION AND FOOLISHNESS

Solomon dies, and his son Rehoboam comes to the throne.

And Rehoboam went to Shechem: for all Israel were come to Shechem to make him king.

And it came to pass, when Jeroboam the son of Nebat, who was yet in Egypt, heard of it, (for he was fled from the presence of king Solomon, and Jeroboam dwelt in Egypt:)

That they sent and called him. And Jeroboam and all the congregation of Israel came, and spake unto Rehoboam, saying,

Thy father made our yoke grievous: now therefore make thou the grievous service of thy father, and his heavy yoke which he put upon us, lighter, and we will serve thee.

And he said unto them, Depart yet for three days, then come again to me. And the people departed [1 Kings 12:1-5].

Solomon had carried on a tremendous building program at great cost. After his death the people asked for their taxes to be lowered. We hear about the government costing so much today. If you want to know *why* it costs so much, go to the capital of any state, or go to any county seat or to our capital in Washington, D.C., and you will see why taxes are like they are. Believe me, government is a fat calf. It is really spending money and putting up many buildings. Spending requires increased taxation; this is something that is always going to cause trouble. Our problem today is one of taxation—our government costs too much. We are seeing the increase in buildings to house more committees and more workers. Before long there will probably be more people working for the government than are working in all other jobs put together. This is the movement today; there was the same problem during the days of Solomon. He kept building and in order to do it, he had to increase the taxes.

Rehoboam was asked by the people to reduce taxes. This young ruler had an opportunity to move in and make himself popular by reducing taxes. If he had done that, the people would have followed him. Where is the man today who has the nerve, after being elected to office, to fire about half of the government workers? If someone would do that and cut down taxes, he would make himself popular. Leaders are afraid to take the first step.

Rehoboam called a meeting of his wise men (only they were very unwise).

And king Rehoboam consulted with the old men, that stood before Solomon his father while he yet lived, and said, How do ye advise that I may answer this people?

And they spake unto him, saying, If thou wilt be a servant unto this people this day, and wilt serve them, and answer them, and speak good words to them, then they will be thy servants for ever [1 Kings 12:6-7].

Rehoboam first turned to the wise men in the kingdom who had coun-
seled Solomon his father. Their advice was good, but Rehoboam did
not follow it.

> But he forsook the counsel of the old men, which they
> had given him, and consulted with the young men that
> were grown up with him, and which stood before him:
>
> And he said unto them, What counsel give ye that we
> may answer this people, who have spoken to me, say-
> ing, Make the yoke which thy father did put upon us
> lighter?
>
> And the young men that were grown up with him spake
> unto him, saying, Thus shalt thou speak unto this peo-
> ple that spake unto thee, saying, Thy father made our
> yoke heavy, but make thou it lighter unto us; thus shalt
> thou say unto them, My little finger shall be thicker than
> my father's loins.
>
> And now whereas my father did lade you with a heavy
> yoke, I will add to your yoke: my father hath chastised
> you with whips, but I will chastise you with scorpions
> [1 Kings 12:8–11].

Then he asked the young men who had grown up with him what they
would advise. They too gave him advice, but it was foolish.

> So Jeroboam and all the people came to Rehoboam the
> third day, as the king had appointed, saying, Come to
> me again the third day.
>
> And the king answered the people roughly, and forsook
> the old men's counsel that they gave him;
>
> And spake to them after the counsel of the young men,
> saying, My father made your yoke heavy, and I will add
> to your yoke: my father also chastised you with whips,
> but I will chastise you with scorpions.

> Wherefore the king hearkened not unto the people; for
> the cause was from the LORD, that he might perform his
> saying, which the LORD spake by Ahijah the Shilonite
> unto Jeroboam the son of Nebat [1 Kings 12:12-15].

Rehoboam heeded what the young men told him rather than what the wise older men said. He told the people, "Instead of decreasing the taxes, I intend to increase them. Instead of being less severe with the people, I intend to be more severe."

JEROBOAM BECOMES ISRAEL'S KING
AND THE KINGDOM IS DIVIDED

> So when all Israel saw that the king hearkened not unto
> them, the people answered the king, saying, What por-
> tion have we in David? neither have we inheritance in
> the son of Jesse: to your tents, O Israel: now see to thine
> own house, David. So Israel departed unto their tents
> [1 Kings 12:16].

This is rebellion. This is the splitting up of the kingdom, and it will result, of course, in civil war.

> Then king Rehoboam sent Adoram, who was over the
> tribute; and all Israel stoned him with stones, that he
> died. Therefore king Rehoboam made speed to get him
> up to his chariot, to flee to Jerusalem [1 Kings 12:18].

All Israel stoned Adoram. That is the way they got rid of the tax collector. And when Rehoboam heard what had happened, he fled to Jerusalem.

> So Israel rebelled against the house of David unto this
> day [1 Kings 12:19].

Israel rebelled against the house of David until the time 1 Kings was written. It was a rebellion that continued on until they returned from the Babylonian captivity. Rehoboam's unwise decision in not listening to the people enabled Jeroboam to take the ten northern tribes and build a northern kingdom.

JEROBOAM'S IDOLATRY

Then Jeroboam built Shechem in mount Ephraim, and dwelt therein; and went out from thence, and built Penuel.

And Jeroboam said in his heart, Now shall the kingdom return to the house of David:

If this people go up to do sacrifice in the house of the LORD at Jerusalem, then shall the heart of this people turn again unto their lord, even unto Rehoboam king of Judah, and they shall kill me, and go again to Rehoboam king of Judah.

Whereupon the king took counsel, and made two calves of gold, and said unto them, It is too much for you to go up to Jerusalem: behold thy gods, O Israel, which brought thee up out of the land of Egypt.

And he set the one in Beth-el, and the other put he in Dan.

And this thing became a sin: for the people went to worship before the one, even unto Dan [1 Kings 12:25–30].

Jeroboam put a golden calf in Bethel and one in Dan. He put them there for the people to worship so that they would not go to Jerusalem to worship in the temple. This marks the division of the kingdom into the northern and southern kingdoms.

We will now follow the account of the divided kingdom and will find that the method used in 1 and 2 Kings is to record some history about Israel and then some history about Judah. The record goes back and forth. We will be looking at both kingdoms as we go along, but the kingdom of Judah will last longer than the kingdom of Israel. Also, almost all of the prophets, except the postcaptivity prophets, prophesied during this period (see Chronological Table of the Kings of the Divided Kingdom, p. 227). The Table shows which kings of Judah and Israel were contemporary—that is, those who ruled at the same time—and which prophets prophesied during each reign.

This brings us to the end of 1 Kings 12. Rehoboam is the king of the southern kingdom following in the Davidic line. Jeroboam is the king of the northern kingdom. He has introduced idolatry into the north by building two golden calves and placing them in Bethel and Dan so that the people would no longer go to Jerusalem to worship. There is a division—soon civil war will break out. It will continue until the northern kingdom goes into captivity. And we will find that eventually the southern kingdom will also go into captivity. This is a sad period in the life of the nation of Israel. It contains many lessons for us and for our government.

In chapter 13 we see God's judgment against the false altar of Jeroboam and the strange incident of the man of God who was deceived by a fellow prophet.

The kingdom has now been divided following the rebellion led by Jeroboam who took the ten northern tribes and formed the kingdom of Israel. Rehoboam, a man who certainly did not have the wisdom nor the diplomacy of his father Solomon, was actually responsible for the splitting of the kingdom. The northern kingdom will eventually go into captivity in Assyria and the southern kingdom into Babylon.

There can be a great deal of confusion as we go through this section and read of king after king. You may wonder whether this king belongs to the northern kingdom or the southern kingdom, and whether he is good or bad. The chronological chart of the kings will give you that information. (See page 227.)

When I was a freshman in college, I took a Bible course that was puerile—it was a weak cup of tea. There were certain questions that were always asked in the class. One of the questions was, "Name the kings of Israel and Judah and briefly describe the reign of each." Well, some freshman in years gone by had made a profound discovery. He found out that if he memorized the names of the kings and wrote after each one—"a bad King"—he could make 95% on the test. What freshman would want to make a better mark than that? So that is what all the freshmen did.

You are going to find that in the northern kingdom every king was bad. There wasn't a good one in the lot. There were only eight kings in the southern kingdom—over a two-hundred-year period—who could be called good. The rest of them were bad kings. This is a dark blot in the history of Israel. Yet, I think you would find a similar record in other lands. If you want to bring all of this down to today, how many good presidents have we had? Party allegiances aside, I believe that history will have to record that we did not do so well either. We have probably had a better percentage of good leaders than Israel, but our batting average hasn't been very good.

The thing that makes Israel's record so bleak is that these people had light from heaven. They had a revelation from God, and their responsibility was greater. But I also feel that the responsibility of our nation is greater than that of other nations because we have, in certain respects, more light from heaven than other nations. Unfortunately our political affairs are a black spot in the life of our nation.

I would like to look back to Solomon for a moment to see why the kingdom was rent. Here is what happened. Solomon was given a special dispensation of wisdom from God to administer the kingdom. Yet that wisdom, apparently, did not enter into his own personal life: Solomon obviously did not have spiritual wisdom or discernment. He did understand certain basic principles and concepts which enabled him to be a very wise ruler, but which did not enter into his personal, private, and certainly not his spiritual life. You begin to see early in his career that he never really broke with false religion. At the beginning, when he came to the throne, there was idolatry, and he closed his eyes to it—he took no particular, definite, positive stand against it. Then he began to engage in that which was the mark of prosperity. He sent ships out to bring back apes and peacocks. There's nothing particularly wrong with apes and peacocks, but such an obsession is wrong if you have been called to glorify God—to witness and live for Him. Solomon had a definite weakness.

The Book of Proverbs reveals the wisdom of Solomon, but the Book of Ecclesiastes reveals his foolishness. You will not find any failure of Solomon's or his father David's in the Book of Chronicles. The two Books of Chronicles cover the same ground as the Books of Kings with one difference: in Kings you have man's viewpoint; you have the history given. Chronicles gives God's viewpoint. God forgave David; and, when God forgave him, He blotted out his sin. Written from God's viewpoint, the sin is not mentioned in Chronicles, but God put it in Kings for men to see. Likewise God forgave Solomon his failure, and his sin is not recorded in Chronicles. In Kings we do see Solomon's weakness—he began to multiply wives. God never approved of polygamy; His wrath was against it.

The interesting thing is that immorality and false religion always go together. John made it very clear for the Christian when he said, "If we say that we have fellowship with him, and walk in darkness, we lie, and do not the truth" (1 John 1:6). Don't kid yourself—you cannot serve God and have fellowship with Him if you live in sin. You can fool the people around you. Unfortunately, we have Christian leaders today who live in sin. They have been proven immoral, and yet people go ahead and support them—I have never quite understood why. But they are not fooling God, and they certainly are not having fellowship with Him.

Solomon was a man who was a great failure. There are two men in the Scripture who had tremendous potential and opportunity: one was Samson, and the other one was Solomon. Both of these men failed God in a tragic way. In Ecclesiastes Solomon said, "Therefore I hated life; because the work that is wrought under the sun is grievous unto me: for all is vanity and vexation of spirit" (Eccl. 2:17). The glory of Solomon was a passing glory. Our Lord could say that Solomon in all his glory is not arrayed like that little flower by the side of the road that you passed unnoticed. May I say to you that the wealth and achievements of this world are also a passing glory.

I have given this background of Solomon at this point—I guess I have more or less preached his funeral service—because now we are seeing a kingdom divided, and it is divided because of the sin of Solomon.

THE PROPHECY AGAINST
JEROBOAM'S FALSE ALTAR

We are going to move rather rapidly through this section—it is history. We will be following the course of the two kingdoms, one following after the other or sometimes together or overlapping.

We find that Jeroboam, who came to the throne in the northern kingdom, was given an opportunity to really serve God. Yet his fear was that the tribes in the north would go back to Jerusalem to worship. That might reunite the kingdom, and he wanted to keep it separate. So Jeroboam set up two golden calves for the people to worship, one in Samaria and one in Bethel.

> **And, behold, there came a man of God out of Judah by the word of the LORD unto Beth-el: and Jeroboam stood by the altar to burn incense.**

> **And he cried against the altar in the word of the LORD, and said, O altar, altar, thus saith the LORD; Behold, a child shall be born unto the house of David, Josiah by name; and upon thee shall he offer the priests of the high places that burn incense upon thee, and men's bones shall be burnt upon thee [1 Kings 13:1–2].**

Let me pause here a moment. It is interesting to note when Josiah reigned. It was almost three hundred years later, but the prophet of God marks him out now. He was a good king and he reigned thirty-one years. Josiah led in one of the five great revivals that took place during the period of the kings. We will consider those revivals in Chronicles. These revivals are not mentioned in Kings but in Chronicles, which gives God's viewpoint. Revival is always from God's viewpoint. Man is interested in numbers, but it is impossible for him to determine the real converts. God knows the hearts and knows whether a spiritual movement has taken place or not.

The prophet of God prophesied against the altar, saying that God was going to raise up a man who would destroy such altars. Josiah was the one who would be raised up to accomplish that task.

> **And he gave a sign the same day, saying, This is the sign which the LORD hath spoken; Behold, the altar shall be rent, and the ashes that are upon it shall be poured out.**

> **And it came to pass, when king Jeroboam heard the saying of the man of God, which had cried against the altar in Beth-el, that he put forth his hand from the altar, saying, Lay hold on him. And his hand, which he put forth against him, dried up, so that he could not pull it in again to him [1 Kings 13:3–4].**

Jeroboam was by the altar when the man of God prophesied. He was making a sacrifice to a golden calf. When the man of God was finished speaking, Jeroboam put out his hand against him. In effect, the king was saying, "Lay hold on him. He is to be slain." When the king pointed to the man of God, his hand dried up; that is, it withered and became paralyzed.

> **The altar also was rent, and the ashes poured out from the altar, according to the sign which the man of God had given by the word of the LORD.**

> **And the king answered and said unto the man of God, Entreat now the face of the LORD thy God, and pray for me, that my hand may be restored me again. And the man of God besought the LORD, and the king's hand was restored him again, and became as it was before.**

> **And the king said unto the man of God, Come home with me, and refresh thyself, and I will give thee a reward [1 Kings 13:5–7].**

The king changes his tune very definitely and begs the man of God to ask the Lord that his arm might be restored. The king's hand is restored to him, and in appreciation he offers to take the man of God home with him and reward him.

> **And the man of God said unto the king, If thou wilt give me half thine house, I will not go in with thee, neither will I eat bread nor drink water in this place:**
>
> **For so it was charged me by the word of the LORD, saying, Eat no bread, nor drink water, nor turn again by the same way that thou camest.**
>
> **So he went another way, and returned not by the way that he came to Beth-el [1 Kings 13:8–10].**

The man of God will not compromise with evil and idolatry. This is quite remarkable.

This is the place to say that there is a lot of double-talk and subterfuge in supposedly fundamentalist Christian circles. I have recently read a statement issued by a certain seminary that claims to be fundamental, and is trying to build a reputation as a conservative school. I have never before read such double-talk in any statement. It claims a super piety and a super intellectualism that is nothing in the world but a denial of the things of God. There is such compromise today in Christian circles! I don't mean that we are to become ugly and cantankerous, or to not speak to certain individuals or have fellowship with them. That is not the point. But what we do need is to have a clear-cut, honest statement of where we stand theologically.

My Christian friend, many believers are supporting organizations that they are not sure are sound. If you don't know whether or not a ministry is giving out the Word of God, you ought to check into it. It is important, and God will hold you responsible for how you invest your money. These are evil days in which we live. They were evil days during the time of Jeroboam, and this prophet was not about to stay and have lunch with the king. He refused to become involved with him.

However, in the next several verses we find that he was deceived by another prophet into disobeying the Lord and suffered the sad consequences. Although he was wary of association with an idolatrous king, he was deceived by a man who claimed to have counter directions from God. My friend, when the church of God today gets involved in the things of the world and makes all kinds of compromises, it is a stench in the nostrils of Almighty God. We are living in days that are much like Jeroboam's, and we need to exercise the same caution and discernment that was needed then by God's man.

You would think that the experience Jeroboam had with the man of God would have changed him. His hand had been withered and healed. Do you think he changed?

> **After this thing Jeroboam returned not from his evil way, but made again of the lowest of the people priests of the high places: whosoever would, he consecrated him, and he became one of the priests of the high places.**
>
> **And this thing became sin unto the house of Jeroboam, even to cut it off, and to destroy it from the face of the earth [1 Kings 13:33–34].**

Chapter 14 describes the reigns of Jeroboam and Rehoboam and sets the pace for the sordid record of the kings of the divided kingdom. There was not one good king in the northern kingdom of Israel—all nineteen of them were bad kings. In the southern kingdom there were twenty kings, of which twelve of them were bad. Only eight of them could be labeled good kings. And of the eight, only five were outstanding. (See Chronological Table of the Kings of the Divided Kingdom on p. 227.)

The chapter opens with Jeroboam sending his wife to inquire to Ahijah the prophet because their son is very sick. The Lord's reply through Ahijah is that the child will die, and in addition He gives a further prophecy regarding His judgment on Jeroboam's family.

GOD'S JUDGMENT ON JEROBOAM

Go, tell Jeroboam, Thus saith the Lord God of Israel,
Forasmuch as I exalted thee from among the people, and
made thee prince over my people Israel,

And rent the kingdom away from the house of David,
and gave it thee: and yet thou hast not been as my servant David, who kept my commandments, and who followed me with all his heart, to do that only which was
right in mine eyes [1 Kings 14:7–8].

David is the standard, you see, for the kings of both the northern and
southern kingdoms from now on. Jeroboam fell far short of the man
David was, and God will set him aside.

And the rest of the acts of Jeroboam, how he warred,
and how he reigned, behold, they are written in the
book of the chronicles of the kings of Israel.

And the days which Jeroboam reigned were two and
twenty years: and he slept with his fathers, and Nadab
his son reigned in his stead [1 Kings 14:19–20].

JUDAH'S APOSTASY UNDER REHOBOAM

You would think things would be better in the southern kingdom
with Rehoboam, but they weren't.

And it came to pass in the fifth year of king Rehoboam,
that Shishak king of Egypt came up against Jerusalem:

And he took away the treasures of the house of the Lord,
and the treasures of the king's house; he even took away
all: and he took away all the shields of gold which Solomon had made.

> And king Rehoboam made in their stead brasen shields
> and committed them unto the hands of the chief of the
> guard, which kept the door of the king's house [1 Kings
> 14:25-27].

Old Rehoboam is now beginning to go down, but he is keeping up a
front. When the golden shields are taken by the king of Egypt, he sub-
stitutes brass shields.

Next we are told that there was civil war.

> And there was war between Rehoboam and Jeroboam
> all their days [1 Kings 14:30].

Finally, we have the death of Rehoboam.

> And Rehoboam slept with his fathers, and was buried
> with his fathers in the city of David. And his mother's
> name was Naamah an Ammonitess. And Abijam his son
> reigned in his stead [1 Kings 14:31].

CHAPTERS 15 AND 16

THEME: Kings of the divided kingdom

In chapter 15 two of Judah's kings are mentioned: Abijam, a sinful king, and Asa, a good king. Also the reigns of two of Israel's kings are given to us: Nadab, the son of Jeroboam, who walked in the sins of his father, and Baasha, who murdered him and reigned in his stead.

Chapter 16 continues with the history of Baasha, then four other kings of Israel—each more wicked than his successor: Elah, Zimri, Omri, and Ahab who compounded his wickedness by marrying the infamous Jezebel.

REHOBOAM IS SUCCEEDED BY ABIJAM

I feel that we need a double portion of the Spirit of God as we go through this section. In the last part of chapter 14 we were told that Rehoboam, a son of Solomon, reigned over the southern kingdom of Judah and Benjamin. Jeroboam reigned over Israel in the north. He is the one who led a rebellion of the ten northern tribes. Civil war continued between the two kingdoms. It was a bitter war with brother fighting brother—there is nothing quite as bad as that.

We have also noted that so far none of the kings have been good. In fact, there is never a good king in Israel, and only eight good kings in the southern kingdom of Judah in the line of David.

We find that after the death of Rehoboam, his son Abijam (also called Abijah) comes to the throne:

> **Now in the eighteenth year of king Jeroboam the son of Nebat reigned Abijam over Judah.**
>
> **Three years reigned he in Jerusalem. And his mother's name was Maachah, the daughter of Abishalom [1 Kings 15:1–2].**

There is something quite interesting that you will find all through this section: every time a king is mentioned his mother is also mentioned. That is unusual. We are generally told who a man's father was and whom he succeeded, but in this portion the mother's name is given again and again. Why? It is because each mother had a great deal to do with influencing the life of her son. My position here is that the reason God recorded the name of the mother along with each king's name (and these are bad kings) is because she is partially responsible for the way he turned out. Also when the king was a good king, the mother was partially responsible. She must accept responsibility for him.

You and I are living in a time when a lot of condemnation and judgment are brought against young people who become vagrants and are dissolute. I recognize that trouble can arise out of a Christian home, but generally the background of a young person has something to do with the way he or she turns out. Ordinarily these troubled young people have a mother who is partially responsible for the way they act and live—you cannot escape it, friend. Now I know that this cuts very deep and very hard, but we need to recognize that a mother has had a great opportunity to influence her little one, and if a little one has grown up to feel neglected, unwanted, and unloved, maybe the mother ought to stop and think. Instead of trying to be president of the missionary society, sing in the choir, and do everything else in the church, a mother would be doing more for the Lord if she would stay home some evening, take the little one up in her arms and love him and let him know how much she really appreciates him. This is something that is being neglected in our day. The biggest problem that most young couples have today is finding a baby sitter. May I say to you that we need a few more "mother sitters" who take time to train little Willie and little Susie. My friend, it takes a lot of time and love to rear a child—this is something that is very important.

I have taken some extra time on this subject because, candidly, it will occur again and again. Every time we have a bad king, his mamma's name is given—I think God is trying to tell us something. If he was a good king, his mother's name is also given; she will get credit for that. I just would not want to be the mother of some of the rascals we are going to find here in Scripture. It would disturb me a great deal to have a son like most of these kings.

> **And he walked in all the sins of his father, which he had done before him: and his heart was not perfect with the LORD his God, as the heart of David his father [1 Kings 15:3].**

Abijam walked in all the sins of his father—he followed his father's pattern. Papa was to blame, also, for the way his son turned out; papa set the example. Abijam was not brought up in a very good home. He was a rotten, corrupt king, and his father and mother are responsible to a certain degree. We are told also that "his heart was not perfect with the LORD his God, as the heart of David his father." David had become the standard for these kings. It is true that David was a human standard, but it was a standard that God accepted.

> **Nevertheless for David's sake did the LORD his God give him a lamp in Jerusalem, to set up his son after him, and to establish Jerusalem [1 Kings 15:4].**

The line of David, friend, never ends until you come to the Lord Jesus Christ. It ended there—you cannot follow the line of David after Christ. God says, "I won't let the lamp go out until the fulfillment of the covenant I made with David." There will come One to sit on his throne who will rule the world—that One is the Lord Jesus Christ.

> **Because David did that which was right in the eyes of the LORD, and turned not aside from any thing that he commanded him all the days of his life, save only in the matter of Uriah the Hittite [1 Kings 15:5].**

Why did God accept David as the standard? Because of his sin? No! That was a black spot on David's record. Although little man is in no position to sit in judgment upon God, we do it nonetheless. But if you are going to judge God about His relationship with David, understand what God really said about David. God listed David's assets and liabilities in this verse: David did not turn aside from anything that He commanded except in the matter of Uriah the Hittite. That was the black spot on David's record. In every other matter he obeyed God. David did not live in sin. The king of Babylon did. What David did one time, the king of Babylon did every day. It was the weekend practice of the king of Egypt to do the thing David did one time. The whole thought is expressed by our Lord in the parable of the prodigal son. Friend, the son can get in the pigpen—we need to recognize that. God's child can get in the pigpen, but by the same token the child of God will not stay in the pigpen. Why won't he? The reason is obvious: he is a son of the father; he is not a pig. Pigs live in pigpens. Sons want to live in the father's house. My friend, if you want to live in a pigpen, that is where you belong! And that tells who you are. However, if you are in the pigpen but you have a desire in your heart to cry out to God for forgiveness, He will hear you. When you turn back to Him, He will receive you. David did a wrong thing, but David confessed his sin. However, obedience to God was the norm for David. I think it behooves us to be very careful about criticizing David—he was a great man. We are not worthy (at least I am not) to tie the strings of his shoes. He was a great man of God and became the earthly standard for the kings.

And there was war between Rehoboam and Jeroboam all the days of his life [1 Kings 15:6].

This was a time of civil strife. It was a time of brother fighting against brother, and it seriously weakened the kingdom.

ABIJAM IS SUCCEEDED BY ASA

Now the rest of the acts of Abijam, and all that he did, are they not written in the book of the chronicles of the kings of Judah? And there was war between Abijam and Jeroboam.

> And Abijam slept with his fathers; and they buried him
> in the city of David: and Asa his son reigned in his stead
> [1 Kings 15:7-8].

Abijam did nothing outstanding during his reign—all was evil. He was a bad king. So he died and was buried with his fathers.

Abijam was succeeded by his son Asa. Now we come to the first good king, and we feel like saying, "Hallelujah, we've found a good king!"

> And in the twentieth year of Jeroboam king of Israel
> reigned Asa over Judah.
>
> And forty and one years reigned he in Jerusalem. And
> his mother's name was Maachah, the daughter of
> Abishalom.
>
> And Asa did that which was right in the eyes of the
> LORD, as did David his father [1 Kings 15:9-11].

You can see that there is an overlapping here of two years. Asa reigned during the last two years of Jeroboam's reign. Asa reigned for forty-one years. He had one of the longest reigns of any king. In fact, the only two kings who reigned longer than Asa were Azariah (or Uzziah) and Manasseh.

Asa's mother's name was Maachah. Isn't that interesting? Asa was a good king, and she gets credit here for the way Asa turned out. Again David is the standard of right and wrong for a king—Asa measured up to David.

Now what did he do?

> And he took away the sodomites out of the land, and
> removed all the idols that his fathers had made [1 Kings
> 15:12].

Asa did not go for the idea that we should be soft on homosexuals. He was opposed to homosexuality. It is not a mark of being civilized when any nation drops to the low level that we have today. God gives up any people who have a permissive society, openly allowing homosexuality. It is a mark of gross degradation—we are going down as a nation. Someone needs to speak out against this today. We need to recognize it as a sin—it is as corrupt, depraved, and degraded as any sin a person can commit. Man cannot sink any lower than this. When a person sinks this low, God gives him up. Our society is moving in that direction. Asa dealt with the problem, and he is called a good king. God has not changed His mind on this issue at all.

WAR WITH BAASHA

And there was war between Asa and Baasha king of Israel all their days [1 Kings 15:16].

Asa made war against Baasha, king of Israel. It was continual civil war.

We are told that Asa did other things also. He had to appease a kingdom that was arising in the north and becoming dominant—that kingdom was Syria.

Then Asa took all the silver and the gold that were left in the treasures of the house of the LORD, and the treasures of the king's house, and delivered them into the hand of his servants: and king Asa sent them to Ben-hadad, the son of Tabrimon, the son of Hezion, king of Syria, that dwelt at Damascus, saying,

There is a league between me and thee, and between my father and thy father: behold, I have sent unto thee a present of silver and gold; come and break thy league with Baasha king of Israel, that he may depart from me [1 Kings 15:18–19].

Asa sent Ben-hadad presents of gold and silver in order to appease him. To keep him from invading his kingdom, Asa made a league with him. This is probably the one thing he did that was wrong.

> Then king Asa made a proclamation throughout all Judah: none was exempted: and they took away the stones of Ramah, and the timber thereof, wherewith Baasha had builded; and king Asa built with them Geba of Benjamin, and Mizpah [1 Kings 15:22].

Asa did all of this for protection, of course.

ASA IS SUCCEEDED BY JEHOSHAPHAT

> The rest of all the acts of Asa, and all his might, and all that he did, and the cities which he built, are they not written in the book of the chronicles of the kings of Judah? Nevertheless in the time of his old age he was diseased in his feet.
>
> And Asa slept with his fathers, and was buried with his fathers in the city of David his father: and Jehoshaphat his son reigned in his stead [1 Kings 15:23–24].

As we shall see, Jehoshaphat was another good king.

NADAB IS SLAIN AND SUCCEEDED BY BAASHA

Now we come back to Nadab, the son of Jeroboam:

> And Nadab the son of Jeroboam began to reign over Israel in the second year of Asa king of Judah, and reigned over Israel two years.
>
> And he did evil in the sight of the Lord, and walked in the way of his father, and in his sin wherewith he made Israel to sin [1 Kings 15:25–26].

Nadab began to reign in the second year of the reign of Asa, king of Judah. Nadab ruled for two years over Israel. We will find in this succession of bad kings that there was a great deal of sin and political intrigue in the northern kingdom.

> **And Baasha the son of Ahijah, of the house of Issachar, conspired against him; and Baasha smote him at Gibbethon, which belonged to the Philistines; for Nadab and all Israel laid siege to Gibbethon [1 Kings 15:27].**

You would think that somewhere along the line there would be peace, but there was not. There was war between Asa and Baasha all their days. The continual civil war depleted the energy and resources of both the kingdoms. It also made both kingdoms subject to the powers round about them. They were invaded again and again by Egypt in the south, by Syria, and finally by Assyria in the north. These people simply would not change their ways.

BAASHA'S DEATH, AND THE REIGNS
OF ELAH AND ZIMRI

Baasha reigned longer than any other king in the north up to this point. He reigned for twenty-four years. But we are told that this man is to be put down because he did evil. The word of the Lord against Baasha came through Jehu:

> **Behold, I will take away the posterity of Baasha, and the posterity of his house; and will make thy house like the house of Jeroboam the son of Nebat.**

> **Him that dieth of Baasha in the city shall the dogs eat; and him that dieth of his in the fields shall the fowls of the air eat [1 Kings 16:3–4].**

This was a sad period in the life of the king. Because Baasha chose to share in the sins of the house of Jeroboam, he would also share in the severe penalty, even to the point of being devoured by dogs.

So Baasha slept with his fathers, and was buried in Tirzah: and Elah his son reigned in his stead.

And also by the hand of the prophet Jehu the son of
Hanani came the word of the LORD against Baasha, and
against his house, even for all the evil that he did in the
sight of the LORD, in provoking him to anger with the
work of his hands, in being like the house of Jeroboam;
and because he killed him.

In the twenty and sixth year of Asa king of Judah began
Elah the son of Baasha to reign over Israel in Tirzah,
two years [1 Kings 16:6-8].

Elah had not reigned but two years until Zimri his captain conspired
and led a rebellion against him:

And his servant Zimri, captain of half his chariots, conspired against him, as he was in Tirzah, drinking himself drunk in the house of Arza steward of his house in
Tirzah.

And Zimri went in and smote him, and killed him, in
the twenty and seventh year of Asa king of Judah, and
reigned in his stead [1 Kings 16:9-10].

When Elah got drunk, Zimri went in and killed him. It seems that
because of the conspirators in the northern kingdom no man was
really safe. After Zimri killed Elah, he began to reign.

However, Zimri did not last very long either—only seven days.

In the twenty and seventh year of Asa king of Judah did
Zimri reign seven days in Tirzah. And the people were
encamped against Gibbethon, which belonged to the
Philistines [1 Kings 16:15].

Another conspiracy and another rebellion got rid of Zimri.

> **And Omri went up from Gibbethon, and all Israel with him, and they besieged Tirzah.**
>
> **And it came to pass, when Zimri saw that the city was taken, that he went into the palace of the king's house, and burnt the king's house over him with fire, and died [1 Kings 15:17–18].**

These were dark days for the kingdom, and there are darker days yet to come.

TIBNI AND OMRI ARE RIVAL KINGS OF ISRAEL

After Omri's conspiracy succeeded in establishing him as king, another problem arose. A rival of Omri's also claimed to be king—his name was Tibni.

> **Then were the people of Israel divided into two parts: half of the people followed Tibni the son of Ginath, to make him king; and half followed Omri.**
>
> **But the people that followed Omri prevailed against the people that followed Tibni the son of Ginath: so Tibni died, and Omri reigned [1 Kings 16:21–22].**

Omri put Tibni to death, and then Omri reigned. He ruled for twelve years. He was a bad king and exceeded the other kings in his evil deeds.

> **But Omri wrought evil in the eyes of the Lord, and did worse than all that were before him [1 Kings 16:25].**

ACCESSION OF AHAB; HIS MARRIAGE TO JEZEBEL

So Omri slept with his fathers, and was buried in Samaria: and Ahab his son reigned in his stead.

And Ahab the son of Omri did evil in the sight of the LORD above all that were before him [1 Kings 16:28, 30].

Omri is succeeded by his son Ahab. Omri had been the most corrupt ruler up to that time, but his son Ahab exceeded him in evil.

And it came to pass, as if it had been a light thing for him to walk in the sins of Jeroboam the son of Nebat, that he took to wife Jezebel the daughter of Ethbaal king of the Zidonians, and went and served Baal, and worshipped him [1 Kings 16:31].

Ahab was evil, and he had a wife that helped him with his evil ways. She was a real helpmeet in the area of evil. What Ahab didn't think of, Jezebel did. What she didn't think of nobody else could—she was a mean woman. The combination of Ahab and Jezebel was the worst possible. You can be sure that Mr. and Mrs. Haman were bad. Herod and Herodias were evil enough. And we know of Ptolemy Dionysius and Cleopatra—they were quite a couple. Philip I of Spain and Bloody Mary also did pretty well together. These are four of the most infamous couples in history. In particular there were also several couples where the wife was dominant in diabolical designs. For example, there was Catherine de'Medici and Henry II of France; Lucrezia Borgia (she was the daughter of a pope) and Alfonso; Macbeth and Lady Macbeth; Louis XVI and Marie Antoinette of France; and finally, coming down to our day, Julius and Ethel Rosenberg. All of these are couples who stand out on the pages of history as being evil, but none can exceed Ahab and Jezebel—they head the list.

Jezebel was the daughter of a king who was also a priest of Baal and who murdered his brother. It is interesting to note that the name

Jezebel means "unmarried" or "without cohabitation." In other words, the marriage of Ahab and Jezebel was not a romance—it was not a love match. Rather than a true marriage, it was just a wedding. Apparently there had never been a real meeting of these two people in a love relationship. She was a masculine woman with strong intellectual powers and a fierce passion for evil. She was strong-willed and possessed a dominant personality, but she had no moral sense. She was hardened into insensibility. She was unscrupulous and the most wicked person in history—bar none.

In the Book of Revelation, our Lord gave a message to the church of Thyatira: "Notwithstanding I have a few things against thee, because thou sufferest that woman Jezebel, which calleth herself a prophetess, to teach and to seduce my servants to commit fornication, and to eat things sacrificed unto idols" (Rev. 2:20). Jezebel was a dominating and domineering woman. Christ gave this message to Thyatira because it was a period without natural affection—it was a picture of Jezebel.

How did Jezebel and Ahab ever get together? I think it was quite easy. For years I went to young people's conferences. It was quite interesting how there could be a boy who was a bad apple and a girl who was a bad egg, and for some strange reason the bad apple and the bad egg always got together and started dating. It always happened that way, and that is the way it was with Ahab and Jezebel.

Something else happened during this period which reveals how ominous and critical those days were:

And he reared up an altar for Baal in the house of Baal, which he had built in Samaria.

And Ahab made a grove; and Ahab did more to provoke the Lord God of Israel to anger than all the kings of Israel that were before him.

In his days did Hiel the Beth-elite build Jericho: he laid the foundation thereof in Abiram his firstborn, and set up the gates thereof in his youngest son Segub, according to the word of the Lord, which he spake by Joshua the son of Nun [1 Kings 16:32–34].

At the time of the destruction of Jericho, Joshua said, ". . . Cursed be the man before the LORD, that riseth up and buildeth this city Jericho . . ." (Josh. 6:26). It had not been rebuilt until the time of Ahab and Jezebel, and the curse that was pronounced by Joshua came upon the builder, Hiel.

CHAPTER 17

THEME: Three years of drought as announced by Elijah

God had to have His man present at the time when Ahab and Jeze-bel sat on the throne of Israel. It would have to be someone who would have the courage to stand up against them. God had that man ready. He was Elijah the prophet, one of the greatest men who ever walked across the pages of Scripture. Also he is probably the man who will return to the earth to witness in the last days—it is predicted that he will return.

ELIJAH ANNOUNCES THE DROUGHT

Elijah is introduced to us in a most dramatic way. He strides into the court of Ahab and Jezebel and makes a very brave announcement.

And Elijah the Tishbite, who was of the inhabitants of Gilead, said unto Ahab, As the LORD God of Israel liveth, before whom I stand, there shall not be dew nor rain these years, but according to my word [1 Kings 17:1].

Elijah walked into the court of Ahab and Jezebel and gave them the latest weather report. He said it was not going to rain except by his word and he was leaving town—he had no intention of saying the word. Then he walked out of the court just as dramatically as he had walked in. I think Ahab and Jezebel were taken aback because they never dreamed anyone could speak out so boldly. They will find out that Elijah has a habit of speaking out. You get the impression that Elijah was a rugged individual, and he was. But there's something else that should be said here about him—God had to train this man. God has always had a method of training the men He uses by taking them to the desert. You will recall that that is where He trained Moses. God took Abraham out of Ur of the Chaldees and placed him in a land with rugged terrain. God did the same for John the Baptist, and the apostle Paul spent at least two full years out in the Arabian desert. This is God's method of training His men. Now He is going to take out this man Elijah and teach him several things he needs to learn.

GOD FEEDS ELIJAH AT CHERITH AND ZAREPHATH

And the word of the LORD came unto him, saying,

Get thee hence, and turn thee eastward, and hide thyself by the brook Cherith, that is before Jordan [1 Kings 17:2–3].

God was telling Elijah to get as far out in the country as he could. So he went out into the desert and came to a little stream.

And it shall be, that thou shalt drink of the brook; and I have commanded the ravens to feed thee there [1 Kings 17:4].

God used two methods of caring for Elijah out in the desert. One was the brook which was a natural means. He was to drink the water. The other was a supernatural means—the ravens were to come and feed him. Well, Elijah stayed there for awhile, and then the brook began to dry up.

And it came to pass after a while, that the brook dried up, because there had been no rain in the land [1 Kings 17:7].

Here is this man out in the wilderness, and he goes to the brook every morning and notices that it is going down a little bit more each day.

All he had to do was put a peg in the water to note how much it went down each day. Then he could figure out how many days it would be before he starved to death or died of thirst. Having the mathematical measurement, anyone with common sense would know that on a certain day the end would come.

This is the sin of statistics. Today the condition of a church is often determined by statistics. If you go to a church meeting and observe that the offering has been good, new members have been received, and there is increased attendance, the church is considered a howling success—and that may not be the true picture at all.

I once heard the story of a preacher who got up at a church business meeting and said, "We are going to call on the treasurer to give a report so that we can know the status quo of our church." One of the members got up and said, "Mr. Preacher, we don't know what the status quo means." The preacher replied, "The 'status quo' means the mess we are in." Interestingly enough, the true status quo of many churches and other organizations often reveals the mess they are in, although the statistics may look healthy.

Now Elijah could have figured very closely the time he was going to die—he could have done it mathematically. But, you see, the cold figures of mathematics do not take into account the spiritual fire that is there. You cannot put the condition of the church in the form of a bank statement. You cannot measure it on a computer. Even a revival is not determined by numbers. When Elijah looked at that little brook which was getting smaller and smaller, he learned a spiritual lesson. He saw that his life was a dried-up brook. He was nothing—he was just a brook, a channel, through which living water *could* flow. The Lord Jesus Christ says, ". . . Whosoever drinketh of this water shall thirst again: but whosoever drinketh of the water that I shall give him shall never thirst; but the water that I shall give him shall be in him a well of water springing up into everlasting life" (John 4:13–14). Sometimes we sing the song, "Make Me A Blessing," and I think that half of the folk don't know the meaning of the words. Why, it means that you are an empty brook and that you do not have any water of life. It is only as the water of life, the Word of God, flows through you that you can be a channel of blessing. Elijah had to learn that ". . . God hath chosen the foolish things of the world to confound the wise; and God hath chosen the weak things of the world to confound the things which are mighty" (1 Cor. 1:27). God was telling Elijah, "You are not a big, strong, rugged individual. You are no stronger or better than that dried-up brook. You will have no strength until the water of life flows through you."

It is said of Hudson Taylor that when he prepared young missionaries for service in his mission, he insisted, "Remember that when you come out here you are *nothing*. It is only what God can and will do through you that will be worth anything." One young missionary replied, "It is hard for me to believe that I am just nothing." And Hudson Taylor said to him, "Take it by faith because it is true—you are nothing." You and I are just dried-up brooks unless the Word of God is flowing through us.

And then God transferred Elijah:

And the word of the LORD came unto him, saying,

Arise, get thee to Zarephath, which belongeth to Zidon, and dwell there: behold, I have commanded a widow woman there to sustain thee.

So he arose and went to Zarephath. And when he came to the gate of the city, behold, the widow woman was there gathering of sticks: and he called to her, and said, Fetch me, I pray thee, a little water in a vessel, that I may drink.

And as she was going to fetch it, he called to her, and said, Bring me, I pray thee, a morsel of bread in thine hand.

And she said, As the LORD thy God liveth, I have not a cake, but an handful of meal in a barrel, and a little oil in a cruse: and, behold, I am gathering two sticks, that I

**may go in and dress it for me and my son, that we may
eat it, and die [1 Kings 17:8–12].**

After the widow told her story, Elijah told her to go into her house and
make the cake. He assured her that she was not going to die.

**And Elijah said unto her, Fear not; go and do as thou
hast said: but make me thereof a little cake first, and
bring it unto me, and after make for thee and for thy son.**

**For thus saith the LORD God of Israel. The barrel of meal
shall not waste, neither shall the cruse of oil fail, until
the day that the LORD sendeth rain upon the earth
[1 Kings 17:13–14].**

You know, Elijah and that widow stuck their heads down in that
empty flour barrel every day and sang the doxology—and God sus-
tained them out of an empty flour barrel. That barrel was as fertile as
the plains of Canada or the corn fields of Iowa. Here is another lesson
Elijah needed to learn.

It is a lesson you and I need to learn: we are nothing but empty
flour barrels. I hear so much today about consecration—we are to
"give our talents to the Lord." My friend, you and I have nothing to
offer God. There was a wedding in Cana of Galilee: what was the most
important thing at that wedding? Was it the bride's dress? No! It was
that there were some empty water crocks there. The Lord filled them
with water, and He was able to serve the guests a delicious refresh-
ment. That was the important thing at the wedding. My friend, we are
nothing but empty flour barrels and empty water crocks. We are nothing until the water of life and the bread of life have been put into us.
And since we do not recognize this, we are having spiritual floor
shows in many of our churches today. They have become religious
nightclubs, and there is no more spiritual life in them than there is in
a Rose Bowl game in Pasadena, California. There is more enthusiasm
and a larger crowd at many activities outside the church than there is

at most church meetings. In fact, many church meetings are pretty sad and silly, if you ask me. We need to remember that we are empty flour barrels.

THE WIDOW'S SON IS RAISED BY ELIJAH

And it came to pass after these things, that the son of the woman, the mistress of the house, fell sick; and his sickness was so sore, that there was no breath left in him [1 Kings 17:17].

The widow's son died. And what did Elijah do?

And he said unto her, Give me thy son. And he took him out of her bosom, and carried him up into a loft, where he abode, and laid him upon his own bed.

And he cried unto the LORD, and said, O LORD my God, hast thou also brought evil upon the widow with whom I sojourn, by slaying her son?

And he stretched himself upon the child three times, and cried unto the LORD, and said, O LORD my God, I pray thee, let this child's soul come into him again.

And the LORD heard the voice of Elijah; and the soul of the child came into him again, and he revived [1 Kings 17:19-22].

Elijah made contact with the boy's body three times. This is the great principle of resurrection—it involves contact with life. Today Christianity needs to be in contact with Jesus Christ. When it is not, it is as dead as a dodo bird. We need to recognize that this is one of the great miracles of Scripture: "and the soul of the child came into him again, and he revived." You and I are dead bodies. We are lost sinners—dead in trespasses and sins. If we have trusted Christ, then we can say that we were crucified with Him nineteen hundred years ago; He died, and we died with Him. He was raised, and we were raised with Him. We are joined to the living Christ today—if we are not joined to Him, we are nothing. The apostle Paul expressed it this way: "I am crucified with Christ: nevertheless I live; yet not I, but Christ liveth in me: and the life which I now live in the flesh I live by the faith of the Son of God, who loved me, and gave himself for me" (Gal. 2:20).

Elijah had to learn that he was a dried-up brook, an empty flour barrel, a dead body. When Elijah recognized this, then God could use him. Martin Luther once said that God creates out of nothing. Until a man recognizes that he is nothing, God can do nothing with him. That is the problem with many of us today: we are too strong, we have too much ability, and God cannot use us.

CHAPTER 18

THEME: Elijah versus the prophets of Baal

This is one of the most spectacular chapters in the Scriptures. Elijah challenges the prophets of Baal to a contest to determine who is really God. The prophets of Baal—all 450 of them—are about an even match for this one man Elijah. He is a great man!

ELIJAH AND OBADIAH

And it came to pass after many days, that the word of the LORD came to Elijah in the third year, saying, Go, shew thyself unto Ahab; and I will send rain upon the earth.

And Elijah went to shew himself unto Ahab. And there was a sore famine in Samaria [1 Kings 18:1–2].

God is ready to use Elijah. This man can now step out with boldness—he has learned that he is nothing and God is everything. He goes out to meet Ahab, and he is prepared.

And Ahab called Obadiah, which was the governor of his house. (Now Obadiah feared the LORD greatly:

For it was so, when Jezebel cut off the prophets of the LORD, that Obadiah took an hundred prophets, and hid them by fifty in a cave, and fed them with bread and water.)

And Ahab said unto Obadiah, Go into the land, unto all fountains of water, and unto all brooks: peradventure we may find grass to save the horses and mules alive, that we lose not all the beasts.

**So they divided the land between them to pass through-
out it: Ahab went one way by himself, and Obadiah went
another way by himself [1 Kings 18:3–6].**

The famine was now in the acute stage. Much of the vegetation had
dried up and the cattle could no longer find places to graze. So Ahab
and his servant, Obadiah, set out in search of possible pasture land.
Ahab went one direction and Obadiah went another. Now Obadiah
was the governor of Ahab's palace. He was a God-fearing man, and he
had hidden one hundred prophets of God from Jezebel's wrath.

**And as Obadiah was in the way, behold, Elijah met him:
and he knew him, and fell on his face, and said, Art
thou that my lord Elijah?**

**And he answered him, I am: go, tell thy lord, Behold,
Elijah is here [1 Kings 18:7–8].**

While Obadiah was looking for grazing sites, he met Elijah. Elijah
told him to tell the king, "Behold, Elijah is here." My, how we need a
voice like Elijah's today. I believe he is coming back in the last days
after the church leaves the earth. This earth will need a strong voice
then, and it will have one in Elijah.

**And he said, What have I sinned, that thou wouldest de-
liver thy servant into the hand of Ahab, to slay me?**

**As the LORD thy God liveth, there is no nation or king-
dom, whither my lord hath not sent to seek thee: and
when they said, He is not there; he took an oath of the
kingdom and nation, that they found thee not.**

**And now thou sayest, Go, tell thy lord, Behold, Elijah is
here.**

**And it shall come to pass, as soon as I am gone from
thee, that the Spirit of the LORD shall carry thee whither**

> I know not; and so when I come and tell Ahab, and he cannot find thee, he shall slay me: but I thy servant fear the LORD from my youth.
>
> Was it not told my lord what I did when Jezebel slew the prophets of the LORD, how I hid an hundred men of the LORD'S prophets by fifty in a cave, and fed them with bread and water? [1 Kings 18:9–13].

Obadiah does not want to deliver Elijah's message as he is afraid that Elijah will disappear before Ahab sees him. Obadiah is fearful for his own life, and he makes it very clear that he does not want to do what Elijah has asked.

> And now thou sayest, Go, tell thy lord, Behold, Elijah is here: and he shall slay me.
>
> And Elijah said, As the LORD of hosts liveth, before whom I stand, I will surely shew myself unto him today.
>
> So Obadiah went to meet Ahab, and told him: and Ahab went to meet Elijah [1 Kings 18:14–16].

We have read the message three times now: "Behold, Elijah is here." With Elijah's assurances that he will certainly meet Ahab, Obadiah goes to the king. And you know what this man said? He said, "Behold, Elijah is here." And that will be the message again some day.

ELIJAH'S CHALLENGE TO AHAB

> And it came to pass, when Ahab saw Elijah, that Ahab said unto him, Art thou he that troubleth Israel?
>
> And he answered, I have not troubled Israel; but thou, and thy father's house, in that ye have forsaken the commandments of the LORD, and thou hast followed Baalim [1 Kings 18:17–18].

Elijah said to Ahab, "I am not the one who is troubling Israel—you are!" Elijah's kind of preaching cannot be misunderstood. It is not double-talk; it is telling is like it is.

Before we go any further, I want to say that the liberal is always blaming the fundamentalist for causing division in the church. But who *really* caused it? The church held very fundamental beliefs at one time. Who brought bifurcation into the church? Who was it that led the church away from its foundation? The liberal did. I have been accused of leaving my former denomination, but I did not—my denomination left me. I still have the same beliefs that I had at the beginning. Unfortunately, my denomination has departed from these historic beliefs.

It has always been the custom of the liberal to blame any trouble in the church on the fundamentalist. The liberal is never to blame.

In the same way Ahab blames Elijah for the problem in the land. He accuses Elijah of stirring things up. The Word of God will always stir up things. The interesting thing is that rats will always scurry to a dark corner when the light is turned on.

Then Elijah challenged Ahab to a contest between himself and the prophets of Baal.

> **Now therefore send, and gather to me all Israel unto mount Carmel, and the prophets of Baal four hundred and fifty, and the prophets of the groves four hundred, which eat at Jezebel's table [1 Kings 18:19].**

The contest was actually one between the Lord and Satan—between the worship of the living God and the worship of Baal. Outwardly it was a battle of Ahab and Jezebel with the 450 prophets against Elijah. Elijah, however, was worth a whole army.

THE LORD VERSUS BAAL AT MOUNT CARMEL

> **So Ahab sent unto all the children of Israel, and gathered the prophets together unto mount Carmel.**

> And Elijah came unto all the people, and said, How long
> halt ye between two opinions? if the Lord be God, follow
> him: but if Baal, then follow him. And the people an-
> swered him not a word [1 Kings 18:20-21].

The people of Israel have assembled at Carmel. It is going to be quite
a contest. Elijah knew what was in the hearts of the people. They were
pretending to worship the living and true God, but they were also
worshiping Baal. The reason the people did not answer Elijah is that
they were guilty of sin. It is that type of double-talk—a two-faced way
of life—that today has become so abhorrent and is a stench in the nostrils of God. The double standard of many Christians has turned off
many people as far as the church is concerned. If the average unsaved
man knew the church as I know it today, I have my doubts that he
would ever darken the door of a church. If there ever was a place
where things should be made clear and plain, simple and forthright, it
is in the church. Unfortunately, that is where there is more double-talk
and beating around the bush than any place else.

> Then said Elijah unto the people, I, even I only, remain a
> prophet of the Lord; but Baal's prophets are four hun-
> dred and fifty men [1 Kings 18:22].

Elijah had what I am pleased to call an Elijah complex—some of us
develop that even today. Many times in my ministry I feel that I am the
only one left. Then I find out that there is a preacher in a hollow in
Tennessee, or on the side of a hill in Georgia, or down around a lake in
Florida, or up in the mountains of California, or in the suburban areas
of Chicago who is standing for God and paying a bigger price than I
have ever paid. Then I just get rid of my Elijah complex and thank God
that there are men standing for God and His Word in these days in
which we are living. Now I recognize that there are many big-name
preachers that you hear about but who are not actually standing for
God. Instead they are pussy-footing around. They are trying to compromise. I heard one preacher give a certain message in one part of the
country and then turn around in another part of the country and prac-

tically reverse his message. There is something wrong when you can't give the same message everywhere. There is something wrong with the message or with the man who gives it.

Elijah says to the people of Israel, "I am the only one who is standing for God." Now he was wrong—there were seven thousand people hiding in the hills who had not bowed the knee to Baal. I never cared too much for that crowd, but at least they did not worship Baal. Elijah did not even know about them. If Elijah had been on the radio in those days, he never would have received a letter from any of those folk. It is too bad that they did not encourage him a little bit, but they did not.

Elijah continues his message to the people and his challenge to the prophets of Baal:

> **Let them therefore give us two bullocks; and let them choose one bullock for themselves, and cut it in pieces, and lay it on wood, and put no fire under: and I will dress the other bullock, and lay it on wood, and put no fire under:**
>
> **And call ye on the name of your gods, and I will call on the name of the LORD: and the God that answereth by fire, let him be God. And all the people answered and said, It is well spoken [1 Kings 18:23–24].**

In other words, Elijah said, "Let us taste of the Lord and see whether He is good or not. If Baal is God, then let us worship him. And if he is not, then let's kick him out. If the Lord God is the living God, we want to know." My friend, today God wants you to know Him. Although you may have doubts, if you're sincere and really want to know Him, He will reveal Himself to you—because God *wants* you to know. Faith is not groping in the dark: our faith rests upon facts. Your salvation depends on your believing those facts and trusting Christ.

Notice what is going to take place. I think this is one of the most dramatic scenes in Scripture.

> And Elijah said unto the prophets of Baal, Choose you one bullock for yourselves, and dress it first; for ye are many; and call on the name of your gods, but put no fire under.
>
> And they took the bullock which was given them, and they dressed it, and called on the name of Baal from morning even until noon, saying, O Baal, hear us. But there was no voice, nor any that answered. And they leaped upon the altar which was made.
>
> And it came to pass at noon, that Elijah mocked them, and said, Cry aloud: for he is a god; either he is talking, or he is pursuing, or he is in a journey, or peradventure he sleepeth, and must be awakened.
>
> And they cried aloud, and cut themselves after their manner with knives and lancets, till the blood gushed out upon them [1 Kings 18:25–28].

The prophets of Baal put on quite a performance. Elijah just sits there and watches them at first with a good deal of cynicism. They begin to call upon Baal. Nothing happens. They jump on the altar—and that doesn't help. They become fanatics. They display a lot of emotion. Their actions become almost hysterical. Finally, they begin to cut themselves, and the blood gushes out. They are sure this will stir Baal to action. Old Elijah says to them, "Say, it may be that he has gone on vacation and you will have to wait until he comes back. Or maybe he is taking his afternoon siesta and you are going to have to yell louder to wake him up." Elijah has a big time during their performance. And all the while the people of Israel are watching.

It is Martin Luther, by the way, who is credited with the statement, "One with God is a majority," and he knew the accuracy of that statement by experience. Elijah also learned this truth through experience in his day when there had been a wholesale departure of the northern kingdom from God. Under Ahab and Jezebel there was almost total apostasy—Elijah pretty much stood alone. It is true that there were

seven thousand people who had not bowed to Baal, but they had re-
treated to the mountains. Not one of them stood with Elijah. He was
not aware that they even existed until God told him. Elijah took a
stand against calf worship. You might say he took a stand against new
morality and rock music in the church. He took exception to many of
the things that were going on and refused to compromise with the
prophets of Baal. When they wrote a new "Confession of Faith" and
rejected the authority of the Word of God, he was opposed to them.

It was Dr. Wilfred Funk who said that the most bitter word in the
English language is "alone." Elijah stood alone. He did not voice public opinion, friend. He was no echo—he was no parrot. He was not
promoting anyone else. He was no politician. He was more concerned
about pleasing God than courting the popularity of the crowd. He
sought divine approval rather than public applause. He was not a
clown in a public parade. He was a fool for God's sake. He was a solo
voice in the wilderness of the world. He carried on an all-out war
against Satan and his hosts. He stood alone, arrayed against the
prophets of Baal. Elijah chose Mount Carmel to take a dramatic stand
for God.

Several years ago I stood in what is probably the exact area where
Elijah and the prophets of Baal held their contest. Mount Carmel overlooks the Bay of Haifa and the blue Mediterranean Sea. It is a long
ridge; and way out yonder to the east is Megiddo in the Valley of
Esdraelon. In this dramatic spot the lone, majestic figure of Elijah
stood apart. He was detached. I think he looked bored after a few minutes of the performance by Baal's prophets. Then that ironic smile
crossed his face and you could hear the acid sarcasm in his voice. He
used the rapier of ridicule. He taunted and jeered at these prophets.
And finally, with wilting scorn, he waved them aside.

**And it came to pass, when midday was past, and they
prophesied until the time of the offering of the evening
sacrifice, that there was neither voice, nor any to answer, nor any that regarded.**

**And Elijah said unto all the people, Come near unto me.
And all the people came near unto him. And he re-**

paired the altar of the LORD that was broken down
[1 Kings 18:29-30].

Elijah is now going to have to depend on God. The altar of the Lord
has been broken, and Elijah spends some time cementing it together.
That was a dramatic move, friend.

What is it that has caused division in our country today? I recognize that there are many explanations being offered, but a departure
from God is basic to the divisions in this nation. There was a time that
there was a measure of unity, and it was a unity based on the fact that
there is a living God—that is written in our constitution—and we are
responsible to Him. There was a time when this nation believed that
the Bible was an authority. Who divided this country? Those, my
friend, who began to cut up the Word of God. That is what caused the
division. It is hypocrisy today when so many are saying, "Let's get
together." Get together on what, my friend? You cannot get together on
nothing. It is like the story that is told about a man who was walking
through the jungle in Africa, and he met an elephant. The elephant
said to him, "Where are you going?" The man replied, "I am not going anywhere." The elephant said, "I'm not going anywhere either.
Let's go together." That is the only way you are going to get together
with today's crowd: you will have to agree on nothing. If you do that,
you can all get together. My friend, you can't get together unless
you've got something to gather around that will hold you together.

The altar was the place of unity. Elijah put it back together.

And Elijah took twelve stones, according to the number
of the tribes of the sons of Jacob, unto whom the word of
the LORD came, saying, Israel shall be thy name:

And with the stones he built an altar in the name of the
LORD: and he made a trench about the altar, as great as
would contain two measures of seed.

And he put the wood in order, and cut the bullock in
pieces, and laid him on the wood, and said, Fill four

> **barrels with water, and pour it on the burnt sacrifice,
> and on the wood [1 Kings 18:31–33].**

Notice that Israel was *one* nation. It was not Israel and Judah, or Samaria and Jerusalem, but all twelve tribes as the one nation, Israel. So
Elijah built an altar in the name of the Lord. Then he made a trench
around the altar, put the wood in order, and cut the bullock in pieces.
Finally he ordered that four barrels be filled with water and poured on
the sacrifice and on the wood. Now it was a long way down to the
water supply. As I stood on Mount Carmel, I wondered how long it
took those who were bringing the water to get four barrels up the side
of that mountain. It was a long route, but Elijah was in no hurry.

> **And he said, Do it the second time. And they did it the
> second time. And he said, Do it the third time. And they
> did it the third time.**

> **And the water ran round about the altar; and he filled
> the trench also with water [1 Kings 18:34–35].**

They fetched the water once, and Elijah said, "Go down and fill it
again." And that was not enough. He said, "Do it the third time," and
they did it the third time. I think if you could have seen Elijah that day
there would have been a wry smile on his face. Do you know what that
wry smile was about? Why did he pour water on that altar? My friend,
only God can do the impossible. A little water won't keep the fire from
falling, so he did not mind pouring the water over everything. He
could have poured water for the next twenty-four hours, and the fire
still would have fallen. Elijah is learning to depend on God—we have
seen that. Remember, as he stood at that little brook and watched it
dry up, he knew he was nothing in the world but a channel through
which water could flow. He had also looked down in an empty flour
barrel and sung the doxology. God fed Elijah, the widow, and her son
out of that empty flour barrel for the period of the drought. And then
he found out he was a dead body. He had learned that if anything is

going to be done, God has to do it. He just stood up there that day, a wry smile on his face—I think Elijah had a sense of humor. And I know God has a sense of humor. Under his breath Elijah probably said, "Lord, if You don't do it, it won't be done."

And it came to pass at the time of the offering of the evening sacrifice, that Elijah the prophet came near, and said, LORD God of Abraham, Isaac, and of Israel, let it be known this day that thou art God in Israel, and that I am thy servant, and that I have done all these things at thy word [1 Kings 18:36].

Friend, I wish we recognized the fact that if God doesn't do it, it's not going to be done. Do you understand Elijah's prayer? This is one of the great prayers of Scripture—it's not long, but it is great. He said, "LORD God of Abraham, Isaac, and of Israel . . ." You will notice that Elijah used the term *Israel*, not *Jacob*. Why *Israel*? Well, Israel is the name that was given not to twelve tribes, but to *one nation*. Also in his prayer Elijah said, "Let it be known this day that thou art God in Israel, and that I am thy servant, and that I have done all these things at thy word." You and I need to be sure that what we are doing is according to the will of God. Don't do something that you want to do and then ask God to bless it. God doesn't move that way. You have to go His route if you want to receive the blessing. We have no right to demand anything of God. It is true that He demands a great deal of us, but we are not to demand anything of Him. He is not a Western Union boy. He will not come at your command. We are to pray according to His will.

Hear me, O LORD, hear me, that this people may know that thou art the LORD God, and that thou hast turned their heart back again [1 Kings 18:37].

Elijah is praying for the glory of God in this verse. That is what moves the arm of God. And do you know what happened?

> Then the fire of the LORD fell, and consumed the burnt
> sacrifice, and the wood, and the stones, and the dust,
> and licked up the water that was in the trench.
>
> And when all the people saw it, they fell on their faces:
> and they said, The LORD, he is the God; the LORD, he is
> the God.
>
> And Elijah said unto them, Take the prophets of Baal;
> let not one of them escape. And they took them: and Eli-
> jah brought them down to the brook Kishon, and slew
> them there [1 Kings 18:38–40].

That was a pretty brutal thing to do, wasn't it? But it sure got rid of the
apostasy and the heresy.

ELIJAH'S PRAYER FOR RAIN

> And Elijah said unto Ahab, Get thee up, eat and drink;
> for there is a sound of abundance of rain [1 Kings
> 18:41].

When the people turned to God, the rain came and the blessings
came.

> So Ahab went up to eat and to drink. And Elijah went
> up to the top of Carmel; and he cast himself down upon
> the earth, and put his face between his knees.
>
> And said to his servant, Go up now, look toward the sea.
> And he went up, and looked, and said, There is nothing.
> And he said, Go again seven times.
>
> And it came to pass at the seventh time, that he said,
> Behold, there ariseth a little cloud out of the sea, like a
> man's hand. And he said, Go up, say unto Ahab, Pre-
> pare thy chariot, and get thee down, that the rain stop
> thee not.

> And it came to pass in the mean while, that the heaven
> was black with clouds and wind, and there was a great
> rain. And Ahab rode, and went to Jezreel [1 Kings
> 18:42–45].

Elijah was a great man! And so that the people might realize that the drought was not just an accident of nature but was a disciplinary measure, it ended the same way that it had begun—by the command of God's man, Elijah. Elijah said that rain was coming, but at first nothing could be seen but blue water and blue sky. When his servant looked for the seventh time, however, a cloud as small as a man's hand could be seen. The cloud rapidly increased in size until the heavens were black and rain flooded the parched earth.

> And the hand of the LORD was on Elijah; and he girded
> up his loins, and ran before Ahab to the entrance of
> Jezreel [1 Kings 18:46].

Elijah had told Ahab to hurry home because the creek would soon rise and he would not be able to cross it. But then Elijah began to run. Why? Because he is a man of like passion as we are. He is very much a human being, and we are going to see just how human he is.

CHAPTER 19

THEME: Elijah under a juniper tree

Ahab reports to Jezebel that Elijah had slain all her prophets of Baal. She vows to kill Elijah. He beats a cowardly retreat to Beersheba, where he leaves his servant and continues on into the wilderness to crawl under a juniper tree, where he requests that he might die. Evidently Elijah is suffering from nervous exhaustion. He is physically and mentally depleted. God gives him nourishing food and plenty of sleep. Then He treats him to a spectacular display: strong wind, earthquake, and fire. Elijah loves all of this. Then comes the still, small voice. Although this is contrary to Elijah's personality, God is in the still, small voice. He sends him back to the scene of action and danger. On the way, Elijah calls Elisha to be his successor.

ELIJAH RUNS FROM JEZEBEL

It is difficult to believe that Elijah is the same man who defied 450 prophets of Baal on the top of Mount Carmel. He seems to be a different man, but there is an explanation for his condition.

And Ahab told Jezebel all that Elijah had done, and withal how he had slain all the prophets with the sword.

Then Jezebel sent a messenger unto Elijah, saying, So let the gods do to me, and more also, if I make not thy life as the life of one of them by tomorrow about this time.

And when he saw that, he arose, and went for his life, and came to Beer-sheba, which belongeth to Judah, and left his servant there [1 Kings 19:1–3].

That was a threatening message Jezebel sent to Elijah. Being before the public defying the false worship in his nation had drained a great deal of his energy and strength. He did a strange thing when he heard Jezebel's message threatening to kill him. Like Simon Peter when he took his eyes off the Lord, looked at those waves, and began to sink, Elijah lost his courage. He began to run. He went to Beer-sheba which is way down south. And friend, take it from someone who has been there, it is way down in the desert. Anyone who got as far away as Beer-sheba could consider himself safe from a ruler in the northern kingdom. But Elijah, when he reached this place in the desert, left his servant there and continued on another day's journey.

But he himself went a day's journey into the wilderness, and came and sat down under a juniper tree: and he requested for himself that he might die; and said, It is enough; now, O LORD, take away my life; for I am not better than my fathers [1 Kings 19:4].

You must admit that this is quite a change for the man who stood on top of Mount Carmel and defied the prophets of Baal. Now he is hiding under a juniper tree way down at the other end of the land, hiding from a woman, Jezebel. Ahab had not made any effort to arrest him or destroy him, but Jezebel hated Elijah, and she was not going to let him live if she could help it.

I think we need to note that Elijah had gone through a traumatic experience when he stood before that altar, prayed to God, and fire from heaven fell. Then there was the execution of the prophets of Baal. Next there was a tremendous rain storm, which was a great victory for Elijah. When Ahab went back and reported to Jezebel all that had happened, she sent a telegram to Elijah saying, "I want you to know that I intend to get you!" She is the most wicked woman in the Bible. Elijah got his eyes off the Lord and ran to an area that was beyond the farthest outpost of civilization. When he got to Beer-sheba, he just kept going. Finally he felt that he was out of her reach. Frankly, when I see him crawling underneath that juniper tree, I am ashamed of him. I am sure that some very pious Christian would have given Elijah a fine little lecture on how to be cheerful and optimistic and smile in his situation. They would tell him that Romans 8:28 was still in the Bible. May

I say to you, I don't think you could have gotten Elijah to smile while he was under that tree.

I heard an English divine who preached a sermon some time ago on the subject, "Brief, Bright, and Brotherly." Elijah did not feel that way underneath that juniper tree. You can criticize Elijah, you can find fault with him, and you can denounce him, and you can say that he is not trusting God as he should. Some might even say he is a disgrace to the Lord. What has happened to our prophet? Is this the man who defied the prophets of Baal? Is this the man who said, "If the Lord be God, follow Him"? What disease has smitten him? What is the diagnosis? Could you give us the etiology of it?

Let me suggest several things. There was a physical cause for the way he acted. He was overworked. He was overwrought. He was over-worried. He was physically exhausted. I think he could have dropped in his tracks after that experience at Mount Carmel. He was worn out after the arduous task of standing for God in the face of such opposition.

The sin of the ministry is not finances, although many people think it is. Unfortunately, there are some preachers who are running a religious racket, but money is not the problem with the average preacher. When I was ordained, I was warned about the three sins of the ministry: pride, being boring, and laziness. I am confident that some folk are never going to get under a juniper tree. Do you know why? They are too lazy. Although there were seven thousand believers who had not bowed a knee to Baal, they were not under the juniper tree. They were hiding in caves up in the hills. They would never have been able to stand the lofty heights of Mount Carmel, and they did not see the fire come down from heaven. Elijah stood alone. He was a prodigal of his own physical strength. Some dear saint, I am sure, whispered in his ear, "You are doing too much. Take it easy." Elijah would never have run away from Jezebel if he had not been exhausted. I think we need men today who are willing to work for God. I hear a lot of talk about folks being dedicated, but they are as lazy and careless in the Lord's work as they possibly can be. This could never be said of Elijah. He was under the juniper tree because he was exhausted.

There is also a psychological factor involved in this situation. This is the day of hypertension, frustration, sterility, frigidity, nervous debilitation, disappointment, discouragement, despondency, let-down, run-down, and breakdown. Perhaps you have misunderstood Elijah. He was rough and rugged. He was a blood-and-thunder man. But that rugged exterior concealed a sensitive soul. He was ruled by his emotions, and he could go from elation to dejection. He possessed the finer sensibilities—he had artistic taste and aesthetic taste. His nature was emotional, and he did things that were emotional. Perhaps he suffered, as the psychologists say, from manic-depressive psychosis. A woman is probably the most delicate of God's creatures, and a woman is emotional. She has a finer sensibility than a man. Elijah had that kind of a nature. Did you ever notice that God put a badger skin around all of the beauty, wealth, and workmanship of the tabernacle? A badger skin was the exterior of something fine and beautiful. The exterior of Elijah was like that. Now he is crying out for God to take his life. He is in bad shape.

And as he lay and slept under a juniper tree, behold, then an angel touched him, and said unto him, Arise and eat.

And he looked, and, behold, there was a cake baken on the coals, and a cruse of water at his head. And he did eat and drink, and laid him down again.

And the angel of the LORD came again the second time, and touched him, and said, Arise and eat; because the journey is too great for thee [1 Kings 19:5–7].

Elijah needed rest. The Lord knew that, so He put him to sleep. Elijah slept like a baby. He also needed some good food—I don't think he had been eating regularly. He awoke to find some bread being baked. Do you know who I think baked that bread? I believe it was the same One who prepared that breakfast on the shore of Galilee one morning after the Resurrection. It was our Lord who comforted Elijah, fed him, and then put him back to sleep. He fed him, the second time, and told Elijah, "The journey is too great for you." This was something that Elijah had learned.

My friend, today may be a very happy day for you. You may think that you are sufficient for the battle of life. But I want to tell you that the journey through life is too great for you. You are going to need a Savior. You are going to need a helper. Elijah, as rugged as he was, needed Him.

ELIJAH AT MOUNT HOREB

And he arose, and did eat and drink, and went in the strength of that meat forty days and forty nights unto Horeb the mount of God [1 Kings 19:8].

Strengthened by the food provided by God, Elijah continued to run. He went clear to Mount Horeb, the mount on which the Law had been given to Moses.

And he came thither unto a cave, and lodged there; and, behold, the word of the LORD came to him, and he said unto him, What doest thou here, Elijah?

And he said, I have been very jealous for the LORD God of hosts: for the children of Israel have forsaken thy covenant, thrown down thine altars, and slain thy prophets with the sword; and I, even I only, am left; and they seek my life, to take it away [1 Kings 19:9–10].

The Lord is dealing with Elijah. He is overwrought and needs real psychological help. I have been asked if I believe in going to a psychologist. I think there are times when a person needs to consult a psychologist. Most of us, however, could solve our problems if we crawled on the couch of the Lord Jesus Christ and told Him everything. We wouldn't have to be running around telling everybody else about our troubles and problems if we would just talk them over with Him. We ought to tell Him everything.

And he said, Go forth, and stand upon the mount before the LORD. And, behold, the LORD passed by, and a great and strong wind rent the mountains, and brake in pieces the rocks before the LORD; but the LORD was not in the wind: and after the wind an earthquake; but the LORD was not in the earthquake [1 Kings 19:11].

First of all there was a great and strong wind that split the mountains and broke the rocks. Oh, did he love a good wind storm! Then the mountain rolled and shook under his feet. He loved it—he was that type of man.

And after the earthquake a fire; but the LORD was not in the fire: and after the fire a still small voice [1 Kings 19:12].

After the earthquake there was a fire. After all, he was the man who brought fire down from heaven on Mount Carmel. He liked that too. But wait a minute. God was not in the strong wind, nor the earthquake, nor the fire. After the fire came a still, small voice. If there was one thing that Elijah did not like, it was a still, small voice. I am sure Elijah did not have that kind of a voice, but he had to learn that God moves in a quiet way—how wonderful it is to see God moving in this way. He was teaching Elijah a great lesson. The battle was not actually won on top of Mount Carmel by fire coming down from heaven. God moves in mysterious and unostentatious ways His wonders to perform. God moves in a quiet way. God uses little things to accomplish His purpose. As someone has said, "Great doors are swung on little hinges." God uses small things to open mighty doors. That is what Elijah had to learn.

And it was so, when Elijah heard it that he wrapped his face in his mantle, and went out, and stood in the entering in of the cave. And, behold, there came a voice unto him, and said, What doest thou here, Elijah?

And he said, I have been very jealous for the LORD God of hosts: because the children of Israel have forsaken thy covenant, thrown down thine altars, and slain thy prophets with the sword; and I, even I only, am left; and they seek my life, to take it away [1 Kings 19:13–14].

Many of us can identify with Elijah. Sometimes with our families or in our communities we are surrounded by unbelievers, and we get the feeling that we are the only ones on earth standing for Christ.

And the LORD said unto him, Go, return on thy way to the wilderness of Damascus: and when thou comest, anoint Hazael to be king over Syria:

And Jehu the son of Nimshi shalt thou anoint to be king over Israel: and Elisha the son of Shaphat of Abelmeholah shalt thou anoint to be prophet in thy room.

And it shall come to pass, that him that escapeth the sword of Hazael shall Jehu slay: and him that escapeth from the sword of Jehu shall Elisha slay [1 Kings 19:15–17].

God is saying to Elijah, "Go back to the north country; I have more work for you to do." He is to anoint Hazael to be king over Syria and Jehu to be king over Israel. Then God tells Elijah about his successor, Elisha.

Yet I have left me seven thousand in Israel, all the knees which have not bowed unto Baal, and every mouth which hath not kissed him [1 Kings 19:18].

Finally, He told Elijah that there was a remnant of seven thousand people who have not bowed to Baal. God always has a remnant, my friend. He had one in Elijah's day, and He has one today. I have been very unkind in my references to the remnant. But they were standing for God. They had not bowed the knee to Baal. They were not out in the open like Elijah; they were the silent ones, but they were true to the God of Israel.

ELISHA'S CALL

God now is preparing to take Elijah home, and He will raise up Elisha to take his place.

> So he departed thence, and found Elisha the son of Shaphat, who was plowing with twelve yoke of oxen before him, and he with the twelfth: and Elijah passed by him, and cast his mantle upon him.

> And he left the oxen, and ran after Elijah, and said, Let me, I pray thee, kiss my father and my mother, and then I will follow thee. And he said unto him, Go back again: for what have I done to thee?

> And he returned back from him, and took a yoke of oxen, and slew them, and boiled their flesh with the instruments of the oxen, and gave unto the people, and they did eat. Then he arose, and went after Elijah, and ministered unto him [1 Kings 19:19–21].

Elisha now becomes the pupil of Elijah. He is being trained to take over his ministry, as we shall see.

CHAPTER 20

THEME: Israel is attacked by Syria

Remember that this event occurs during the time the kingdom of Israel is divided. The ten northern tribes bear the name of Israel. Because of the repeated sin of both king and people, God is permitting their enemies to attack them. However, again God is gracious and gives them opportunity to repent and return to Him. In this chapter God delivers Israel, though pitifully outnumbered, from the mighty army of Syria.

AHAB'S FIRST SYRIAN CAMPAIGN AND HIS VICTORY

And Ben-hadad the king of Syria gathered all his host together: and there were thirty and two kings with him, and horses, and chariots: and he went up and besieged Samaria, and warred against it [1 Kings 20:1].

God is now permitting the enemy to come in from the outside. Up to this time God had not permitted it at all. We are told, however, that God promised victory even to Ahab.

And, behold, there came a prophet unto Ahab king of Israel, saying, Thus saith the LORD, Hast thou seen all this great multitude? behold, I will deliver it into thine hand this day; and thou shalt know that I am the LORD.

And Ahab said, By whom? And he said, Thus saith the LORD, Even by the young men of the princes of the provinces. Then he said, Who shall order the battle? And he answered, Thou [1 Kings 20:13–14].

The promise of God's deliverance in this situation was not based upon Ahab's fidelity but on God's love for His people. God gave this man an opportunity to change. We hear a great deal today about lost opportunities and about opportunity knocking only once at the door of every man. I think opportunity stands at the door and keeps knocking. Now Ahab was promised a victory, and God gave him a great victory over the Syrians.

> **And they slew every one his man: and the Syrians fled; and Israel pursued them: and Ben-hadad the king of Syria escaped on an horse with the horsemen.**

> **And the king of Israel went out, and smote the horses and chariots, and slew the Syrians with a great slaughter [1 Kings 20:20–21].**

AHAB'S SECOND SYRIAN CAMPAIGN AND HIS REBUKE FOR SPARING BEN-HADAD'S LIFE

> **And the prophet came to the king of Israel, and said unto him, Go, strengthen thyself, and mark, and see what thou doest: for at the return of the year the king of Syria will come up against thee [1 Kings 20:22].**

God was telling Ahab, "I have given you a victory now, but you be careful that you don't return to the worship of Baal. I have demonstrated that I am your God—the living God. The king of Syria is going to come against you again at the return of the year." It was not the end of the struggle; Ben-hadad was going to renew his effort to defeat Israel. This is a very vivid picture.

> **And the children of Israel were numbered, and were all present, and went against them: and the children of Israel pitched before them like two little flocks of kids; but the Syrians filled the country.**

> And there came a man of God, and spake unto the king
> of Israel, and said, Thus saith the LORD, Because the
> Syrians have said, The LORD is God of the hills, but he is
> not God of the valleys, therefore will I deliver all this
> great multitude into thine hand, and ye shall know that
> I am the LORD [1 Kings 20:27–28].

Once again God gave Ahab victory over the enemy, but unfortunately, Ahab made the mistake of sparing Ben-hadad's life.

> And Ben-hadad said unto him, The cities, which my
> father took from thy father, I will restore; and thou shalt
> make streets for thee in Damascus, as my father made
> in Samaria. Then said Ahab, I will send thee away with
> this covenant. So he made a covenant with him, and sent
> him away [1 Kings 20:34].

Ahab was told to eliminate the enemy, but he did not obey. There can be no compromise, friend, with sin. God never permits that, and that is exactly what Ahab had done.

> And he said unto him, Thus saith the LORD, Because
> thou hast let go out of thy hand a man whom I appointed
> to utter destruction, therefore thy life shall go for his
> life, and thy people for his people [1 Kings 20:42].

Why is it today that judges are so lenient with criminals? It is because they have a guilt complex themselves, my friend. They feel guilty themselves, and they know they are sinners. It is almost like pointing the finger at themselves to convict someone else. It is very hard for one sinner to judge another sinner. This was the case with Ahab—that is why he spared Ben-hadad's life.

CHAPTER 21

THEME: Ahab and Naboth's vineyard

The chapter before us is a page out of the lives of the wicked king and queen of Israel, Ahab and Jezebel, which reveals their covetous and ruthless characters.

NABOTH'S VINEYARD IS COVETED BY AHAB

And it came to pass after these things, that Naboth the Jezreelite had a vineyard, which was in Jezreel, hard by the palace of Ahab king of Samaria [1 Kings 21:1].

A few years ago I was in Samaria, and I must confess that it is one of the most beautiful spots in the land of Palestine. You can stand on the hill of Samaria where Ahab and Jezebel's palace stood (Omri built it), and you can see Jerusalem to the south, the valley of Esdraelon and the Sea of Galilee to the north, the Jordan River on the east, and the Mediterranean Sea on the west. It is a beautiful view on all four sides. There are not many places like that. If I were living in that land, that would be the spot where I would like to have my home.

And Ahab spake unto Naboth, saying, Give me thy vineyard, that I may have it for a garden of herbs, because it is near unto my house: and I will give thee for it a better vineyard than it; or, if it seem good to thee, I will give thee the worth of it in money.

And Naboth said to Ahab, The LORD forbid it me, that I should give the inheritance of my fathers unto thee [1 Kings 21:2–3].

Naboth had a vineyard in this area. And as I stood on that beautiful hill, I wondered what side it was on. We do know it was nearby. And with as lovely a palace as Ahab had, you would think he would be satisfied. But, no, he wants that vineyard. Naboth does not want to sell it for the very simple reason that the vineyard is his patrimony. It is what God had given to his ancestors, and it had been passed down from father to son. But now here is a king who wants it, and it takes a pretty brave man to turn him down.

> And Ahab came into his house heavy and displeased because of the word which Naboth the Jezreelite had spoken to him: for he had said, I will not give thee the inheritance of my fathers. And he laid him down upon his bed, and turned away his face, and would eat no bread [1 Kings 21:4].

Ahab doesn't get his way, so he goes home and pouts like a little boy. Ahab, wicked as he is, is like a spoiled brat and won't eat now because he cannot have what he wants—he can't have that vineyard!

JEZEBEL'S MURDEROUS PLOT TO OBTAIN NABOTH'S VINEYARD

Ahab did not have any ideas about how to get Naboth's vineyard, but Jezebel did. I can assure you that she is going to work out something that will enable her husband to get it.

> But Jezebel his wife came to him, and said unto him, Why is thy spirit so sad, that thou eatest no bread?

> And he said unto her, Because I spake unto Naboth the Jezreelite, and said unto him, Give me thy vineyard for money; or else, if it please thee, I will give thee another vineyard for it: and he answered, I will not give thee my vineyard.

> And Jezebel his wife said unto him, Dost thou now govern the kingdom of Israel? arise, and eat bread, and let

> thine heart be merry: I will give thee the vineyard of
> Naboth the Jezreelite [1 Kings 21:5-7].

Jezebel was absolutely masculine in her manner—she was a dominant
and domineering woman. I would have been afraid of her myself, I
must confess. She is a wicked woman, and she *is* going to get the
vineyard. She contrives a nice little plot and arranges to have two law-
less men witness against Naboth. They say that he blasphemed God
and the king. Naboth is then carried out of the city and stoned to
death. Can you think of anything more unjust than this? Well, it has
happened many times in the history of the world. Many times the man
on top who has everything has taken advantage of the little man.

Naboth was stoned to death. Did Ahab get by with it? My friend,
you don't get by with sin. I don't care who you are—the day will come
when you are going to have to settle up. And the day came when Ahab
had to settle up.

> And it came to pass, when Jezebel heard that Naboth
> was stoned, and was dead, that Jezebel said to Ahab,
> Arise, take possession of the vineyard of Naboth the
> Jezreelite, which he refused to give thee for money: for
> Naboth is not alive, but dead.

> And it came to pass, when Ahab heard that Naboth was
> dead, that Ahab rose up to go down to the vineyard of
> Naboth the Jezreelite, to take possession of it [1 Kings
> 21:15-16].

So Jezebel came in and announced to her husband Ahab, "Naboth is
dead, and you can have the vineyard." It looks like Ahab has gotten by
with his wickedness, doesn't it? No, God has a man there. Thank God
that there is a man around who will declare the Word of God!

AHAB'S AND JEZEBEL'S DOOM IS PREDICTED

> And the word of the LORD came to Elijah the Tishbite,
> saying,

> Arise, go down to meet Ahab king of Israel, which is in
> Samaria: behold, he is in the vineyard of Naboth,
> whither he is gone down to possess it.
>
> And thou shalt speak unto him, saying, Thus saith the
> LORD, Hast thou killed, and also taken possession? And
> thou shalt speak unto him, saying, Thus saith the LORD,
> In the place where dogs licked the blood of Naboth shall
> dogs lick thy blood, even thine [1 Kings 21:17–19].

Remember that God has said, "Be not deceived; God is not mocked:
for whatsoever a man soweth, that shall he also reap" (Gal. 6:7). If you
and I could speak with men from the past—whether they were God's
men or Satan's—they would tell us that this is an immutable law of
God; it cannot be changed.

Jacob found out the truth of this law. Pharaoh of Egypt, who killed
the little Hebrew boys, thought he got by with his crime, but one day
he found that his firstborn was dead. David committed an awful sin,
but he did not get by with it. The same thing he did came back to him.
Saul of Tarsus was a leader in the stoning of Stephen, but there came a
day in Asia Minor, at Antioch of Pisidia, when he was stoned and left
for dead. The fact of the matter is that he was dead, and God raised
him from the dead.

Now here is the judgment that is pronounced on Ahab and Jezebel:

> Behold, I will bring evil upon thee, and will take away
> thy posterity, and will cut off from Ahab him that piss-
> eth against the wall, and him that is shut up and left in
> Israel,
>
> And will make thine house like the house of Jeroboam
> the son of Nebat, and like the house of Baasha the son of
> Ahijah, for the provocation wherewith thou hast pro-
> voked me to anger, and made Israel to sin [1 Kings
> 21:21–22].

God says to Ahab, "I'm removing your house. Your line will not reign here." Now God is not through:

And of Jezebel also spake the LORD, saying, The dogs shall eat Jezebel by the wall of Jezreel [1 Kings 21:23].

Both of these judgments very definitely come to pass.

CHAPTER 22

THEME: Ahab and the prophet Micaiah

Now in chapter 22 we will see the fulfillment of the Lord's judgment against Ahab. While we have been following the career of this king of the northern kingdom, down in the south Jehoshaphat has come to the throne. He is a good king, but now he is going to make an alliance with Ahab.

> **And they continued three years without war between Syria and Israel.**
>
> **And it came to pass in the third year, that Jehoshaphat the king of Judah came down to the king of Israel [1 Kings 22:1–2].**

What has happened that would cause a good king like Jehoshaphat to make an alliance with a king as wicked as Ahab? Why would he fraternize with his natural enemy? It's an abnormal alliance, an unnatural confederacy. At this point it seems strange, but we will find out later that Jehoram, the son of Jehoshaphat, had married Athaliah, the daughter of Ahab and Jezebel. This was a case of the "sons of God marrying the daughters of men"; that is, a boy with a godly heritage married a girl with a very wicked one. And the wicked influence prevailed. When the believer and the unbeliever get married, my friend, you can always be sure that the believer is going to have trouble. When you marry a child of the Devil, your father-in-law sees to it that you have trouble.

> **And the king of Israel said unto his servants, Know ye that Ramoth in Gilead is ours, and we be still, and take it not out of the hand of the king of Syria?**

> And he said unto Jehoshaphat, Wilt thou go with me to
> battle to Ramoth-gilead? And Jehoshaphat said to the
> king of Israel, I am as thou art, my people as thy people,
> my horses as thy horses [1 Kings 22:3–4].

Ramoth-gilead was one of the chief cities of the tribe of Gad, and it had
been lost to Syria. The best thing to do would have been to leave
things as they were—status quo. At least Jehoshaphat should have
stayed out of it. He should have followed the advice given to him by
the prophet of the Lord. It was too bad that the Devil's man and God's
man made an alliance. This was not Jehoshaphat's fight anyway. Gilead did not belong to him—it belonged to Ahab, and it was Ahab's
quarrel, not his.

AHAB IS PROMISED VICTORY
BY HIS LYING PROPHETS

> And Jehoshaphat said unto the king of Israel, Inquire, I
> pray thee, at the word of the LORD today [1 Kings 22:5].

Jehoshaphat is God's man. He wants to know what the will of God is.

> Then the king of Israel gathered the prophets together,
> about four hundred men, and said unto them, Shall I go
> against Ramoth-gilead to battle, or shall I forbear? And
> they said, Go up; for the LORD shall deliver it into the
> hand of the king.
>
> And Jehoshaphat said, Is there not here a prophet of the
> LORD besides, that we might inquire of him? [1 Kings
> 22:6–7].

Jehoshaphat wants to know the mind of the Lord, and he suspects that
they are not getting it through these false prophets. He has a real spiritual discernment, and so he asks, "Is there not here a prophet of the
LORD besides, that we might inquire of him?"

**And the king of Israel said unto Jehoshaphat, There is
yet one man, Micaiah the son of Imlah, by whom we
may inquire of the LORD: but I hate him; for he doth not
prophesy good concerning me, but evil. And Jehoshaphat said, Let not the king say so [1 Kings 22:8].**

Ahab then introduces Micaiah, the after-dinner speaker. And he does
so in a most unusual way—he says, "I hate him." Then Jehoshaphat
says to Ahab, "You really don't mean that you hate a man of God."
Someone has said that a man is not really known by his friends.
Rather, he is known by his enemies. Every man ought to make sure
that he has the right enemies. The best compliment that could be paid
to Micaiah was for Ahab to say, "I hate him."

In the Lord's work I have always prided myself on the fact that I
had the right enemies. I like the enemies I have because they do not
stand for the Word of God. It is well to have the right enemies as well
as the right friends. I can truthfully say that I thank God for my
friends. I can also thank God for my enemies.

A toastmaster once said about a preacher he was introducing, "He
doesn't have an enemy." God have mercy on him! You only had to
listen to him for three minutes, and you could see why he had no
enemies. He was Mr. Milquetoast—he didn't stand for anything. Micaiah actually was the best friend Ahab ever had. Ahab just didn't
know it. Micaiah could say as Paul did, "Am I therefore become your
enemy, because I tell you the truth?" (Gal. 4:16).

**Then the king of Israel called an officer, and said, Has-
ten hither Micaiah the son of Imlah [1 Kings 22:9].**

They brought Micaiah in. After all, he was very close at hand: Ahab
was keeping him in prison. This is another of these great dramatic
scenes:

**And the king of Israel and Jehoshaphat the king of Ju-
dah sat each on his throne, having put on their robes, in**

a void place in the entrance of the gate of Samaria; and
all the prophets prophesied before them.

And Zedekiah the son of Chenaanah made him horns of
iron: and he said, Thus saith the LORD, With these shalt
thou push the Syrians, until thou have consumed them.

And all the prophets prophesied so, saying, Go up to
Ramoth-gilead, and prosper: for the LORD shall deliver
it into the king's hand [1 Kings 22:10–12].

You can just imagine those four hundred prophets running around
saying to Ahab, "Go up against the king of Syria." One of the prophets
was especially dramatic. Zedekiah ran around with iron horns, push-
ing at everyone with them, saying, "This is the way you are going to
do it." What a scene—two kings on their thrones and all those
prophets running about crying, "Go up and fight. You will win."

DEFEAT IS PROPHESIED BY MICAIAH

And the messenger that was gone to call Micaiah spake
unto him, saying, Behold now, the words of the prophets
declare good unto the king with one mouth: let thy
word, I pray thee, be like the word of one of them, and
speak that which is good [1 Kings 22:13].

The messenger that brought forth Micaiah said, "I'd just like to put a
bug in your ear: all of the prophets are prophesying something good.
They are telling the king to fight because he will win. That is what he
wants to hear. You should join with them. Then you could get back
into the king's favor. Here's your chance, Micaiah." And, I suppose,
this guard thought he was helping Micaiah.

And Micaiah said, As the LORD liveth, what the LORD
saith unto me, that will I speak [1 Kings 22:14].

Micaiah's answer was not only dramatic, it was humorous. He said, "Whatever the Lord tells me to say, that is what I am going to say. I will tell it like it is." Then Micaiah came in and sized up the situation. He saw the two kings on their thrones and all of the false prophets of Baal running around the room. They were all saying nice things to Ahab. They had all read the book, *How to Win Friends and Influence People.* Micaiah had not read that book. Neither had he read *The Power of Positive Thinking.* In fact, he was pretty negative. There is a lot of power in negative thinking, friend. We need more of it today.

> **So he came to the king. And the king said unto him, Micaiah, shall we go against Ramoth-gilead to battle, or shall we forbear? And he answered him, Go, and prosper: for the LORD shall deliver it into the hand of the king [1 Kings 22:15].**

Notice what Micaiah says to the kings. To him it is a humorous scene, so he joins in just for fun. I think he was as sarcastic as any man could be—just as sarcastic as Elijah could be. They were cut out of the same piece of cloth, by the way. Micaiah said, "Go, and prosper: for the LORD shall deliver it into the hand of the king." Immediately the king saw that he was being ridiculed.

> **And the king said unto him, How many times shall I adjure thee that thou tell me nothing but that which is true in the name of the LORD? [1 Kings 22:16].**

The king said to Micaiah, "I know you are kidding me because you have never been on the side of the false prophets."
Suddenly Micaiah becomes very serious and solemn.

> **And he said, I saw all Israel scattered upon the hills, as sheep that have not a shepherd: and the LORD said,**

> These have no master: let them return every man to his
> house in peace.
>
> And the king of Israel said unto Jehoshaphat, Did I not
> tell thee that he would prophesy no good concerning
> me, but evil? [1 Kings 22:17–18].

And the king of Israel says to Jehoshaphat, "I told you so—I told you
he would say nothing but evil about me."

Then Micaiah said, "I'm not through. I have something else to say
to you that you ought to hear." And he gives a parable. You could call it
a parable that is the *reductio ad absurdum*. It is a preposterous parable, a parable by contrast. (You will not find parables like this until
you come to our Lord's teaching as recorded by Luke. Take, for example, the parable of the unjust judge: God is not an unjust judge.)

Notice what Micaiah says here:

> And he said, Hear thou therefore the word of the Lord: I
> saw the Lord sitting on his throne, and all the host of
> heaven standing by him on his right hand and on his
> left.
>
> And the Lord said, Who shall persuade Ahab, that he
> may go up and fall at Ramoth-gilead? And one said on
> this manner, and another said on that manner [1 Kings
> 22:19–20].

Isn't that ridiculous? Can you imagine God calling a meeting of the
board of directors or of the church board to ask them what He should
do in a case like this? God already knows what He is going to do, and
He does not need any advice.

> And there came forth a spirit, and stood before the
> Lord, and said, I will persuade him.

> And the LORD said unto him, Wherewith? And he said, I
> will go forth, and I will be a lying spirit in the mouth of
> all his prophets. And he said, Thou shalt persuade him,
> and prevail also: go forth, and do so [1 Kings 22:21–22].

Imagine this! God says, "My, you smart little fellow! I wish I had
thought of that."

> Now therefore, behold, the LORD hath put a lying spirit
> in the mouth of all these thy prophets, and the LORD hath
> spoken evil concerning thee [1 Kings 22:23].

This was the nicest way Micaiah could call these prophets a bunch of
liars.

> But Zedekiah the son of Chenaanah went near, and
> smote Micaiah on the cheek, and said, Which way went
> the Spirit of the LORD from me to speak unto thee?
>
> And Micaiah said, Behold, thou shalt see in that day,
> when thou shalt go into an inner chamber to hide thy-
> self.
>
> And the king of Israel said, Take Micaiah, and carry
> him back unto Amon the governor of the city, and to
> Joash the king's son:
>
> And say, Thus saith the king, Put this fellow in the
> prison, and feed him with bread of affliction and with
> water of affliction, until I come in peace [1 Kings
> 22:24–27].

Zedekiah, the false prophet, struck Micaiah on the cheek. This was an
extreme insult. In response to the insult Micaiah said by implication
that the day would come when the false prophets would hide them-

selves in terror. That time would come when Ahab was dead and Israel was defeated. Then Zedekiah would know what the truth was.

And Micaiah said, If thou return at all in peace, the LORD hath not spoken by me. And he said, Hearken, O people, every one of you [1 Kings 22:28].

Micaiah told Ahab that he was not coming back. If he did, then the Lord had not spoken by him. Then Micaiah said, "In view of the fact the you won't be coming back, Ahab, I want the people to witness that what I have spoken is the truth."

AHAB'S DEFEAT AND DEATH

Israel went to battle. They listened to the false prophets, and what happened? Israel lost the battle. And Ahab proved he was a deceiver all the way through. You see, the only man in the battle who had on king's robes was Jehoshaphat, which made him a marked man, because Ahab had disguised himself. You might say that Ahab set Jehoshaphat up as a clay pigeon to be slain in the battle. It was not Jehoshaphat's fight at all, but he almost didn't come out of it alive.

But the king of Syria commanded his thirty and two captains that had rule over his chariots, saying, Fight neither with small nor great, save only with the king of Israel.

And it came to pass, when the captains of the chariots saw Jehoshaphat, that they said, Surely it is the king of Israel.

And they turned aside to fight against him: and Jehoshaphat cried out.

And it came to pass, when the captains of the chariots perceived that it was not the king of Israel, that they turned back from pursuing him [1 Kings 22:31–33].

Poor Jehoshaphat almost lost his life in the battle because of Ahab's deception.

> **And a certain man drew a bow at a venture, and smote the king of Israel between the joints of the harness: wherefore he said unto the driver of his chariot, Turn thine hand, and carry me out of the host; for I am wounded.**
>
> **And the battle increased that day: and the king was stayed up in his chariot against the Syrians, and died at even: and the blood ran out of the wound into the midst of the chariot [1 Kings 22:34–35].**

Ahab was not slain by a soldier that aimed at him. The king was not a target, and the soldier did not shoot at Ahab—yet that arrow found him. You might say it was the first guided missile. I imagine that he was just an ordinary soldier with one last arrow left in his quiver. He pulled it out, put it in his bow, and simply let it go. He didn't know where it was going. Ahab's death would have to be listed as accidental, but in God's record it was providential: that arrow was aimed.

And you know, God still uses a very crude form of weapon—He's still back in the bow and arrow days. In Psalm 64:7, we read: "But God shall shoot at them with an arrow; suddenly shall they be wounded." There are those today who think they have escaped the hand of God. But I want to tell you that God has an arrow with your name on it; it will find you one of these days. No matter how much you try to deceive and cover up, that arrow will find you. That is what happened to Ahab.

> **So the king died, and was brought to Samaria; and they buried the king in Samaria.**
>
> **And one washed the chariot in the pool of Samaria; and the dogs licked up his blood; and they washed his ar-**

mour; according unto the word of the LORD which he spake [1 Kings 22:37–38].

That which God had predicted through Elijah came to pass: Ahab died, and his blood was licked up by dogs in the same place that Naboth had died. Of course, Ahab had tried to stay away from that place, but his chariot was brought into Naboth's vineyard, and the blood was washed out of it. The dogs were right there to lick it up. The prophecy was literally fulfilled. Whatever a man sows, my friend, he will reap. Why? Because God is not mocked. You cannot get by with sin; no one gets by with it. God sees to that; He is still on the throne.

Now we turn briefly to the reign of Jehoshaphat, and we find that he made a big mistake.

And he walked in all the ways of Asa his father; he turned not aside from it, doing that which was right in the eyes of the LORD: nevertheless the high places were not taken away; for the people offered and burnt incense yet in the high places [1 Kings 22:43].

This was a token of compromise that God could not nor did He bless in the life of Jehoshaphat. It is quite obvious here that this man is a compromiser, and yet he is rated as a good king because he did serve God in his own personal life.

And Jehoshaphat made peace with the king of Israel [1 Kings 22:44].

This was a mistake also—he should not have done this. We read in 2 Chronicles that Jehu the prophet met Jehoshaphat as he returned from his visit with Ahab: "And Jehu the son of Hanani the seer went out to meet him, and said to king Jehoshaphat, Shouldest thou help the ungodly, and love them that hate the LORD? therefore is wrath upon thee from before the LORD. Nevertheless there are good things found in thee, in that thou hast taken away the groves out of the land, and hast prepared thine heart to seek God" (2 Chron. 19:2–3). Now the groves were a place of great immorality, but the high places where sacrifices offered to Baal were not taken away. Jehoshaphat had compromised.

> **Jehoshaphat made ships of Tharshish to go to Ophir for gold: but they went not; for the ships were broken at Ezion-geber.**
>
> **Then said Ahaziah the son of Ahab unto Jehoshaphat, Let my servants go with thy servants in the ships. But Jehoshaphat would not [1 Kings 22:48–49].**

The son of Ahab who had come to the throne in the northern kingdom wanted Jehoshaphat to join him in a business deal—it would be a peaceful mission this time—but Jehoshaphat would not compromise again. He had learned his lesson. He said, "No, thank you. I don't care for this kind of an arrangement at all."

> **And Jehoshaphat slept with his fathers, and was buried with his fathers in the city of David his father: and Jehoram his son reigned in his stead [1 Kings 22:50].**

Jehoshaphat died and was succeeded by his son Jehoram.

> **Ahaziah the son of Ahab began to reign over Israel in Samaria the seventeenth year of Jehoshaphat king of Judah, and reigned two years over Israel.**
>
> **And he did evil in the sight of the LORD, and walked in the way of his father, and in the way of his mother, and in the way of Jeroboam the son of Nebat, who made Israel to sin:**
>
> **For he served Baal, and worshipped him, and provoked to anger the LORD God of Israel, according to all that his father had done [1 Kings 22:51–53].**

Ahaziah, the son of Ahab, began to reign over Israel in Samaria. He reigned for two years and followed in the footsteps of Ahab and Jezebel.

(For Bibliography to 1 Kings, see Bibliography at the end of 2 Kings.)

The Book of
2 KINGS

For introductory material and outline, see the Book of 1 Kings.

CHAPTER 1

THEME: Fire from heaven protects Elijah from Ahaziah

First Kings 22:51 tells us that "Ahaziah, the son of Ahab, began to reign over Israel in Samaria. . . ." We pick up the story in 2 Kings at this point. In fact, there does not seem to be a proper division between 1 and 2 Kings. Ahaziah's reign in Israel is begun in 1 Kings and concluded in 2 Kings.

The king and the prophet take the place of the priest as God's instruments of communication.

In 2 Kings, the first chapter, Ahaziah, king of Israel and son of Ahab and Jezebel, fell down through a lattice and seriously injured himself.

Then Moab rebelled against Israel after the death of Ahab.

And Ahaziah fell down through a lattice in his upper chamber that was in Samaria, and was sick: and he sent messengers, and said unto them, Go, inquire of Baal-zebub the god of Ekron whether I shall recover of this disease [2 Kings 1:1–2].

I would be inclined to say he fell because he was drunk. This is only a guess. Then instead of going to the Lord God for help, Ahaziah—greatly influenced by his mother Jezebel—went to inquire of Baal-zebub, the god of Ekron. Ahaziah's request for an oracle was a direct challenge to the Lord God of Israel. He wanted to know if he would recover from the effects of the accident.

But the angel of the LORD said to Elijah the Tishbite, Arise, go up to meet the messengers of the king of Sa-

maria, and say unto them, Is it not because there is not a
God in Israel, that ye go to inquire of Baal-zebub the god
of Ekron?

Now therefore thus saith the LORD, Thou shalt not come
down from that bed on which thou art gone up, but shalt
surely die. And Elijah departed [2 Kings 1:3–4].

This was one of Elijah's last missions. He went to meet the messengers
and gave them this challenge. "Is it not because there is not a God in
Israel, that ye go to inquire of Baal-zebub the God of Ekron?" Then he
gave them God's unwelcome prognosis: Ahaziah would not recover,
he would die. The messengers went back and reported to the king
what Elijah had said.

ELIJAH IS PROTECTED BY GOD

And he said unto them, What manner of man was he
which came up to meet you, and told you these words?

And they answered him, He was an hairy man, and girt
with a girdle of leather about his loins. And he said, It is
Elijah the Tishbite [2 Kings 1:7–8].

This furnishes us an interesting description of the physical appear-
ance of Elijah.

Then the king sent unto him a captain of fifty with his
fifty. And he went up to him: and, behold, he sat on the
top of an hill. And he spake unto him, Thou man of
God, the king hath said, Come down.

And Elijah answered and said to the captain of fifty, If I
be a man of God, then let fire come down from heaven,
and consume thee and thy fifty. And there came down
fire from heaven, and consumed him and his fifty
[2 Kings 1:9–10].

Remember that Ahaziah the king was the son of Jezebel, the woman who had tried to kill Elijah. Apparently there was still a price on his head.

Elijah is quite a man, is he not? He simply did not fit in with the compromises of court life in that day.

There is much talk today about the fact that we should learn to communicate and learn to get along with everybody. May I say to you that this is *not* God's method. The compromise of the church and its leaders has not caused the world to listen to the church. As a matter of fact, the world is not listening at all. They pass the church right by. Why? The world will not listen until the church declares the Word of God. If the church preached God's Word, there would be communication.

Elijah managed to communicate. He was heard. People listened to him. He was a pretty rough type of an individual. The king sent another captain with fifty men, and he also ordered Elijah to come down from the top of the hill. What came down was fire from heaven which consumed the captain and his men.

And he sent again a captain of the third fifty with his fifty. And the third captain of fifty went up, and came and fell on his knees before Elijah, and besought him, and said unto him, O man of God, I pray thee, let my life, and the life of these fifty thy servants, be precious in thy sight [2 Kings 1:13].

This man asks for mercy, and God will extend mercy to him.

And the angel of the LORD said unto Elijah, Go down with him: be not afraid of him. And he arose, and went down with him unto the king.

And he said unto him, Thus saith the LORD, Forasmuch as thou hast sent messengers to inquire of Baal-zebub the god of Ekron, is it not because there is no God in Israel to inquire of his word? therefore thou shalt not

come down off that bed on which thou art gone up, but shalt surely die [2 Kings 1:15-16].

Elijah boldly repeated God's pronouncement.

So he died according to the word of the LORD which Elijah had spoken. And Jehoram reigned in his stead in the second year of Jehoram the son of Jehoshaphat king of Judah; because he had no son.

Now the rest of the acts of Ahaziah which he did, are they not written in the book of the chronicles of the kings of Israel? [2 Kings 1:17-18].

This ends the line of Omri and Ahab.

CHAPTER 2

THEME: The translation of Elijah

This chapter brings us to the conclusion of Elijah's life. He is translated into heaven in a chariot of fire. Then Elisha comes into prominence. The chapter closes with the incident of irreverent hoodlums being attacked by bears.

ELIJAH'S DEPARTURE

And it came to pass, when the LORD would take up Elijah into heaven by a whirlwind, that Elijah went with Elisha from Gilgal.

And Elijah said unto Elisha, Tarry here, I pray thee; for the LORD hath sent me to Beth-el. And Elisha said unto him, As the LORD liveth, and as thy soul liveth, I will not leave thee. So they went down to Beth-el.

And the sons of the prophets that were at Beth-el came forth to Elisha, and said unto him, Knowest thou that the LORD will take away thy master from thy head today? And he said, Yea, I know it; hold ye your peace.

And Elijah said unto him, Elisha, tarry here, I pray thee; for the LORD hath sent me to Jericho. And he said, As the LORD liveth, and as thy soul liveth, I will not leave thee. So they came to Jericho [2 Kings 2:1–4].

Elijah is trying to get Elisha to stay back. Elisha will not leave Elijah because he knows that Elijah is going to leave the earth that day. Elisha wants to be present when the Lord takes him home.

And the sons of the prophets that were at Jericho came to Elisha, and said unto him, Knowest thou that the LORD

> will take away thy master from thy head today? And he
> answered, Yea, I know it; hold ye your peace [2 Kings
> 2:5].

The interesting thing is that people, then as well as today, were turning to all kinds of people and places for information. This is the day
when the fortunetellers and those who deal with the zodiac and the
occult are handing out many suggestions. People are turning everywhere except to God. You won't get any information from these areas
that you cannot get from God. The sons of the prophets had information that Elijah was going to leave, but Elisha already knew it. They
could not tell him anything new.

> And Elijah said unto him, Tarry, I pray thee, here; for
> the LORD hath sent me to Jordan. And he said, As the
> LORD liveth, and as thy soul liveth, I will not leave thee.
> And they two went on.
>
> And fifty men of the sons of the prophets went, and
> stood to view afar off: and they two stood by Jordan.
>
> And Elijah took his mantle, and wrapped it together,
> and smote the waters, and they were divided hither and
> thither, so that they two went over on dry ground
> [2 Kings 2:6–8].

The Lord had parted the River Jordan for Joshua and the people of
Israel at least five hundred years before this; now He repeats the miracle for Elijah and Elisha.

> And it came to pass, when they were gone over, that Eli-
> jah said unto Elisha, Ask what I shall do for thee, before
> I be taken away from thee. And Elisha said, I pray thee,
> let a double portion of thy spirit be upon me.
>
> And he said, Thou hast asked a hard thing: neverthe-
> less, if thou see me when I am taken from thee, it shall

be so unto thee; but if not, it shall not be so [2 Kings 2:9–10].

Now don't miss that. Elisha actually was a greater prophet than Elijah. He had a double portion of the Spirit of God upon him.

And it came to pass, as they still went on, and talked, that, behold, there appeared a chariot of fire, and horses of fire, and parted them both asunder; and Elijah went up by a whirlwind into heaven [2 Kings 2:11].

This is a spectacular conclusion of a spectacular life!

ELISHA RECEIVES A DOUBLE PORTION OF ELIJAH'S SPIRIT

And Elisha saw it, and he cried, My father, my father, the chariot of Israel, and the horsemen thereof. And he saw him no more: and he took hold of his own clothes, and rent them in two pieces.

He took up also the mantle of Elijah that fell from him, and went back, and stood by the bank of Jordan;

And he took the mantle of Elijah that fell from him, and smote the waters, and said, Where is the LORD God of Elijah? and when he also had smitten the waters, they parted hither and thither: and Elisha went over [2 Kings 2:12–14].

This man Elisha is taking Elijah's place, and he demonstrates his faith. He takes Elijah's robe and smites the waters just as Elijah had done. The power is not in the robe nor in Elijah; the power is in God, and Elisha knows that. Elisha had the faith Elijah had, and it is faith in the *God* of Elijah. He asks the question, "Where is the LORD God of Elijah?"

This is the important question today. Instead of looking to men or women, methods or some nostrum for help, as many people do, why not look to the Lord God of Israel? He is the *living* God. He is the God and Father of the Lord Jesus Christ. Look to Him, my friend.

Elisha took Elijah's mantle, smote the waters, and they parted. He crossed over the river to begin a new phase in his life.

ELISHA SUCCEEDS ELIJAH

And when the sons of the prophets which were to view at Jericho saw him, they said, The spirit of Elijah doth rest on Elisha. And they came to meet him, and bowed themselves to the ground before him.

And they said unto him, Behold now, there be with thy servants fifty strong men; let them go, we pray thee, and seek thy master: lest peradventure the spirit of the LORD hath taken him up, and cast him upon some mountain, or into some valley. And he said, Ye shall not send [2 Kings 2:15–16].

The sons of the prophets (the theological students of that day) were still watching and they saw Elisha part the waters and return across the Jordan River. They doubted that Elijah had really gone up. They suspected that the Lord had dumped him in some abandoned area. What a peculiar idea they had of God!

And when they urged him till he was ashamed, he said, Send. They sent therefore fifty men; and they sought three days, but found him not.

And when they came again to him, (for he tarried at Jericho,) he said unto them, Did I not say unto you, Go not? [2 Kings 2:17–18].

Elijah was indeed gone, and there was no need to investigate. Elisha said, "I told you so!"

Then the men of the city of Jericho came to Elisha with a problem.

And the men of the city said unto Elisha, Behold, I pray thee, the situation of this city is pleasant, as my lord seeth: but the water is naught, and the ground barren.

And he said, Bring me a new cruse, and put salt therein. And they brought it to him.

And he went forth unto the spring of the waters, and cast the salt in there, and said, Thus saith the LORD, I have healed these waters; there shall not be from thence any more death or barren land.

So the waters were healed unto this day, according to the saying of Elisha which he spake [2 Kings 2:19–22].

Elisha made the bitter waters sweet. This was his *second* miracle. Today you can see those waters in the valley at Jericho. I did not drink the water when I visited there because water out in the open in that land is apt to be contaminated. I am told, however, by those who were brave enough to drink it, that the water was sweet and delicious to drink.

Next followed an incident which has been criticized as much as anything in the Scriptures. This incident is pointed out with glee by the enemies of the Word of God who bemoan the brutal slaying of these poor little children.

First, let's look at the background. Elisha was returning from Elijah's translation when this event took place. The word had gone before him concerning what had taken place. As he went up to Bethel, "little children" mocked him. Elisha cursed them in the name of the Lord, and two female bears came out of the woods and "tare forty and two children."

Not only the critics but also many sincere believers have been stumped by this portion of Scripture. The scorner says, "You don't mean to tell me that God would destroy little children like that!" What is recorded here seems to contradict other portions of Scripture.

First of all we need to recognize that when we come into the world our human minds are more or less neutral. They are neutral on practically every subject but one, and that is an innate streak of rebellion against God. Man has an inborn bias against God. Man, first of all, is skeptical about the Bible. Man will believe anybody or anything except God. If you don't believe this statement, notice how people fall for the "scientific approach." Let a man on television put on a white coat and pince-nez glasses, make a statement about mouthwash, deodorant, or toothpaste, and everybody runs and buys it because it is "scientific." Well, my friend, that reveals the nature of man.

If a man is an honest doubter, he will find there is an answer to all the problems and questions that concern the Word of God. That does not mean that I can answer all of the problems, because I cannot. This is one question, however, that I can answer, and I want to spend a little time with it.

Now Elijah was succeeded by Elisha. In many respects Elisha was greater than Elijah. This will undoubtedly be a surprise to many people who consider Elijah one of the greatest prophets, and possibly one of the witnesses who will one day return to earth during the Tribulation (Rev. 11:3–7). If you want to measure these two men by the miracles they performed, Elisha performed the most miracles. Elijah was the man for the public. Elisha was the one who ministered personally to individuals. Because his ministry was largely in this area, it was not quite as exciting and dramatic as Elijah's ministry. He was a gentle man in contrast to Elijah.

Elisha was a young man at the beginning of his ministry. On this occasion he was returning from beyond Jordan where Elijah had been caught up in a chariot of fire and taken to heaven. News of this event had spread like wildfire over the countryside. Many people knew about it as Elisha returned to Bethel. Probably the news media of the day carried the news about Elijah. I guess the *Bethel Bugle* had a headline about the prophet and the chariot of fire. The *Bugle* would not confirm the story, but they did report that there were those who had seen the event take place.

Bethel means "house of God." It was first mentioned by Abraham, then by Jacob. Bethel, however, did not continue to live up to its name. At the time of the division of the kingdom, Jeroboam, you will recall, placed one of the golden calves in Bethel for the people to worship so that they would not continue to go to Jerusalem to worship. There was also a school for false prophets at Bethel. It was, of course, an imitation of the school of prophets in Judah. It was in this atmosphere that the children of Bethel were educated. They were godless. They had no training. They had no discipline at home. I think Bethel was a great deal like Los Angeles, where I live. How ironical it is: *Los Angeles* means "the city of angels," and we have everything else but angels here.

Now Elisha is on his way to Bethel.

And he went up from thence unto Beth-el: and as he was going up by the way, there came forth little children out of the city, and mocked him, and said unto him, Go up, thou bald head; go up, thou bald head [2 Kings 2:23].

Then "little children" came out of the city. The accepted opinion is that these were precious little children. All of us are moved by children. I have a little grandson, and he has grandpa wrapped around his finger. These little ones really get to you. When you read this portion of Scripture, it touches your heart. If these "children" were beginners, primaries, juniors, or even junior high young people, I would have to admit that Elisha was rather cruel because what happened would be contrary to the teaching of the rest of Scripture.

The Lord Jesus said, ". . . Suffer little children, and forbid them not, to come unto me: for of such is the kingdom of heaven" (Matt. 19:14). As you read the Bible, you will discover God's tender care of the little ones.

Remember that at Kadesh-Barnea the people of Israel refused to go into the land, and they gave the following excuse: "And wherefore hath the LORD brought us unto this land, to fall by the sword, that our wives and our children should be a prey? were it not better for us to return into Egypt?" (Num. 14:3). They felt that their little ones would be in danger. But God said to them in essence, "You should have trusted Me. You thought that I would not take care of your little ones. Well, although you will die in the wilderness, your little ones, who you thought were in danger, are going to inherit the land and dwell in it."

"Little children" is *naar* or *nahar* in Hebrew. It is used of Isaac when he was twenty-eight, of Joseph when he was thirty-nine, also for the Sodomites who attacked the home of Lot. You will find it used in other places in Scripture, and it does not refer to little children as we think of them. For example, 1 Kings 12:8 says, "But he forsook the counsel of the old men, which they had given him, and consulted with the young men that were grown up with him, and which stood before him." This verse is speaking about the time Rehoboam forsook the wisdom of the older men, the wise men, and consulted with the younger men who had grown up with him. The word translated "young men" is the same word translated "little children" in 2 Kings 2:23. I am sure no one believes that Rehoboam was consulting with little juniors, or that he went to nursery school and talked things over with the little ones. They were young men. When Samuel came to anoint as king one of the sons of Jesse, you will remember that his sons were grown. As they passed by Samuel one by one, he said to Jesse, "Are these all thy children?" Well, the word *children* is the same word used in 2 Kings 2:23. It is used to describe Jesse's grown sons. The youngest son, David, was not even there. The hoodlums who were taunting Elisha were young men, not little children. You will find this word used in many places in Scripture, and in every other place it is translated "young men." This was a crowd of young fellows.

They were students of the false prophets. They were a gang that mocked and ridiculed Elisha. They said, "Go up, thou bald head." What did they mean by that? They were telling him to do the same thing Elijah had done. They were saying, "Why don't you take off like Elijah did?" They were ridiculing the truth in Scripture that God will take a people out of this world.

This is the same attitude, Peter says, that will appear on the earth again in the last days. This incident in 2 Kings is given to us to let us know that God intends to judge those who ridicule the second coming of Christ. Second Peter 3:3–4 says, "Knowing this first, that there shall come in the last days scoffers, walking after their own lusts, and saying, Where is the promise of his coming? for since the fathers fell asleep, all things continue as they were from the beginning of the creation." During the last days on earth there will be those who will ridicule believers about the coming of Christ. They will say something like, "Well, what is the matter? You haven't gone up yet. You are still hanging around. I thought you were going to leave us." This is the type of thing scoffers will say to believers. Many are already saying, "Where is the sign of His coming?" For this reason we ought to be careful today in the way that we teach the second coming of Christ. We should not go out on a limb. We should not become fanatics on the subject. We should handle it with care, even in a manner in which the Word of God handles it. So 2 Kings is just a little picture of the judgment that will come upon those who will ridicule Christ's return to earth. It is a fearful judgment.

And he turned back, and looked on them, and cursed them in the name of the LORD. And there came forth two she bears out of the wood, and tare forty and two children of them [2 Kings 2:24].

It is an awful thing for a preacher to deny the deity of Christ and the work He did at His first coming. It is a terrible thing to deny and ridicule the second coming of Christ. This brings a very severe judgment.

Notice that they called Elisha "bald head." We do know something about this man: he had a bald head.

There is a great deal about judgment in the Word of God. We need, therefore, to get our facts squared away. When you understand what we are talking about in this section, there is nothing here that is out of line with the rest of Scripture. He pronounced a curse upon them. Elisha sounds like Elijah here. He also sounds like the Lord Jesus Christ who said, "Woe unto thee, Chorazin! woe unto thee, Bethsaida!

for if the mighty works, which were done in you, had been done in Tyre and Sidon, they would have repented long ago in sackcloth and ashes" (Matt. 11:21). He went on to say, "And thou, Capernaum, which art exalted unto heaven, shalt be brought down to hell . . ." (Matt. 11:23). That is judgment, friends.

We are living in a day when there is a great deal of pussy-footing in our legal system. The lack of the enforcement of law on the part of some judges is a scandal; it is responsible for the lawlessness on every hand. It is responsible for the shooting down of policemen. It is not safe to walk our streets any more. The minds of people in this country have been brainwashed. When are we going to wake up? When gangs of young hoodlums terrorize our neighborhoods, there should be punishment. I personally heard a leading attorney recently tell a small group, privately, that these young lawbreakers should be taken out and publicly whipped, as they used to do in the early days. He said if that were done it would break up a lot of the lawlessness. May I say to you that after the bears did their work, nobody else around Bethel ridiculed Elisha—you may be sure of that.

CHAPTERS 3 AND 4

THEME: Miracles of Elisha

Now Jehoram the son of Ahab began to reign over Israel in Samaria the eighteenth year of Jehoshaphat king of Judah, and reigned twelve years [2 Kings 3:1].

Jehoram was the son of Ahab and Jezebel and successor of his brother Ahaziah, who died without having any children.

And he wrought evil in the sight of the LORD; but not like his father, and like his mother: for he put away the image of Baal that his father had made.

Nevertheless he cleaved unto the sins of Jeroboam the son of Nebat, which made Israel to sin; he departed not therefrom [2 Kings 3:2–3].

He did not sin as Ahab had sinned, but he did cleave "unto the sins of Jeroboam" which was calf worship.

And Mesha king of Moab was a sheepmaster, and rendered unto the king of Israel an hundred thousand lambs, and an hundred thousand rams, with the wool.

But it came to pass, when Ahab was dead, that the king of Moab rebelled against the king of Israel [2 Kings 3:4–5].

Moab was in subjection to Israel and paid tribute. When Ahab died, Moab attempted to regain her freedom, refusing to pay the tribute. Jehoram, therefore, gathered his troops together and made an alliance with Jehoshaphat to join forces with him to bring Moab back into subjection. When they were unable to find water for their troops, their campaign not only was halted, but they were in danger of being conquered by the Moabites. King Jehoshaphat, being a God-fearing man, suggested they call a prophet of God to give them direction. (We could wish he had asked for God's guidance before he formed this alliance with Israel's godless king.) Elisha's response is interesting and reveals his contempt for Jehoram.

> **And Elisha said unto the king of Israel, What have I to do with thee? get thee to the prophets of thy father, and to the prophets of thy mother. And the king of Israel said unto him, Nay: for the LORD hath called these three kings together, to deliver them into the hand of Moab.**

> **And Elisha said, As the LORD of hosts liveth, before whom I stand, surely, were it not that I regard the presence of Jehoshaphat the king of Judah, I would not look toward thee, nor see thee [2 Kings 3:13–14].**

WATER AND VICTORY

Then God promises that there will be victory—they will be given water and they will completely subjugate Moab.

Notice the remarkable way God accomplishes this.

> **And he said, Thus saith the LORD, Make this valley full of ditches [2 Kings 3:16].**

The ditches are pits to retain the water that is coming.

> **And it came to pass in the morning, when the meat offering was offered, that, behold, there came water by the way of Edom, and the country was filled with water [2 Kings 3:20].**

The Moabite troops which are mustered to defend their country against Israel now look out toward the advancing armies.

> And they rose up early in the morning, and the sun
> shone upon the water, and the Moabites saw the water on
> the other side as red as blood:
>
> And they said, This is blood: the kings are surely slain,
> and they have smitten one another: now therefore,
> Moab, to the spoil [2 Kings 3:22-23].

Thinking that the confederate kings had come to blows and the troops
had destroyed each other, the Moabites forget about warfare and each
man takes off to get his share of the spoil. This, of course, gives Israel
a distinct advantage.

> And when the king of Moab saw that the battle was too
> sore for him, he took with him seven hundred men that
> drew swords, to break through even unto the king of
> Edom: but they could not.
>
> Then he took his eldest son that should have reigned in
> his stead, and offered him for a burnt offering upon the
> wall. And there was great indignation against Israel:
> and they departed from him, and returned to their own
> land [2 Kings 3:26-27].

Human sacrifice was widely practiced by the Moabites. Undoubtedly
he offered the sacrifice to his god Chemosh, hoping that by offering
his heir, Chemosh would save him from the enemy. However, it was a
signal victory for Israel, and certainly must have impressed them with
the power and graciousness of the Lord God of Israel.

Chapter 4 contains five miracles performed by Elisha. While there
is a similarity between the miracles of Elisha and Elijah, the miracles
performed by Elisha are more extensive.

INCREASE OF THE WIDOW'S OIL

> Now there cried a certain woman of the wives of the sons
> of the prophets unto Elisha, saying, Thy servant my hus-

> band is dead; and thou knowest that thy servant did fear
> the LORD: and the creditor is come to take unto him my
> two sons to be bondmen [2 Kings 4:1].

Elisha apparently had known her husband. She reminds him that her husband was a true believer. When he died he left an unpaid debt which the creditor had now come to collect. If a borrower did not have personal property as security, his own person and that of his dependents would serve as security. Therefore the creditor could legally take the widow's sons as payment.

> And Elisha said unto her, What shall I do for thee? tell
> me, what hast thou in the house? And she said, Thine
> handmaid hath not any thing in the house, save a pot of
> oil [2 Kings 4:2].

Elisha recognizes his responsibility to help this little family. The Mosaic Law insists that widows and fatherless children be cared for.

> Then he said, Go, borrow thee vessels abroad of all thy
> neighbours, even empty vessels; borrow not a few.
>
> And when thou art come in, thou shalt shut the door
> upon thee and upon thy sons, and shalt pour out into all
> those vessels, and thou shalt set aside that which is full.
>
> So she went from him, and shut the door upon her and
> upon her sons, who brought the vessels to her; and she
> poured out [2 Kings 4:3–5].

They had a regular oil well going in that house!

> And it came to pass, when the vessels were full, that she
> said unto her son, Bring me yet a vessel. And he said
> unto her, There is not a vessel more. And the oil stayed.

Then she came and told the man of God. And he said, Go, sell the oil, and pay thy debt, and live thou and thy children of the rest [2 Kings 4:6–7].

This is actually a greater miracle than the widow of Zarephath's unfailing cruse of oil in Elijah's day.

A SON FOR THE "GREAT WOMAN" OF SHUNEM

This gracious woman, living in Shunem, entertained Elisha whenever he passed through her town.

And she said unto her husband, Behold now, I perceive that this is an holy man of God, which passeth by us continually.

Let us make a little chamber, I pray thee, on the wall; and let us set for him there a bed, and a table, and a stool, and a candlestick: and it shall be, when he cometh to us, that he shall turn in thither [2 Kings 4:9–10].

Since then, there have been many believers who have in their homes what they call the "prophet's chamber." As I have traveled about from place to place, holding Bible conferences, I've stayed in many prophet's chambers. I could tell you about people all across this country today, wonderful Christian folk, who have a room where preachers and missionaries are entertained and feel at home. You do not know what that means in the lives of many of God's people today.

Now Elisha appreciated this home that was always open to him. Lying on the bed one day, he determined to somehow reward this thoughtful woman for her kindness. Elisha summons his servant Gehazi:

And he said, What then is to be done for her? and Gehazi answered, Verily she hath no child, and her husband is old.

And he said, Call her. And when he had called her, she stood in the door.

And he said, About this season, according to the time of life, thou shalt embrace a son. And she said, Nay, my lord, thou man of God, do not lie unto thine handmaid.

And the woman conceived, and bare a son at that season that Elisha had said unto her, according to the time of life [2 Kings 4:14–17].

LIFE RESTORED TO THE SHUNAMMITE'S SON

Years later when her son was a grown child, he died. Elisha restored him to life, using the same method that Elijah had used (1 Kings 17); that is, personal contact with the dead child which brought life. The great principle here is that when we are dead in trespasses and sins, personal contact with Jesus Christ brings life. In Him we have life. He is life.

POISONOUS POTTAGE

The fourth miracle in this chapter concerns food for the sons of the prophets, who were actually students—theological students. This was during a time of famine and one of the boys went out to gather any wild fruits or vegetables that he could find. They concocted a stew of what they found.

So they poured out for the men to eat. And it came to pass, as they were eating of the pottage, that they cried out, and said, O thou man of God, there is death in the pot. And they could not eat thereof.

> But he said, Then bring meal. And he cast it into the pot; and he said, Pour out for the people, that they may eat. And there was no harm in the pot [2 Kings 4:40–41].

Elisha, you see, makes it harmless.

ONE HUNDRED MEN FED MIRACULOUSLY

A man, attempting to be faithful to the Mosaic Law, brought the firstfruits of his harvest to the sons of the prophets since Jeroboam had driven the Levitical priests from the country. Because it was a small amount, the servant balked at inviting one hundred men to dinner!

> And his servitor said, What, should I set this before an hundred men? He said again, Give the people, that they may eat: for thus saith the LORD, They shall eat, and shall leave thereof.
>
> So he set it before them, and they did eat, and left thereof, according to the word of the LORD [2 Kings 4:43–44].

This reminds us of the times our Lord fed crowds of four thousand and five thousand with a few loaves and fish.

CHAPTER 5

THEME: Naaman the Syrian

THE HEALING OF NAAMAN

Chapter 5 is one of the most interesting chapters in the life of Elisha the prophet. It reveals that he was probably as rugged as Elijah and that he had a good sense of humor. I believe the Lord has a sense of humor and likes to use men who have a sense of humor. You cannot help but smile when you read this episode although it deals with a man in a very desperate situation.

> **Now Naaman, captain of the host of the king of Syria, was a great man with his master, and honourable, because by him the LORD had given deliverance unto Syria: he was also a mighty man in valour, but he was a leper [2 Kings 5:1].**

This first verse gives us a thumbnail sketch of Naaman. He was captain of the host of Syria. Although he was a pagan, he was both a great man and an honorable man. By him the Lord had given Syria deliverance—this is a remarkable thing. I am sure that you will agree that he was a man the Lord had used. You will find that the Lord uses men in this world who are not Christian. That may seem strange to you, but you don't have to read very far in the Word of God to find that He used men like Pharaoh, Nebuchadnezzar, Cyrus, and Alexander the Great. Here we are told He used Naaman. We are also told that Naaman was a mighty man of valor. All of these things mentioned count in the high court of heaven. God does not despise these things. This heathen man was used of God: "By him the LORD had given deliverance unto Syria." Even though we find all of these fine things are said of him, we have this to add, ". . . but he was a leper." There are many folks in the world today about whom nice things can be said although they are not Christians. You can say that they are fine men and women and have done fine things. But you have to conclude it all by saying that they are sinners—"For all have sinned, and come short of the glory of God" (Rom. 3:23). No matter how nice people might be, they are all sinners in God's sight.

Lepers were not excluded from society in pagan nations. It is interesting that God gave Israel a law about segregating lepers because it kept the disease from spreading. Today lepers are put in a colony and kept separate from society. God put these instructions in His Book centuries before any pagan nation realized they were necessary. This is something for you to think about, friend. It is not until you come into what we would call a "civilized day" that men decided to separate lepers from the rest of society.

Leprosy in Scripture is a type of sin. One reason is that it was incurable by human means. Only God can cure sin and save a sinner. Naaman had many fine points, but he was a sinner. He tried to cover up his leprosy, but he could not cure it. Many people today whitewash sin. What they need is to be washed white, and only Christ can do that.

And the Syrians had gone out by companies, and had brought away captive out of the land of Israel a little maid; and she waited on Naaman's wife [2 Kings 5:2].

This is one of those unknown, unnamed characters in the Bible. She was a young maid, a little Hebrew girl, and a great person. To me she is as great as Queen Esther, Ruth the Moabite girl, Bathsheba, Sarah, Rebekah, and Rachel. This little maid "waited on Naaman's wife."

And she said unto her mistress, Would God my lord were with the prophet that is in Samaria! for he would recover him of his leprosy [2 Kings 5:3].

This little Hebrew maid was in no position to give orders, but one day she uttered a sigh and said, "Oh, that my master would go down and see the prophet in Samaria. He would recover him of his leprosy"—

Elisha, you see, had quite a reputation. Well, someone—probably his wife—heard what she said, and it reached the ears of the king of Syria.

And one went in, and told his lord, saying, Thus and thus said the maid that is of the land of Israel [2 Kings 5:4].

The king of Syria was delighted to hear that something could be done for this very valuable man, and he immediately sent him to the king of Israel with a letter of introduction and a very handsome reward.

And the king of Syria said, Go to, go, and I will send a letter unto the king of Israel. And he departed, and took with him ten talents of silver, and six thousand pieces of gold, and ten changes of raiment.

And he brought the letter to the king of Israel, saying, Now when this letter is come unto thee, behold, I have therewith sent Naaman my servant to thee, that thou mayest recover him of his leprosy.

And it came to pass, when the king of Israel had read the letter, that he rent his clothes, and said, Am I God, to kill and to make alive, that this man doth send unto me to recover a man of his leprosy? wherefore consider, I pray you, and see how he seeketh a quarrel against me [2 Kings 5:5–7].

This letter from the king of Syria requesting that the captain of his army be healed of leprosy greatly disturbed the king of Israel. He exclaimed, "I am not God. I cannot heal him!" The message had been sent to the wrong person. The king of Israel read the message, but it should have gone to Elisha. I always feel like anyone who claims to have a gift of healing is almost being blasphemous, friend. The king of Israel said, "I don't claim to be able to heal anyone." Elisha did not claim to be a healer either, but he was in contact with the Great Physician. The king of Israel, however, came to the conclusion that the king of Syria was trying to start a quarrel with him—why else would he send the captain of his army with this impossible request?

And it was so, when Elisha the man of God had heard that the king of Israel had rent his clothes, that he sent to the king, saying,

Wherefore hast thou rent thy clothes? let him come now to me, and he shall know that there is a prophet in Israel [2 Kings 5:8].

Elisha said, "Send Naaman down to me."

So Naaman came with his horses and with his chariot, and stood at the door of the house of Elisha.

And Elisha sent a messenger unto him, saying, Go and wash in Jordan seven times, and thy flesh shall come again to thee, and thou shalt be clean [2 Kings 5:9-10].

Naaman was from a great kingdom in the north. In fact, his nation was at that time bearing down upon the nation Israel. Syria had already gained victories over Israel, and Naaman expected the red carpet to be rolled out for him. And what happened?

Elisha told him to go and wash in the Jordan River seven times! Of course this hurt the pride of Naaman. Elisha actually received this man rudely. In fact, Elisha did not receive him at all—he did not even go to the door to receive him. You would think the prophet would bow and scrape to this great captain of the hosts of Syria. Instead, Elisha sent his servant to tell Naaman to go and wash seven times in the Jordan River. Do you think Naaman is going to accept this advice?

But Naaman was wroth, and went away, and said, Behold, I thought, He will surely come out to me, and stand, and call on the name of the LORD his God, and

**strike his hand over the place, and recover the leper
[2 Kings 5:11].**

Naaman was upset because he was a very proud man. He had never
received treatment like this before. The Lord is not only going to heal
his leprosy, He is also going to heal him of pride. When God saves
you, He generally takes out of your life that thing which offends. Pride
just happens to be one of the things God hates.

We hear a great deal about the fact that "God is love," but God also
hates. You cannot love without hating. You cannot love the good without hating the evil. If you love your children, you would hate a mad
dog that would come into the yard to bite your little ones. You would
want to kill that mad dog. It is true that God loves man, and in unmis-
takable language God declares that He hates the pride in man's heart.
Proverbs 6:16–19 lists seven things that God hates. First on His list are
these: "A proud look, a lying tongue, and hands that shed innocent
blood." Do you see what is number one on God's hate parade? It is a
proud look. God says He hates that. He hates that as much as He hates
murder. James 4:6 says, "But he giveth more grace. Wherefore he
saith, God resisteth the proud, but giveth grace unto the humble."
Pride is the undoing of man. It is a great sin. In Proverbs 16:18 we
read, "Pride goeth before destruction, and an haughty spirit before a
fall." Proverbs 11:2 says, "When pride cometh, then cometh shame:
but with the lowly is wisdom." Finally, Proverbs 29:23 says, "A man's
pride shall bring him low: but honour shall uphold the humble in
spirit." Why does God hate pride? The definition of pride is "excessive self-esteem." It is inordinate self-esteem. It is more than reasonable delight in one's position and achievement. Paul put it like this,
"For I say, through the grace given unto me, to every man that is
among you, not to think of himself more highly than he ought to
think; but to think soberly, according as God hath dealt to every man
the measure of faith" (Rom. 12:3). Pride is placing an excessive price
on self. It is demanding more than you are worth. Have you ever heard
it said, "I wish I could buy that man for what he is worth and sell him
for what he thinks he is worth"? Pride is the difference between what
you are and what you think you are. It was the pride of Satan that

brought him down. That was his sin. Pride was also the sin of Edom. Of Edom God said, "Though thou exalt thyself as the eagle, and though thou set thy nest among the stars, thence will I bring thee down, saith the LORD" (Obad. 4).

Man's pride runs counter to God's plan; and, whenever they meet, there is friction. There is no compromise. It is always a head-on collision. You see, God's plan of salvation is the supreme answer to man's pride. God lays man low. God takes *nothing* from man. Paul could say of himself when he met Jesus Christ, "But what things were gain to me, those I counted loss for Christ" (Phil. 3:7). Paul gave up religion. Paul gave up everything he had been; he rated it as dung—he said, "I just flushed it down." Christ and pride do not go together. You cannot be proud and at the same time trust Christ as your Savior. If you trust Him, my friend, you will lay all of your pride in the dust.

The story of Naaman is the finest example that we have of a man being shorn of his pride. He was a great man, to be sure. God listed all the things that marked him out as a man of character and ability. But he was a leper. He was a sinner. God not only healed him of leprosy, He healed him of his pride. Believe me, Elisha insulted him. Naaman thought Elisha would come out to him, stand, and call on the name of the Lord his God, strike his hand over the place, and recover the leper. You know, that is religion. It is as if Naaman were saying, "Oh, if only I could have gotten into a healing line, and had him put his hand on me, and call upon God and pray. If only he had poured a little oil on me. That would be great." That is religion, friend. When God heals a person, it is by faith. He lays your pride in the ground. You do not go to a man for healing; you go to God, the Great Physician.

Are not Abana and Pharpar, rivers of Damascus, better than all the waters of Israel? may I not wash in them, and be clean? So he turned and went away in a rage [2 Kings 5:12].

This is one place where I agree with Naaman. I saw those beautiful rivers in Lebanon. I went up to the city of Byblos from Beirut, and I stopped at a place called, "Calling Cards of the Great Men of the

Earth," because it is a place where many notable men have left inscriptions on the side of a cliff. I walked along a river there about half a mile and looked at the beautiful clear water rippling over the rocks. The Jordan is a muddy little stream, friend. It is not nearly as pretty as some of the streams in Lebanon. I rather agree with Naaman. He said, "Why in the world should I go and dip in the Jordan? Why not dip in a stream with clean water?"

This has an application for us. A lot of folks hate to come to the Cross of Christ. It is a place of ignominy. It is a place of shame. People don't want to come to the Cross. Instead they want to do something great. That is what Naaman wanted to do. Oh, the pride of Naaman! He said the rivers of Damascus were better, and they were. He was disgusted with the impudence and impertinence of the prophet to tell him to wash in the Jordan. But, my friend, you will have to come to the Cross of Christ. You do not come to Jesus and stand before Him as a proud man. You cannot say that you have something you are resting on when you come to Him. You come, "just as I am without one plea, but that Thy blood was shed for me," and shed for every person. All you have to do is accept His work on the Cross.

> **And his servants came near, and spake unto him, and said, My father, if the prophet had bid thee do some great thing, wouldest thou not have done it? how much rather then, when he saith to thee, Wash, and be clean? [2 Kings 5:13].**

As Naaman was riding away in a rage, his servants attempted to reason with him, "If the prophet had asked you to do something great, you would have done it." How many people today would like to do some great thing for salvation? You don't have to do anything; He has already done it for us. All we have to do is receive it. We come as beggars. Naaman would have to come that way also.

> **Then went he down, and dipped himself seven times in Jordan, according to the saying of the man of God: and**

his flesh came again like unto the flesh of a little child,
and he was clean [2 Kings 5:14].

Naaman went down to the Jordan and dipped in the water seven times
according to Elisha's instructions. I would give almost anything in the
world if I could have been there and watched him. I think every time
he went down into the water he would come up and look at himself.
He probably said, "This is absurd. I am not getting clean—I am not
getting rid of my leprosy!" Then he went down into the water again.
But he did dip himself in the Jordan seven times, and he was healed.

GEHAZI'S SIN AND THE PENALTY

And he returned to the man of God, he and all his company, and came, and stood before him: and he said, Behold, now I know that there is no God in all the earth,
but in Israel: now therefore, I pray thee, take a blessing
of thy servant.

But he said, As the LORD liveth, before whom I stand, I
will receive none. And he urged him to take it; but he
refused.

And Naaman said, Shall there not then, I pray thee, be
given to thy servant two mules' burden of earth? for thy
servant will henceforth offer neither burnt offering nor
sacrifice unto other gods, but unto the LORD.

In this thing the LORD pardon thy servant, that when my
master goeth into the house of Rimmon to worship
there, and he leaneth on my hand, and I bow myself in
the house of Rimmon: when I bow down myself in the
house of Rimmon, the LORD pardon thy servant in this
thing.

And he said unto him, Go in peace. So he departed from
him a little way [2 Kings 5:15–19].

Now, deeply grateful for his healing, Naaman is pressing Elisha to accept these rich gifts he has brought as a token of his appreciation. But Elisha will not accept payment for what God has done.

Now Elisha had a servant named Gehazi. He hated to see that handsome reward slip by, so he took out after Naaman.

> So Gehazi followed after Naaman. And when Naaman saw him running after him, he lighted down from the chariot to meet him, and said, Is all well?
>
> And he said, All is well. My master hath sent me, saying, Behold, even now there be come to me from mount Ephraim two young men of the sons of the prophets: give them, I pray thee, a talent of silver, and two changes of garments.
>
> And Naaman said, Be content, take two talents. And he urged him, and bound two talents of silver in two bags, with two changes of garments, and laid them upon two of his servants; and they bare them before him [2 Kings 5:21–23].

Why did Gehazi take the offering from Naaman? Greed!

> And when he came to the tower, he took them from their hand, and bestowed them in the house: and he let the men go, and they departed.
>
> But he went in, and stood before his master. And Elisha said unto him, Whence comest thou, Gehazi? And he said, Thy servant went no whither [2 Kings 5:24–25].

Gehazi allowed the servants to carry the gifts as far as the tower; then he took them himself and sent the servants back to Naaman so that Elisha would not see them. With the gifts safely stowed away, Gehazi rushes back to his job, acting as if nothing had happened.

And he said unto him, Went not mine heart with thee, when the man turned again from his chariot to meet thee? Is it a time to receive money, and to receive garments, and oliveyards, and vineyards, and sheep, and oxen, and menservants, and maidservants?

The leprosy therefore of Naaman shall cleave unto thee, and unto thy seed for ever. And he went out from his presence a leper as white as snow [2 Kings 5:26–27].

The great sin of Naaman was pride. The great sin of Gehazi was greed. My beloved, greed is leprosy of the soul.

CHAPTER 6

THEME: The floating ax head and danger at Dothan

In chapter 6 we will see two more thrilling experiences that Elisha had. Elisha was an outstanding prophet, although he was different from Elijah, Elijah's ministry was public; Elisha's ministry was more private (we have just seen how he dealt with Naaman, the captain of the Syrian host). Elijah was spectacular—he brought down fire and rain from heaven. Elisha was a quiet man; he shunned the spotlight. However, both prophets were God's men at God's time.

THE AX HEAD

Our attention will center now on Elisha. I do not think that any miracle so reveals the character of a person and a prophet as the miracle of the floating ax head.

And the sons of the prophets said unto Elisha, Behold now, the place where we dwell with thee is too strait for us [2 Kings 6:1].

Now this reveals something of the popularity of Elisha. He taught in a theological seminary, the school of the prophets. The school grew, and they needed larger quarters. This was due to the presence and the popularity of Elisha. The strength, I feel, and the value of any school is the character and the ability of those who teach. It is not the methods but the men that are important, especially in a Christian school.

Now notice what they did. In order to enlarge the school they said,

Let us go, we pray thee, unto Jordan, and take thence every man a beam, and let us make us a place there, where we may dwell. And he answered, Go ye [2 Kings 6:2].

The students built their own school. That would be an unusual thing in our day. Today everything has to be given to the students in order to get them through school and, if it doesn't suit them, they rebel. But these students went out to work, and Elisha encouraged them in it.

And one said, Be content, I pray thee, and go with thy servants. And he answered, I will go [2 Kings 6:3].

This is a refreshing and thrilling verse. It is an insight into the winsome character of Elisha. It reveals that he was popular with the students. By the way, do students ordinarily want to take their teacher with them beyond the boundary of the campus? They'd like to leave him there. But these asked Elisha to go with them.

So he went with them. And when they came to Jordan, they cut down wood [2 Kings 6:4].

Now a small tragedy takes place. I say "small" because the ordinary person would call this a trivial incident.

But as one was felling a beam, the axe head fell into the water: and he cried, and said, Alas, master! for it was borrowed [2 Kings 6:5].

There is something here that is quite interesting. It reveals that God is concerned about the small events in our lives. You remember that Paul said to the Philippians, "Pray about everything," and he did not mean to leave anything out.

The loss of an ax head may seem insignificant to us, but to this poor student it is not so small. The fact of the matter is, it is pretty big. In our day of gadgets when we can go down to the hardware store and get an ax head of about fifteen different shapes, this does not seem important. But in that day it was of tremendous importance because any kind of iron tool or weapon was scarce. And if you want to know something about that period, notice just one verse from 1 Samuel: "So it came to pass in the day of battle, that there was neither sword nor spear found in the hand of any of the people that were with Saul and Jonathan: but with Saul and with Jonathan his son was there found" (1 Sam. 13:22). Two swords for an entire army! It lets you know something of the scarcity of weapons and of tools in that day. So you can understand that the loss of an ax head was very important to this young man—and, of course, he had borrowed it.

Most commentators, I have discovered, romp all over this student. They give him a demerit for carelessness and a demerit for the fact that he borrowed something. Well, if this man were guilty, why did not Elisha, his teacher, rebuke him? Elisha did not. Elisha absolved him from all charges. He was not careless, but actually was very careful. Obviously there was a danger of an ax head coming off, and it happened often enough so that God included it in the Mosaic Law: "And this is the case of the slayer, which shall flee thither, that he may live: Whoso killeth his neighbour ignorantly, whom he hated not in time past; As when a man goeth into the wood with his neighbour to hew wood, and his hand fetcheth a stroke with the axe to cut down the tree, and the head slippeth from the helve and lighteth upon his neighbour, that he die; he shall flee unto one of those cities, and live" (Deut. 19:4–5).

God made this law because it evidently was something that occurred quite frequently. Now this man revealed his carefulness by cutting the wood so that there was nobody out in front of him. He was standing so that if the ax head came off it would go into the Jordan River. He was aiming it in a safe direction.

The second fault they find with him is that he borrowed it. Well, I think that I am qualified to speak for this fellow here. He was a poor seminary student, and he could not afford an ax in that day—no more than I could have owned a Cadillac when I was in seminary. He just could not have done it. He had to borrow it. I do not think that this poor fellow should be criticized on these two points.

In fact, I have a question to ask. Who loaned this student an old ax with a head that would come off? That's the fellow I would like to talk to. I imagine that fellow is the same one who today gives secondhand clothes and old Christmas cards to missionaries and thinks he is serving the Lord.

Now this boy was distressed, and he could not reimburse the owner. He would have to face him without the ax and he didn't know what to do. Now notice Elisha's concern. "And the man of God said, Where fell it?" Let's stop there for just a moment because there have been those who have said, "Why did Elisha ask that question if he was a prophet? He would have known where the ax head fell." He knew, and he knew something else also. He knew that he needed to test that young man. By the Spirit of God he needed to test him. Notice that this young man knew exactly where that ax head went into the water. Don't tell me he was careless. Elisha is not doing it only for a test but for another reason. The Spirit of God knew that in the twentieth century there would be critics of this miracle, and, as they've explained away every other miracle, they would say, "Well, after all, the water was clear, and anybody could see where it was." The question Elisha asked precludes anyone saying that the water was clear. And if you know anything about the Jordan River, you know it was muddy. I have heard many romantic, wonderful things about that river, but to me it was the most disappointing thing that I saw. You talk about polluted water! You talk about a muddy little stream! You talk about a dirty thing! That's the Jordan River. Because it was muddy, Elisha said, "Where did it fall?" The young man knew right where it was, but he could not get it out because he could not see it. The water was not clear. Now notice what took place.

> And the man of God said, Where fell it? And he shewed him the place. And he cut down a stick, and cast it in thither; and the iron did swim [2 Kings 6:6].

This was a miracle, and I do not think that you can explain it away. This is one miracle—not sensational, not as spectacular as going to heaven in a chariot of fire—that is great in its simplicity. It is a miracle when iron swims. It is contrary to all known physical laws. I recognize that since the day that the first iron ship was launched, ships of iron and steel now float on the seven seas. And that's no miracle. But, my friend, it was a miracle for an ax head on the bottom of the Jordan River to float to the top like a cork! I know it is not startling, not sensational; it's simple. This is Elisha's method. Elijah would have never done it this way. In fact, I don't think Elijah would have bothered with a thing like that. He would have said, "Son, forget it." But not Elisha.

An ax head, dormant on the bottom of the muddy Jordan, is raised, resurrected, if you please, restored to the owner, replaced on the handle, and it becomes useful again, utilitarian and functional. That's really a greater miracle than these others because there is a tremendous spiritual message here for us today. Man today is like that ax head. He has slipped off the handle. He has fallen. He is totally depraved.

So Elisha cut down a stick. He cast it into the waters of death. That stick is the Cross of Christ. Our Lord came down to that Cross, and He went down into the waters of death for you and me. "Who his own self bare our sins in his own body on the tree, that we, being dead to sins, should live unto righteousness: by whose stripes ye were healed" (1 Pet. 2:24).

Man today can rise from the waters of death and judgment through Christ. He can be placed back on the handle of God's plan and purpose for him, and he can be geared into God's program. Paul testifies, "I can do all things through Christ which strengtheneth me" (Phil. 4:13). And further, ". . . this one thing I do, forgetting those things which are behind, and reaching forth unto those things which are before, I press toward the mark for the prize of the high calling of God in Christ Jesus" (Phil. 3:13–14). It is no longer necessary for any person to live an aimless and useless life. Having no purpose in life is the thing that is driving literally thousands of people to suicide. This past week a half dozen college students committed suicide, and the whole explanation was, "It isn't worth living." My friend, of course it's not worth living when you are an old ax head down at the bottom of the muddy Jordan. It is not until Christ lifts you by His Cross (His death for you and me) and places us back in His plan and purpose that life becomes worthwhile. A young man (not yet twenty-one years old) said to me, "My life is a failure." I said to him, "Your life hasn't even begun, and you are talking about being a failure!" How we need God today! The greatest miracle today, friend, is not to go to the moon. It is not even to go to heaven in a chariot of fire. Rather it is to go to the highest heaven when we are still sinners and have trusted Christ. That's the greatest miracle there is—to be lifted out of the muck and mire of this world and to be given meaning for our lives and enabled to live for God.

> **Therefore said he, Take it up to thee. And he put out his hand, and took it [2 Kings 6:7].**

All you have to do is reach out the hand of faith today and take it, for He died for you. He rose again in order that He might lift you up. All you have to do from your position is to reach out the hand of faith and trust Him.

DANGER AT DOTHAN

The next episode begins with a very familiar ring. It sounds like a page out of the morning newspaper: "Then the king of Syria warred against Israel." They have been at it for a long time; actually, it was an old conflict even at that time. The present conflict between Israel and the Arab world has a definite Bible background.

Now notice the situation.

> **Then the king of Syria warred against Israel, and took counsel with his servants, saying, In such and such a place shall be my camp.**

> **And the man of God sent unto the king of Israel, saying, Beware that thou pass not such a place; for thither the Syrians are come down.**

> And the king of Israel sent to the place which the man of
> God told him and warned him of, and saved himself
> there, not once nor twice.
>
> Therefore the heart of the king of Syria was sore trou-
> bled for this thing; and he called his servants, and said
> unto them, Will ye not shew me which of us is for the
> king of Israel? [2 Kings 6:8-11].

The king of Syria was disturbed because every plan he made and
every place he went was discovered by the king of Israel. He came to
the conclusion that there was a spy in his camp. He called together his
military and attempted to ferret out the traitor. "Which one of you is
for the king of Israel?" Honestly there was no one—all of them were
loyal to him.

> And one of his servants said, None, my lord, O king: but
> Elisha, the prophet that is in Israel, telleth the king of
> Israel the words that thou speakest in thy bedchamber
> [2 Kings 6:12].

The prophet Elisha had "bugged" even the bedroom of the king of
Syria and knew everything he said. And the way he "bugged" them in
that day was that the Lord revealed this to him.

So the king of Syria decided to eliminate Elisha. He first sent out
those to spy out where he was and they located him in Dothan. Dothan
is a place north of Jerusalem about sixty miles. It means "two wells"
and was a place where there was good pasture, a place where flocks
were brought. At the present time and for several years Dr. Joseph
Free, of Wheaton College, has been carrying on an excavation in that
place. I am told that there is really not much to see there because it
never was a very prominent place. But it was the headquarters of
Elisha at this particular time. The king of Syria sends in the military,
and they entirely surround the place. The servant of Elisha goes out in
the morning, I suppose to get water out of one of those wells (which

are still there today); he looks around and sees that the city of Dothan is surrounded by the hosts of Syria. You can be sure of one thing, he is alarmed. He comes back and reports to Elisha, and he says to him, "Alas, my master! What shall we do? The city is surrounded. We might just as well give up. It looks hopeless for us! What can we do under these circumstances?"

And he answered, Fear not: for they that be with us are more than they that be with them [2 Kings 6:16].

And I want to tell you, that seemed rather unrealistic because here were the hosts of Syria outside, and Elisha was very much alone with his servant—and that servant was frightened to death. So Elisha prayed, and his prayer is interesting.

And Elisha prayed, and said, LORD, I pray thee, open his eyes, that he may see. And the LORD opened the eyes of the young man; and he saw: and, behold, the mountain was full of horses and chariots of fire round about Elisha [2 Kings 6:17].

The question now arises: Is this the stated policy of God in dealing with His own?

Well, I have discovered that a great many Christians today have become great escape artists. They are sort of spiritual Houdinis. They can tell you about miraculous instances of God delivering them and leading them. But many other saints have to bow their heads in shame and say, "I've had no such experience, and I have had no such leading from God. It must mean that either I am out of touch with Him, or He is not for me at all." My friend, let's go back to Dothan. The answer, I believe, is here. Dothan is mentioned only two times in the Bible, and I think for a definite reason.

Another man approaches Dothan, a young man. In fact, he is a boy seventeen years of age, and danger and destiny await him there. Actually he is walking like a helpless and unsuspecting animal into a trap, and I feel like warning him, "Don't go to Dothan!" But that foolish "Houdini" Christian I referred to is apt to say, "You don't need to worry, preacher. No harm is going to come to him. He's not going to be hurt at Dothan. He will be home next week because God will deliver him. After all, there are chariots of fire around Dothan, and he will be delivered." But is he? Joseph's brothers conspire against him. They want to murder him and, after they cool off just a little, the wiser of the brothers recommends that he be sold into slavery. My friend, that was worse than death in that day. It was a living hell to be sold into slavery, yet that is what is happening to this boy, seventeen years of age—and he happens to be God's man! Where are the chariots of fire? Just because you cannot see the chariots of fire does not mean they are not there. They are there. I see more evidences of the hand of God in the life of Joseph than I see in the life of Elisha who performed miracles, yet God never appeared to Joseph, never performed a miracle for him. But I see that God used this seeming disaster, and Joseph recognized it later on at the end of his life. He could say to his brothers, ". . . ye thought evil against me; but God meant it unto good . . ." (Gen. 50:20). And at Dothan the chariots of fire are there, but they are going to be used in a different way.

SYRIAN SOLDIERS ARE BLINDED

And when they came down to him, Elisha prayed unto the LORD and said, Smite this people, I pray thee, with blindness. And he smote them with blindness according to the word of Elisha [2 Kings 6:18].

Elisha did a very unusual thing. He asked God to smite the hosts of the Syrians with blindness, and God did just that. Then Elisha led them all the way into Samaria and told them that he was leading them where Elisha was! When they got to Samaria, he turned them over to the king of Samaria. The king wanted to slay them, but Elisha said, "Don't do that. Feed them and send them home."

And he prepared great provision for them: and when
they had eaten and drunk, he sent them away, and they
went to their master. So the bands of Syria came no
more into the land of Israel [2 Kings 6:23].

Both the power and graciousness of Israel's God, as represented by
Elisha, must have really shaken the Syrian king. He abandoned his
war against Israel. However, at a later date Ben-hadad (this, by the
way, is a title rather than a proper name) again besieged Samaria, as
we shall see in the next episode.

BEN-HADAD BESIEGES SAMARIA

And it came to pass after this, that Ben-hadad king of
Syria gathered all his host, and went up, and besieged
Samaria.

And there was a great famine in Samaria: and, behold,
they besieged it, until an ass's head was sold for fourscore pieces of silver, and the fourth part of a cab of
dove's dung for five pieces of silver [2 Kings 6:24–25].

The famine was so severe that a donkey's head (imagine how little
meat there would be on that, and it could only be boiled, I guess, and
made into soup or stew!) was sold for a ridiculous price. They were
really having inflation!

The next few verses reveal the horrible fact that they were actually
eating their children because of the desperate shortage of food.

Then he said, God do so and more also to me, if the head
of Elisha the son of Shaphat shall stand on him this day
[2 Kings 6:31].

We don't know why the king considered Elisha as responsible for the
horrors of the siege. Probably he thought it was in Elisha's power to

provide food in a miraculous way and was going to execute him because he did not.

The episode is continued without a break in the next chapter. This is another thrilling incident in the life of this man Elisha.

CHAPTER 7

THEME: Elisha's promise of plenty is fulfilled

Chapter 7 continues the narrative of chapter 6. Holding Elisha responsible for the siege, the king of Israel sends an executioner to slay him. However, God forewarns Elisha and gives him the good news that the famine will end on the following day.

> Then Elisha said, Hear ye the word of the LORD; Thus saith the LORD, Tomorrow about this time shall a measure of fine flour be sold for a shekel, and two measures of barley for a shekel, in the gate of Samaria [2 Kings 7:1].

A measure of fine flour actually means about four pecks, which would be about a bushel. One shekel would probably be worth about sixty-five cents. That means the inflation would be over. They would be having a real discount sale on flour. How could such a thing come to pass? How could food be brought into the city when the Syrian host was camped outside the walls allowing no one in or out? Apparently the king believed Elisha's audacious prophecy because he spared his life at this time. However, his right-hand man scoffed at the idea.

> Then a lord on whose hand the king leaned answered the man of God, and said, Behold, if the LORD would make windows in heaven, might this thing be? And he said, Behold, thou shalt see it with thine eyes, but shalt not eat thereof [2 Kings 7:2].

This prediction was literally fulfilled the next day.

Now the scene shifts to a pathetic group of hopeless men outside the city gates.

> And there were four leprous men at the entering in of the
> gate: and they said one to another, Why sit we here until
> we die?
>
> If we say, We will enter into the city, then the famine is in
> the city, and we shall die there: and if we sit still here,
> we die also. Now therefore come, and let us fall unto the
> host of the Syrians: if they save us alive, we shall live;
> and if they kill us, we shall but die.
>
> And they rose up in the twilight, to go unto the camp of
> the Syrians: and when they were come to the uttermost
> part of the camp of Syria, behold, there was no man
> there [2 Kings 7:3–5].

Because they were lepers, they were excluded from society and were
dependent upon relatives or friends bringing them food. Now that
everyone inside the city was starving, of course, there was no surplus
for them.

As we have said, leprosy is a type of sin. The application for us is
that before we came to Christ we were in a predicament equally as
desperate. We were like the lepers, sitting among the dead, having no
hope and without God in the world.

The lepers, realizing they had nothing to lose, decided to throw
themselves upon the mercy of the enemy. When they reached the
camp of the Syrians, they found it deserted. What had happened to
that great host—probably a hundred thousand or more?

> For the LORD had made the host of the Syrians to hear a
> noise of chariots, and a noise of horses, even the noise of
> a great host: and they said one to another, Lo, the king of
> Israel hath hired against us the kings of the Hittites, and
> the kings of the Egyptians, to come upon us.
>
> Wherefore they arose and fled in the twilight, and left
> their tents, and their horses, and their asses, even the
> camp as it was, and fled for their life [2 Kings 7:6–7].

The sound of an approaching army had put them in panic. The Syrians did not march in an orderly way. When they took off, it was every man for himself. They were traveling at night and they were traveling fast.

And when these lepers came to the uttermost part of the camp, they went into one tent, and did eat and drink, and carried thence silver, and gold, and raiment, and went and hid it; and came again, and entered into another tent, and carried thence also, and went and hid it [2 Kings 7:8].

In that day, the army carried with it all the food they would need. This was a long campaign—they were besieging Samaria, the city there on the hill. In their scramble to get away, they had left everything, all the supplies they had. After the Syrian army had fled, the lepers went into the camp and gorged themselves on gourmet food for as long as they could eat. Then they found and hid more gold and silver than they would ever need.

Then they said one to another, We do not well: this day is a day of good tidings, and we hold our peace: if we tarry till the morning light, some mischief will come upon us: now therefore come, that we may go and tell the king's household [2 Kings 7:9].

Now the excitement is over, and they begin to come to themselves. "Here we are gorging ourselves when the people in the city are starving. We've got to go tell them the good news!"

There is a great spiritual lesson for us here. At this moment you and I are enjoying the Word of God. Today is a day of good tidings, and we sit here and enjoy it. What about getting the Word out to others? What are you doing to share the Word of God with those who are starving spiritually? You ought to be busy getting the Word of God out to needy hearts. One man told me, "I can't speak, I can't teach, I can't sing, I can't do much of anything except make money." Believe me,

God has given him a talent for making money. He simply cannot lose money. Everything he touches turns to gold. I believe his ability is a gift from God, and he certainly is using it to get the Word of God out. God expects each of us to use the talents He has given us to publish the good tidings which are the Word of God. We must not hold our peace in this desperate hour!

After the lepers told the king the good news, the children of Israel went into the abandoned Syrian camp and found enough food to feed an army of several thousand. There was an abundance of food. The supermarkets in Samaria had a big sale; you could buy food cheap. You did not have to buy animal heads for food anymore. You could buy filet mignon instead! The prophecy of Elisha was literally fulfilled.

CHAPTERS 8—10

THEME: Judgment of the wicked

The people of Israel soon forgot God's marvelous deliverance and returned to their sin. So again they suffer the judgment of a famine.

ELISHA'S PREDICTION OF FAMINE

Then spake Elisha unto the woman, whose son he had restored to life, saying, Arise, and go thou and thine household, and sojourn wheresoever thou canst sojourn: for the LORD hath called for a famine; and it shall also come upon the land seven years.

And the woman arose, and did after the saying of the man of God: and she went with her household, and sojourned in the land of the Philistines seven years [2 Kings 8:1–2].

Elisha told the Shunammite woman to leave the land and go to another place because there was going to be a seven-year famine in the land. She believed and obeyed Elisha. She took her household into the land of the Philistines and lived there during the period of the famine. The famine, once again, was a judgment of God upon the northern kingdom.

Frankly I believe that the different tragedies that have struck our land in recent years have been a warning to our nation. The earthquakes, hurricanes, storms, and other tragedies that have swept across our land have, I think, been warnings from God to stop and think and change our ways.

THE SHUNAMMITE'S LAND RESTORED

And it came to pass at the seven years' end, that the woman returned out of the land of the Philistines: and she went forth to cry unto the king for her house and for her land.

And the king talked with Gehazi the servant of the man of God, saying, Tell me, I pray thee, all the great things that Elisha hath done.

And it came to pass, as he was telling the king how he had restored a dead body to life, that, behold, the woman, whose son he had restored to life, cried to the king for her house and for her land. And Gehazi said, My lord, O king, this is the woman, and this is her son, whom Elisha restored to life.

And when the king asked the woman, she told him. So the king appointed unto her a certain officer, saying, Restore all that was hers, and all the fruits of the field since the day that she left the land, even until now [2 Kings 8:3-6].

When the famine was over and the Shunammite woman returned to her former home, she apparently found others living on her land. At the same time, in God's providence, the king was inquiring about some of the lesser known acts of the prophet Elisha, and Gehazi was telling him about Elisha raising the Shunammite woman's son from the dead. The king made a ruling that her property was to be restored to her as well as all the fruit of the land.

ELISHA PREDICTS HAZAEL'S TREASON

Here is another incident in the life of Elisha that is quite remarkable. You will recall that the king of Syria had attempted to capture Elisha and slay him. But now the king is an old man, and he is sick.

And Elisha came to Damascus; and Ben-hadad the king
of Syria was sick; and it was told him, saying, The man
of God is come hither [2 Kings 8:7].

The king thought that Elisha would restore him to health. In view of
the fact that his own life might hang in the hands of Elisha, of course
the king would not touch one hair of his head.

And the king said unto Hazael, Take a present in thine
hand, and go, meet the man of God, and inquire of the
LORD by him, saying, Shall I recover of this disease?
[2 Kings 8:8].

Hazael went to meet Elisha. He is the captain of Ben-hadad's hosts.
There is a reference to him in 1 Kings 19:15 which says, "And the
LORD said unto him [Elijah], Go, return on thy way to the wilderness of
Damascus: and when thou comest, anoint Hazael to be king over
Syria." So Hazael had been anointed king many years earlier; he is just
waiting around for old Ben-hadad to die. You can well understand that
it would be very difficult for the king's successor—whether it be a son,
a general, or someone else—to shed very many tears at his funeral
because it was his funeral that would bring his successor to power. So
Hazael went out to meet Elisha, but I don't think he went with a great
deal of enthusiasm. He took an impressive gift to Elisha, which was
from the king.

So Hazael went to meet him, and took a present with
him, even of every good thing of Damascus, forty cam-
els' burden, and came and stood before him, and said,
Thy son Ben-hadad king of Syria hath sent me to thee,
saying, Shall I recover of this disease?

And Elisha said unto him, Go, say unto him, Thou mayest certainly recover: howbeit the LORD hath shewed me
that he shall surely die [2 Kings 8:9-10].

Notice the message that Elisha gave: "You will surely live, but you won't live." That sounds like double-talk. Can't you just see Hazael when he hears that the king is going to die? A smirk comes over his face, and then a smile because he is going to be king.

And he settled his countenance stedfastly, until he was ashamed: and the man of God wept [2 Kings 8:11].

Elisha's knowing eyes bored into him until Hazael felt embarrassed. Then Elisha began to weep.

And Hazael said, Why weepeth my lord? And he answered, Because I know the evil that thou wilt do unto the children of Israel: their strong holds wilt thou set on fire, and their young men wilt thou slay with the sword, and wilt dash their children, and rip up their women with child [2 Kings 8:12].

Hazael is amazed, "Why weepeth my lord? Why are you weeping about this man who sought your life?" Elisha was not weeping for the king. Elisha loved his people. He loved his God. He loved the service God had given to him—he was a prophet. The heartbreak because of Ben-hadad had been bad enough, but Hazael is going to bring even more heartbreak to the people. Although Elijah had anointed Hazael king, and Hazael professes that he isn't going to do evil, Elisha knows better.

And Hazael said, But what, is thy servant a dog, that he should do this great thing? And Elisha answered, The Lord hath shewed me that thou shalt be king over Syria [2 Kings 8:13].

I don't know whether or not he was a dog, but he *did* it.

So he departed from Elisha, and came to his master; who said to him, What said Elisha to thee? And he answered, He told me that thou shouldest surely recover.

> And it came to pass on the morrow, that he took a thick
> cloth, and dipped it in water, and spread it on his face,
> so that he died: and Hazael reigned in his stead [2 Kings
> 8:14–15].

This is what Elisha foresaw. In substance he had said, "Of course the
king will be glad to hear he is going to recover, and that's what you are
going to tell him, but you won't let him recover."

The rest of this chapter will be less confusing if you follow along
carefully the Chronological Table of the Kings on page 227.

> And in the fifth year of Joram the son of Ahab king of
> Israel, Jehoshaphat being then king of Judah, Jehoram
> the son of Jehoshaphat king of Judah began to reign.

> Thirty and two years old was he when he began to
> reign; and he reigned eight years in Jerusalem.

> And he walked in the way of the kings of Israel, as did
> the house of Ahab: for the daughter of Ahab was his
> wife: and he did evil in the sight of the LORD [2 Kings
> 8:16–18].

Now you can see *why* God doesn't go for mixed marriages. Although
Jehoram was the son of the God-fearing king Jehoshaphat, he married
the daughter of Ahab and Jezebel, and under her evil influence, "he
walked in the ways of the kings of Israel."

Now we begin to see that Israel is going downhill as a great nation.
Both Edom and Libnah revolted against them. Then Jehoram died,
and Ahaziah became the new king of Judah. He joined forces with
Joram, king of Israel, to war against the Syrians. Joram was wounded
and went back to Jezreel to be healed from the wounds which he suffered at the hands of the Syrians.

> And king Joram went back to be healed in Jezreel of the
> wounds which the Syrians had given him at Ramah,
> when he fought against Hazael king of Syria. And Aha-

ziah the son of Jehoram king of Judah went down to see
Joram the son of Ahab in Jezreel, because he was sick
[2 Kings 8:29].

In the next chapter we shall see what happened to him while he was
in Jezreel recovering from his wounds.

JEHU IS ANOINTED KING OVER ISRAEL

As we begin this chapter, we need to keep in mind that Ahaziah, the
king of Judah, went up to visit Joram at Jezreel because Joram was
wounded in battle and was in Jezreel recovering. Apparently he was a
very sick man.

And Elisha the prophet called one of the children of the
prophets, and said unto him, Gird up thy loins, and
take this box of oil in thine hand, and go to Ramoth-
gilead:

And when thou comest thither, look out there Jehu the
son of Jehoshaphat the son of Nimshi, and go in, and
make him arise up from among his brethren, and carry
him to an inner chamber;

Then take the box of oil, and pour it on his head, and
say, Thus saith the LORD, I have anointed thee king over
Israel. Then open the door, and flee, and tarry not.

So the young man, even the young man the prophet,
went to Ramoth-gilead [2 Kings 9:1–4].

The young prophet did the thing Elisha commanded him to do. You
will notice that Elisha is not spectacular in what he does. You would
think he would not have sent a young prophet to anoint a king but that
Elisha would have done it himself. Samuel, you remember, had
anointed Saul as king, and he also came to David and anointed him

king. You would naturally think that Elisha would want to be the one to anoint the king, but he did not. He sent a young prophet to anoint Jehu king, and he did it secretly and privately. This is probably the reason he sent a young man to do it—no one would suspect the motives of a young prophet.

So Jehu was anointed king. He was one of the bloodiest rascals you will meet on the pages of Scripture, and yet he did the will of God in many respects. God said that He would cut off from Ahab every male member and none would be left in Israel.

And I will make the house of Ahab like the house of Jeroboam the son of Nebat, and like the house of Baasha the son of Ahijah:

And the dogs shall eat Jezebel in the portion of Jezreel, and there shall be none to bury her. And he opened the door, and fled [2 Kings 9:9-10].

Jezebel will not escape God's judgment for her wickedness.

Then Jehu came forth to the servants of his lord: and one said unto him, Is all well? wherefore came this mad fellow to thee? And he said unto them, Ye know the man, and his communication.

And they said, It is false; tell us now. And he said, Thus and thus spake he to me, saying, Thus saith the LORD, I have anointed thee king over Israel.

Then they hasted, and took every man his garment, and put it under him on the top of the stairs, and blew with trumpets, saying, Jehu is king [2 Kings 9:11-13].

When it was known that Jehu had been anointed king, it put everyone in a flurry, and they began to move. They blew the trumpets and said, "Jehu is king." Joram is sick in Jezreel and Ahaziah is there visiting him. What is going to happen in Jezreel now?

JEHU EXECUTES JORAM

Now Joram down there in Jezreel doesn't know that God has removed him from his throne and has anointed Jehu king over Israel. As Joram and Ahaziah, king of Judah, are there visiting, the watchman reports that a company of horsemen is coming. Joram sends a messenger to meet them with the question: "Is it peace?"—are you bringing good news or bad? Instead of answering his question, Jehu tells him to fall in line behind him. Now the second watchman reports to Joram.

> **And the watchman told, saying, He came even unto them, and cometh not again: and the driving is like the driving of Jehu the son of Nimshi; for he driveth furiously [2 Kings 9:20].**

The messengers who were sent out to meet Jehu never came back to report to the king because Jehu is coming to exterminate this king. So Joram and Ahaziah themselves ride out to meet Jehu.

> **And it came to pass, when Joram saw Jehu, that he said, Is it peace, Jehu? And he answered, What peace, so long as the whoredoms of thy mother Jezebel and her witchcrafts are so many? [2 Kings 9:22].**

Obviously no loyal subject would dare make such a statement about the queen mother. Joram instantly recognizes that Jehu is leading a revolt.

> **And Joram turned his hands, and fled, and said to Ahaziah, There is treachery, O Ahaziah.**
>
> **And Jehu drew a bow with his full strength, and smote Jehoram between his arms, and the arrow went out at his heart, and he sunk down in his chariot [2 Kings 9:23-24].**

As Joram was trying to escape, Jehu drew his bow and put an arrow through his heart. Notice that Joram is called Jehoram in this instance. Both names have the same meaning in Hebrew and are used interchangeably for both the king of Israel and the king of Judah.

JEHU EXECUTES AHAZIAH

Jehu had come to Jezreel to exterminate Joram. Ahaziah, as we have already seen, was visiting Joram. He was keeping bad company, by the way, with those of the house of Ahab. Ahaziah was in the wrong place at the wrong time!

> But when Ahaziah the king of Judah saw this, he fled by the way of the garden house. And Jehu followed after him, and said, Smite him also in the chariot. And they did so at the going up to Gur, which is by Ibleam. And he fled to Megiddo, and died there [2 Kings 9:27].

Jehu's followers pursued and mortally wounded Ahaziah.

> And his servants carried him in a chariot to Jerusalem, and buried him in his sepulchre with his fathers in the city of David [2 Kings 9:28].

JEHU EXECUTES JEZEBEL

> And when Jehu was come to Jezreel, Jezebel heard of it; and she painted her face, and tired her head, and looked out at a window [2 Kings 9:30].

Now we come to the slaying of Jezebel, the queen mother, which was indeed a frightful thing. She was a bloody, mean, terrible woman. She was a member of a royal family, the beautiful daughter of Ethbaal, king of Zidon. Probably she had been one of the most beautiful women of her day and of all history. As a young woman I think Jezebel could compare with Helen of Troy, Salome, Cleopatra, and Catherine de Medici. When Ahab and Jezebel married, it was the society event of the year. The best people of the two kingdoms were there. There was a surplus of royalty gathered. It was respectful and dignified—even Elijah could not find fault with the event. The common people of both realms celebrated. It should also be added that the demons of hell joined the festivities. They laughed with glee, and the Devil was glad. However, crepe was on the gate of heaven and the angels wept. Instead of wedding bells, it was a funeral dirge. That was heaven's view of this marriage. The world saw things differently, as it always does. Why is the world optimistic and heaven pessimistic? God looks on the heart. Man has only a limited view of things.

Jezebel is one of the most remarkable women in history. She was capable, she was influential, and she had a dominant personality. Her evil influence was felt in three kingdoms and extended beyond her lifetime. Her notorious life became a proverb. She poured a stream of poison into history. Scripture never mentions her again until you come to the Book of Revelation at the conclusion of the Bible.

Her name is suggestive. It means "unmarried, chaste." You have here a veiled suggestion of an abnormality and a perversion. She was probably cold and sexless, yet she was beautiful and alluring. Strong men yielded to her seductive charms. No one resisted her, not even Ahab. She dominated him and ruled the northern kingdom.

She introduced the worship of Baal. She imported 450 prophets of Baal and 400 prophets of Astarte. She was reckless, violent, rapacious, and ferocious. She killed God's prophets. God's people went underground. She engineered the marriage of her daughter to the house of David. During her long reign as the consort of Ahab, her will was supreme; no person dared to oppose her—except Elijah. She is the Lady Macbeth of Shakespeare and the Clytemnestra of Greek tragedy. Her crimes were many. Blood flowed freely from her influence. None resisted her. For a time it seemed as if God was in hiding and doing nothing.

Finally Jezebel committed her crowning crime. She arranged the death of Naboth so that Ahab might possess his vineyard. Her deed was high-handed, cold-blooded murder. It was a dastardly deed, and heaven could no longer remain silent. God's patience was exhausted, and He sent Elijah to announce His judgment. The day of reckoning came. First Ahab was killed, and the dogs licked up his blood just as the prophet had said they would. Now it is Jezebel's turn. She will be trodden underfoot, and the dogs will eat her to the point that there will not even be enough left for a decent burial. Fourteen years had elapsed since the death of Ahab and undoubtedly Jezebel did not believe that God's word would ever be fulfilled in her case. She was unmoved. She defied God. She stayed on in Jezreel, thinking perhaps that the death of Ahab was just a coincidence. She felt that she could get by and nothing would happen to her. But, you know, there is a law of God written in neon lights in every sphere on the crossroads of life: "Be not deceived; God is not mocked: for whatsoever a man soweth, that shall he also reap" (Gal. 6:7). ". . . For with the same measure that ye mete withal it shall be measured to you again" (Luke 6:38).

This is one of the most sordid and sadistic chapters in history. It is gruesome, it is ghastly, and it is a gory sight. Added to that, it is grizzly. It is one of the most revolting and repulsive scenes on the pages of Scripture. Jezebel is the queen mother. She has been living in luxury in the palace at Jezreel. The terrible prophecy of that horrible man Elijah has not been fulfilled. Suddenly out of the north came a swift chariot. It was Jehu driving furiously. He had just slain two kings, the king of Judah and the king of Israel—her own son, Joram. What does she do? She paints her eyes and arranges her hair, and looks out of a window. This proud queen still thinks she can seduce her captor—captivate him with her charms. She had a grandson twenty-three years old. She is no longer young; she is an old woman. No secret formulas for lotions, powders, sprays, and creams can make this faded queen look attractive. As she looks from an upstairs window at Jehu, she begins with flattery.

And as Jehu entered in at the gate, she said, Had Zimri peace, who slew his master? [2 Kings 9:31].

Her inference is, "Can't we get together and talk this over? Come up and see me sometime."

And he lifted up his face to the window, and said, Who is on my side? who? And there looked out to him two or three eunuchs.

And he said, Throw her down. So they threw her down: and some of her blood was sprinkled on the wall, and on the horses: and he trode her under foot [2 Kings 9:32–33].

Jehu is unmoved and untouched by Jezebel's words. He is without pity or mercy. Jezebel did not awe Jehu. She had no appeal for him. He did not even respect her. He said, "Throw her down!" And the eunuchs threw her down and she broke open like a ripe watermelon. This is the most frightful, terrible, and vivid picture in all of the annals of tragedy. Hammond says that history presents no parallel to such an indignity. It is truly unprecedented. A queen mother was customarily treated with respect.

And when he was come in, he did eat and drink, and said, Go, see now this cursed woman, and bury her: for she is a king's daughter [2 Kings 9:34].

How could Jehu enjoy a hearty meal after he had done this awful thing? As someone has said, he was "a fiend in human form." He was a rough soldier with no courtesy and certainly no chivalry. All he had was crude ambition. He did not shrink from any crime. He was depraved and degraded.

And they went to bury her: but they found no more of her than the skull, and the feet, and the palms of her hands.

Wherefore they came again, and told him. And he said, This is the word of the LORD, which he spake by his servant Elijah the Tishbite, saying, In the portion of Jezreel shall dogs eat the flesh of Jezebel:

And the carcase of Jezebel shall be as dung upon the face of the field in the portion of Jezreel; so that they shall not say, This is Jezebel [2 Kings 9:35-37].

When Jehu sent servants out to bury Jezebel, the dogs had already devoured her. The dogs had a big gourmet meal. But, my friend, there was no laughter in heaven because of this. There was no mourning, either. Perhaps in heaven it was being said—as the Book of Revelation tells us that it will be said in the future—"For true and righteous are his judgments: for he hath judged the great whore, which did corrupt the earth with her fornication, and hath avenged the blood of his servants at her hand" (Rev. 19:2). The horrible death of Jezebel illustrates again the truth of Galatians 6:7: "Be not deceived; God is not mocked: for whatsoever a man soweth, that shall he also reap."

Chapter 10 continues the judgment on the house of Ahab through the murderous heart of Jehu.

AHAB'S HOUSE IS JUDGED

And Ahab had seventy sons in Samaria. And Jehu wrote letters, and sent to Samaria, unto the rulers of Jezreel, to the elders, and to them that brought up Ahab's children, saying,

Now as soon as this letter cometh to you, seeing your master's sons are with you, and there are with you chariots and horses, a fenced city also, and armour;

Look even out the best and meetest of your master's sons, and set him on his father's throne, and fight for your master's house [2 Kings 10:1-3].

Jehu is giving the sons of Ahab the privilege of fighting for the throne of Israel. Not one of the seventy sons is willing to tackle Jehu.

Then the elders of Israel—to save their own necks—prove their allegiance to Jehu by slaying these seventy sons of Ahab.

So Jehu slew all that remained of the house of Ahab in
Jezreel, and all his great men, and his kinsfolks, and
his priests, until he left him none remaining [2 Kings
10:11].

JEHU MASSACRES THE ROYAL PRINCES OF JUDAH

And he arose and departed, and came to Samaria. And
as he was at the shearing house in the way,

Jehu met with the brethren of Ahaziah king of Judah,
and said, Who are ye? And they answered, We are the
brethren of Ahaziah: and we go down to salute the children of the king and the children of the queen.

And he said, Take them alive. And they took them alive,
and slew them at the pit of the shearing house, even two
and forty men; neither left he any of them [2 Kings
10:12–14].

After dealing with the house of Ahab, Jehu was on his way to assume
the throne in Samaria. He met forty-two sons (or nephews) of Ahaziah, the king of Judah. He slew them also. It is interesting to note,
however, that one of them was spared, and he was a descendant of the
house of Saul.

And when he was departed thence, he lighted on Jehonadab the son of Rechab coming to meet him: and he
saluted him, and said to him, Is thine heart right, as my
heart is with thy heart? And Jehonadab answered, It is.
If it be, give me thine hand. And he gave him his hand;
and he took him up to him into the chariot [2 Kings
10:15].

Jehu, still on his way to Samaria, met Jehonadab, the Rechabite. The
question he put to him was, "Are you friend or foe?" Jehonadab was
the founder of the very strict sect of Rechabites mentioned by Jere-

miah. He was undoubtedly a man of influence. Apparently he heartily approved of Jehu's anti-Ahab policy and was willing to lend his support by being seen in Jehu's chariot.

JEHU EXTERMINATES BAAL'S WORSHIPERS

And Jehu gathered all the people together, and said unto them, Ahab served Baal a little; but Jehu shall serve him much.

Now therefore call unto me all the prophets of Baal, all his servants, and all his priests; let none be wanting: for I have a great sacrifice to do to Baal; whosoever shall be wanting, he shall not live. But Jehu did it in subtilty, to the intent that he might destroy the worshippers of Baal [2 Kings 10:18–19].

The next thing Jehu did was to bring together all of the prophets of Baal by issuing a false statement that he would offer a great sacrifice to Baal. Jehu had no intention of worshiping Baal. When all the prophets came together, he slew them. His sacrifice to Baal was a trap and the prophets fell right into it.

JEHU FOLLOWS THE SINS OF JEROBOAM

While it is true that Jehu slew the prophets of Baal, he did not turn to the prophets of God.

Howbeit from the sins of Jeroboam the son of Nebat, who made Israel to sin, Jehu departed not from after them, to wit, the golden calves that were in Beth-el, and that were in Dan [2 Kings 10:29].

Jehu went back to the calf worship that Jeroboam had established. He did not worship Baal, nor the gods of the Zidonians, but he engaged in the calf worship that apparently came out of the land of Egypt.

Jehu did not turn to the Lord, but because he was zealous for the Lord, God gave him an earthly reward—that is, He extended the reign of his house for four generations.

And the LORD said unto Jehu, Because thou hast done well in executing that which is right in mine eyes, and hast done unto the house of Ahab according to all that was in mine heart, thy children of the fourth generation shall sit on the throne of Israel [2 Kings 10:30].

Although Jehu was a very brutal man, God makes the wrath of man to praise Him!

ISRAEL IS SMITTEN BY HAZAEL OF SYRIA

In those days the LORD began to cut Israel short: and Hazael smote them in all the coasts of Israel [2 Kings 10:32].

What is happening here? The northern kingdom is getting ready to go into captivity. From now on there will be a decline which will ultimately end in disaster. They will be carried away into captivity by Assyria.

The chapter concludes with the death of Jehu who had been king of Israel for twenty-eight years.

CHAPTERS 11 AND 12

THEME: Joash, the boy king

The story of Ahab and Jezebel is not a pretty section, and you probably thought we were through with them, but we are not. While it is true that Jehu had eliminated all the line of Ahab in the northern kingdom of Israel, a daughter of Ahab and Jezebel had married into the southern kingdom of Judah and was at this time the queen mother. Believe me, she took after mama and papa and was the meanest of them all. Her name is Athaliah, and she is going to perform an unbelievably terrible act.

ATHALIAH MURDERS HER GRANDCHILDREN

And when Athaliah the mother of Ahaziah saw that her son was dead, she arose and destroyed all the seed royal [2 Kings 11:1].

As long as Ahaziah had lived Athaliah actually had been the queen because she controlled her son. She was very much like Jezebel. Now that Ahaziah was dead, a grandson would come to the throne and Athaliah did not want that. She was afraid that she would not be able to control him, and she would lose her position. So what did she do? She slew all the line of David that she could get her hands on. Talk about a bloodthirsty act! She tried to exterminate the line of David. This was another attempt of Satan to destroy the line that is leading to the Lord Jesus Christ. Satan attempted to wipe out the line of David so that the Savior would not be born. Down through the ages the Devil has tried to eliminate the Jews. In Egypt the Lord preserved Moses, and the Jews were not slain but allowed to leave Egypt. Haman, in the Book of Esther, attempted to exterminate the Jews but was foiled. Satan was behind each of these attempts. Now here is this woman Athaliah attempting to exterminate the line of David.

Although she thought she had killed all of them, she missed one, as we are told here.

> **But Jehosheba, the daughter of king Joram, sister of Ahaziah, took Joash the son of Ahaziah, and stole him from among the king's sons which were slain; and they hid him, even him and his nurse, in the bedchamber from Athaliah, so that he was not slain.**

> **And he was with her hid in the house of the LORD six years. And Athaliah did reign over the land [2 Kings 11:2–3].**

She came to the throne after her son was killed and for years she was ruling alone—that was the way she wanted it. But all the while this little boy Joash was growing up.

JOASH COMES TO THE THRONE OF JUDAH

> **And the seventh year Jehoiada sent and fetched the rulers over hundreds, with the captains and the guard, and brought them to him into the house of the LORD, and made a covenant with them, and took an oath of them in the house of the LORD, and shewed them the king's son [2 Kings 11:4].**

When Joash (sometimes called Jehoash) was about seven years old, Jehoiada sent for the rulers, the captains, and the guard. He revealed to them that the king had a son. When they discovered that there was a son in the line of David it brought encouragement, joy, and hope to their hearts. They had had enough of this woman Athaliah anyway, and they jumped at the chance to dethrone her.

> **And he commanded them, saying, This is the thing that ye shall do; A third part of you that enter in on the sab-**

> bath shall even be keepers of the watch of the king's
> house;
>
> And a third part shall be at the gate of Sur; and a third
> part at the gate behind the guard: so shall ye keep the
> watch of the house, that it be not broken down.
>
> And two parts of all you that go forth on the sabbath,
> even they shall keep the watch of the house of the LORD
> about the king [2 Kings 11:5–7].

They were to "compass the king round about, every man with his
weapons in his hand." Extra precautions were taken to preserve the
life of this little fellow because his life would not have been worth a
plugged nickel if Athaliah had been able to get to him. She would
have slain him without a qualm although he was her grandson! This
woman was as heartless as Jezebel. So the young boy was well pro-
tected until the time he could be brought before the people.

> And the guard stood, every man with his weapons in his
> hand, round about the king, from the right corner of the
> temple to the left corner of the temple, along by the altar
> and the temple.
>
> And he brought forth the king's son, and put the crown
> upon him, and gave him the testimony; and they made
> him king, and anointed him; and they clapped their
> hands, and said, God save the king [2 Kings 11:11–12].

This was a great day for the southern kingdom to crown a king in the
line of David. Things had looked very discouraging there for a time.

ATHALIAH IS SLAIN

> And when Athaliah heard the noise of the guard and of
> the people, she came to the people into the temple of the
> LORD [2 Kings 11:13].

Of course Athaliah had not been invited to the coronation of the king. She evidently was in the palace of David on Mount Zion, which was situated right above the temple area. When she heard the clamor and noise in the temple area, she went there to see what was going on.

> **And when she looked, behold, the king stood by a pillar, as the manner was, and the princes and the trumpeters by the king, and all the people of the land rejoiced, and blew with trumpets: and Athaliah rent her clothes, and cried, Treason, Treason [2 Kings 11:14].**

This, of course, was Athaliah's idea of treason.

> **But Jehoiada the priest commanded the captains of the hundreds, the officers of the host, and said unto them, Have her forth without the ranges: and him that followeth her kill with the sword. For the priest had said, Let her not be slain in the house of the LORD.**

> **And they laid hands on her; and she went by the way by the which the horses came into the king's house: and there was she slain [2 Kings 11:15–16].**

Athaliah tried to flee. There was no way in the world for her to have her trial transferred to another district where she could be expected to receive a fair trial. They just executed her as she fled and saved an appeal to the supreme court. They got rid of her, which was, in my opinion, the proper thing to do at that time.

REVIVAL

The removal of Athaliah took a dark cloud off the southern kingdom. There was a new king, but naturally this little boy had to have counselors to rule in his stead because he was so young. One of them was Jehoiada who had engineered bringing Joash to the throne and executing Athaliah.

And Jehoiada made a covenant between the LORD and
the king and the people, that they should be the LORD'S
people; between the king also and the people [2 Kings
11:17].

This is the beginning of a return to God. Jehoiada the priest now leads
in a movement to return to the worship of Jehovah. The worship of
Baal was prevalent; it had penetrated even into Judah. Probably the
people were still going to the temple of the Lord, but they were worshiping Baal at the same time.

The same thing is going on today. Many people are religious on
Sunday and then live for the Devil the rest of the week. There are
many church members doing that today, and they wonder why the
church is dead! The explanation is not found in a building; it is found
in people. That is where the deadness lies at the present time.

And all the people of the land went into the house of
Baal, and brake it down; his altars and his images
brake they in pieces thoroughly, and slew Mattan the
priest of Baal before the altars. And the priest appointed
officers over the house of the LORD [2 Kings 11:18].

This is the beginning of a great spiritual movement that is nothing
short of a revival.

And he took the rulers over hundreds, and the captains,
and the guard, and all the people of the land; and they
brought down the king from the house of the LORD, and
came by the way of the gate of the guard to the king's
house. And he sat on the throne of the kings.

And all the people of the land rejoiced, and the city was
in quiet: and they slew Athaliah with the sword beside
the king's house.

Seven years old was Jehoash when he began to reign
[2 Kings 11:19–21].

What a day of rejoicing this was to have a descendant of David back on the throne and the wicked foreign usurper and her temple of Baal gone from the land!

THE REIGN OF JEHOASH (JOASH)

In the twelfth chapter we have the reign of Jehoash, and we will see that it is Jehoiada the high priest who is engineering it. This is the beginning of a great spiritual movement that I would call revival.

At this juncture I would like to have a roll call of kings. There was a total of nineteen kings who reigned over the northern kingdom of Israel. There was a total of twenty kings who reigned over the southern kingdom of Judah. Among the nineteen kings who ruled over Israel, not one of them could be labeled a righteous king. Actually the only thing you could say about them was that every one of them was a *bad* king—there was not a good one in the lot. In the southern kingdom of Judah there were twenty kings, and only ten of them could be considered good. Five of the kings were exceptional, and during their reigns there were five periods of reformation and revival. All of the reformation and blessing was incubated in the nest of spiritual revival. These brief periods of respite kept the fires burning on the altars that were all but extinguished at other times. Five times revival flared up and swept through the nation—not a fire of destruction but of construction and instruction. God visited His people with the heaven-sent times of refreshing. There was a turning to the Word of God and a return to the worship of God. There was power and prosperity.

When a revival comes, my friend, there will be new joy in the church. There will be renewed power in the church. There will be a new love. First, however, there must be a return to the Bible. A return to the Word of God has brought about every great spiritual revival. I personally believe that we can have a true revival today. Years ago Dr. Griffith Thomas said, "I cannot see anywhere in Scripture that revival of the true church is contrary to the will of God." Dr. R. A. Torrey also said, "There is no such teaching in Scripture that revival is contrary to the will of God." Dr. James M. Gray said, "We recall nothing in the epistles justifying the conclusion that the experiences of the early church may not be repeated today." My friend, let's do our part in getting out the Word of God so that God will be able to do a real work of grace in our time.

In chapter 12 we see Joash (also called Jehoash) as an adult.

In the seventh year of Jehu Jehoash began to reign; and forty years reigned he in Jerusalem. And his mother's name was Zibiah of Beer-sheba [2 Kings 12:1].

Joash (or Jehoash) began his reign as a child of seven and continued until he was forty-seven years old. His mother was Zibiah of Beer-sheba. Remember how the mother's names are often given because mothers have a tremendous influence on their sons.

And Jehoash did that which was right in the sight of the LORD all his days wherein Jehoiada the priest instructed him [2 Kings 12:2].

Joash was taught in the Word of God. My friend, what we need today are not empty-headed politicians who are everlastingly coming up with nostrums and criticizing all other parties and politicians, thinking only *they* have the answer. May I say to you, we need men today who are instructed in the Word of God and who *know* God today. We need a spiritual renewing in this land, and it can only come through the Word of God.

But the high places were not taken away: the people still sacrificed and burnt incense in the high places [2 Kings 12:3].

"Revival" did not mean that everyone had turned to God. Many were still sacrificing and offering incense in the high places. Even among the priests there were those who were not revived.

> And Jehoash said to the priests, All the money of the dedicated things that is brought into the house of the LORD, even the money of every one that passeth the account, the money that every man is set at, and all the money that cometh into any man's heart to bring into the house of the LORD,
>
> Let the priests take it to them, every man of his acquaintance: and let them repair the breaches of the house, wheresoever any breach shall be found [2 Kings 12:4–5].

The temple was in disrepair. It needed to be repaired. The priests took the money that was supposed to be used to repair the breaches of the temple and used it for other things.

> But it was so, that in the three and twentieth year of king Jehoash the priests had not repaired the breaches of the house.
>
> Then king Jehoash called for Jehoiada the priest, and the other priests, and said unto them, Why repair ye not the breaches of the house? now therefore receive no more money of your acquaintance, but deliver it for the breaches of the house.
>
> And the priests consented to receive no more money of the people, neither to repair the breaches of the house [2 Kings 12:6–8].

It is the same old story today. I think, very candidly, that you can test Christians and churches by their use or abuse of money. Many people in churches say, "Let's make So-and-So the treasurer or put him on the board of deacons because he is a good business man." May I say to you that you had better find out whether or not he is a spiritual man. That is the important thing.

What did they do? They had to prepare a locked box so that the money would be safe and the priests could not get their hands on it.

> But Jehoiada the priest took a chest, and bored a hole in the lid of it, and set it beside the altar, on the right side as one cometh into the house of the LORD: and the priests that kept the door put therein all the money that was brought into the house of the LORD [2 Kings 12:9].

I think this box was a good idea. Anyone can juggle figures, and I have seen officers who handle the money do just that—it is an absolute disgrace. "Joash's chest" is used today by many organizations to raise money. I wonder sometimes if people who use it recognize its background. The chest was secured so that some deacons and preachers and other religious racketeers could not get their hands on the offerings. This was a good idea that you might want to use sometime.

TEMPLE TREASURES BUY OFF HAZAEL

Although there had been a great spiritual movement in the land, the nation was beginning to go downhill.

> Then Hazael king of Syria went up, and fought against Gath, and took it: and Hazael set his face to go up to Jerusalem.
>
> And Jehoash king of Judah took all the hallowed things that Jehoshaphat, and Jehoram, and Ahaziah, his fathers, kings of Judah, had dedicated, and his own hallowed things, and all the gold that was found in the treasures of the house of the LORD, and in the king's house, and sent it to Hazael king of Syria: and he went away from Jerusalem [2 Kings 12:17–18].

In other words, Joash was buying time. He was trying to buy off Hazael, king of Syria.

> And the rest of the acts of Joash, and all that he did, are they not written in the book of the chronicles of the kings of Judah?

And his servants arose, and made a conspiracy, and slew Joash in the house of Millo, which goeth down to Silla [2 Kings 12:19–20].

We will talk more about revival when we get to the two Books of Chronicles. Joash was just forty-seven years old when he died. His servants killed him, and he was buried with his fathers in the city of David. Joash had been a good king. We will find that his son Amaziah will also be a good king.

CHRONOLOGICAL TABLE OF THE KINGS OF THE DIVIDED KINGDOM

JUDAH

King	Reign		Character	Prophet
1. Rehoboam	931–913 B.C.	(17 yrs.)	Bad	Shemaiah
2. Abijah	913–911	(3 yrs.)	Bad	
3. Asa	911–870	(41 yrs.)	Good	
4. Jehoshaphat	870–848*	(25 yrs.)	Good	
5. Jehoram	848–841*	(8 yrs.)	Bad	
6. Ahaziah	841	(1 yr.)	Bad	
7. Athaliah	841–835	(6 yrs.)	Bad	
8. Joash	835–796	(40 yrs.)	Good	Joel
9. Amaziah	796–767	(29 yrs.)	Good	
10. Azariah (or Uzziah)	767–740*	(52 yrs.)	Good	Isaiah
11. Jotham	740–732*	(16 yrs.)	Good	Micah
12. Ahaz	732–716	(16 yrs.)	Bad	
13. Hezekiah	716–687	(29 yrs.)	Good	
14. Manasseh	687–642*	(55 yrs.)	Bad	Nahum
15. Amon	642–640	(2 yrs.)	Bad	{ Habakkuk Zephaniah
16. Josiah	640–608	(31 yrs.)	Good	Jeremiah
17. Jehoahaz	608	(3 mo.)	Bad	
18. Jehoiakim	608–597	(11 yrs.)	Bad	
19. Jehoiachin	597	(3 mo.)	Bad	
20. Zedekiah	597–586	(11 yrs.)	Bad	

(Destruction of Jerusalem and captivity of Judah)

ISRAEL

King	Reign		Character	Prophet
1. Jeroboam I	931–910 B.C.	(22 yrs.)	Bad	Ahijah
2. Nadab	910–909	(2 yrs.)	Bad	
3. Baasha	909–886	(24 yrs.)	Bad	
4. Elah	886–885	(2 yrs.)	Bad	
5. Zimri	885	(7 days)	Bad	
6. Omri	885–874*	(12 yrs.)	Bad	
7. Ahab	874–853	(22 yrs.)	Bad	{ Elijah Micaiah
8. Ahaziah	853–852	(2 yrs.)	Bad	
9. Joram	852–841	(12 yrs.)	Bad	Elisha
10. Jehu	841–814	(28 yrs.)	Bad	
11. Jehoahaz	814–798	(17 yrs.)	Bad	
12. Jehoash	798–782	(16 yrs.)	Bad	
13. Jeroboam II	782–753*	(41 yrs.)	Bad	{ Jonah Amos Hosea
14. Zechariah	753–752	(6 mo.)	Bad	
15. Shallum	752	(1 mo.)	Bad	
16. Menahem	752–742	(10 yrs.)	Bad	
17. Pekahiah	742–740	(2 yrs.)	Bad	
18. Pekah	740–732*	(20 yrs.)	Bad	
19. Hoshea	732–721	(9 yrs.)	Bad	

(Capture of Samaria and captivity of Israel)

*Co-regency

CHAPTER 13

THEME: The final acts of Elisha

Friend, this is a rugged portion of Scripture; yet it can minister to our hearts. This is an especially good section for the rulers of nations. We are following both kingdoms of Israel and Judah. In the north the ten tribes constitute the northern kingdom, and in the south the tribes of Judah and Benjamin constitute the southern kingdom. In the south the line of David is reigning. That is the line that will be followed right on into the New Testament to the birth of the Lord Jesus Christ. As we have seen, the line of David was almost eliminated by Athaliah, the daughter of Ahab and Jezebel, who married into the family of David.

JEHOAHAZ REIGNS OVER ISRAEL

In chapter 13 we find that Jehoahaz, the son of Jehu, reigned over Israel for seventeen years. He followed in the sinful steps of Jeroboam. Actually, there is nothing very sensational or interesting about his reign. Many people feel that sin brings excitement into life. There is nothing quite as boring as sin after a while. The man who starts drinking reaches the day when he is a drunkard; and, at that point, he is as boring as anyone can possibly be. And his life loses its purpose. The same thing is true of any individual who indulges in sin. This period of history is very boring. There is excitement only when God is moving. How we need Him today on the scene!

In the three and twentieth year of Joash the son of Ahaziah king of Judah Jehoahaz the son of Jehu began to reign over Israel in Samaria, and reigned seventeen years.

> And he did that which was evil in the sight of the LORD,
> and followed the sins of Jeroboam the son of Nebat,
> which made Israel to sin; he departed not therefrom
> [2 Kings 13:1-2].

Jeroboam is the one who instituted calf worship in Israel. He led Israel away from the worship of the true God and led them into sin. When Ahab and Jezebel came to the throne, they went way beyond that. They began an active worship of Baal, which actually was demonism. Now Jehoahaz, like his father Jehu, does not go into Baal worship, nor sink into the depths of sin like Ahab and Jezebel did. He does go as far as Jeroboam did, however, and that is bad enough.

REPENTANCE OF JEHOAHAZ

Because of Israel's sin, God allowed the king of Syria to come against Israel.

> And the anger of the LORD was kindled against Israel,
> and he delivered them into the hand of Hazael king of
> Syria, and into the hand of Ben-hadad the son of Ha-
> zael, all their days.

> And Jehoahaz besought the LORD, and the LORD hear-
> kened unto him: for he saw the oppression of Israel,
> because the king of Syria oppressed them [2 Kings
> 13:3-4].

This man knew he was in danger and in trouble. So in fear he turns to the Lord.

> (And the LORD gave Israel a saviour, so that they went
> out from under the hand of the Syrians: and the chil-
> dren of Israel dwelt in their tents, as beforetime [2 Kings
> 13:5].

Notice how gracious God is. The minute the king called upon Him, He heard and answered prayer! He delivered the people from Syria's oppression. My friend, you and I today do not realize how good God is and how good He is to you and me today. Oh, how wonderful He is!

Nevertheless they departed not from the sins of the house of Jeroboam, who made Israel sin, but walked therein: and there remained the grove also in Samaria).

Neither did he leave of the people to Jehoahaz but fifty horsemen, and ten chariots, and ten thousand footmen; for the king of Syria had destroyed them, and had made them like the dust by threshing [2 Kings 13:6-7].

We see the goodness of the Lord in the life of Jehoahaz. The king called upon God and He answered. But the king and his people went on in sin, and they continued their idol worship. The king of Syria so destroyed the defense of Jehoahaz that he was never able to properly defend his kingdom again.

Now the rest of the acts of Jehoahaz, and all that he did, and his might, are they not written in the book of the chronicles of the kings of Israel?

And Jehoahaz slept with his fathers; and they buried him in Samaria: and Joash his son reigned in his stead [2 Kings 13:8-9].

Here we have the record of the death of Jehoahaz. This is the record of man: The king is dead, long live the king.

JEHOASH REIGNS OVER ISRAEL

Another king comes to the throne of the northern kingdom.

In the thirty and seventh year of Joash king of Judah began Jehoash the son of Jehoahaz to reign over Israel in Samaria, and reigned sixteen years [2 Kings 13:10].

Now we come to a very confusing period because the names of the kings in both kingdoms are similar, if not identical. It is difficult to know who is reigning, where he is reigning, and the circumstances of the reign. I am not so sure but what the Lord left it that way for a definite reason.

> **And he did that which was evil in the sight of the LORD; he departed not from all the sins of Jeroboam the son of Nebat, who made Israel sin: but he walked therein [2 Kings 13:11].**

Jeroboam was the standard. When a king reached his level of sin, God always judged.

ELISHA'S DEATH: HIS PROPHECY IS FULFILLED

It was at this time that Elisha fell sick; it was the illness that brought death to him.

> **Now Elisha was fallen sick of his sickness whereof he died. And Joash the king of Israel came down unto him, and wept over his face, and said, O my father, my father, the chariot of Israel, and the horsemen thereof [2 Kings 13:14].**

Elisha had been a tower of strength to the northern kingdom in a way that Elijah had not been. (When the news of Elijah's translation reached the palace, I imagine there was a celebration party!) However, Elisha had been a tremendous help to the king, and he was heartbroken when the prophet became ill.

> **And Elisha said unto him, Take bow and arrows. And he took unto him bow and arrows [2 Kings 13:15].**

When the king visits him, Elisha does not just accept his sympathy and flowers. He is still a prophet of God, and he is giving God's message to him.

> And he said to the king of Israel, Put thine hand upon
> the bow. And he put his hand upon it: and Elisha put his
> hands upon the king's hands.
>
> And he said, Open the window eastward. And he
> opened it. Then Elisha said, Shoot. And he shot. And he
> said, The arrow of the LORD's deliverance, and the ar-
> row of deliverance from Syria: for thou shalt smite the
> Syrians in Aphek, till thou have consumed them
> [2 Kings 13:16–17].

Well, Joash is not noted for his faith. Although he is weeping over the
prophet who is dying, he is not a man of great faith, and he doesn't
believe God is going to give him the victory over Syria.

> And he said, Take the arrows. And he took them. And
> he said unto the king of Israel, Smite upon the ground.
> And he smote thrice, and stayed.
>
> And the man of God was wroth with him, and said,
> Thou shouldest have smitten five or six times; then hadst
> thou smitten Syria till thou hadst consumed it: where-
> as now thou shalt smite Syria but thrice [2 Kings
> 13:18–19].

Because he didn't have the faith that God would give him deliverance,
discouragement caused him to quit.

Many wonderful projects for God never come to fruition, are never
executed, because a child of God meets opposition or discouragement. He gives up, and says, "The project is not in God's will." That is
the attitude of Joash—he smote only three times. He is saying by this,
"I don't think God will see me through." Today I see so much soft
"faith." Folk sit on the sidelines and engage in wishful thinking. They
say, "Oh, I want to do something for God." And the next time I see

them, they are still sitting there. God expects you to get on the move for Him. If you believe God can use you, then get busy! Elisha gives us a very practical lesson here.

THE MIRACLE AT HIS TOMB

And Elisha died, and they buried him. And the bands of the Moabites invaded the land at the coming in of the year.

And it came to pass as they were burying a man, that, behold, they spied a band of men; and they cast the man into the sepulchre of Elisha: and when the man was let down, and touched the bones of Elisha, he revived, and stood up on his feet [2 Kings 13:20–21].

Even in death Elisha was a miracle-working individual. What a tremendous tower of strength he had been in that nation.

But Hazael king of Syria oppressed Israel all the days of Jehoahaz.

And the LORD was gracious unto them, and had compassion on them, and had respect unto them, because of his covenant with Abraham, Isaac, and Jacob, and would not destroy them, neither cast he them from his presence as yet [2 Kings 13:22–23].

While God is punishing Israel with the word of Hazael, He does not allow the oppression to go too far.

So Hazael king of Syria died; and Ben-hadad his son reigned in his stead.

And Jehoash the son of Jehoahaz took again out of the hand of Ben-hadad the son of Hazael the cities, which he

had taken out of the hand of Jehoahaz his father by war.
Three times did Joash beat him, and recovered the cities
of Israel [2 Kings 13:24–25].

In other words, as his faith, so was it done unto him—*three* times God
gave him victory.

CHAPTERS 14—16

THEME: Good and bad kings of Israel and Judah

AMAZIAH'S REIGN OVER JUDAH

Now we come to the reign of Amaziah over Judah. As was indicated before, Amaziah was a good king. He reigned for twenty-nine years.

> **In the second year of Joash son of Jehoahaz king of Israel reigned Amaziah the son of Joash king of Judah [2 Kings 14:1].**

The fact that there are two kings by the same name is certainly confusing. The chronological table will help clear up the confusion.

> **He was twenty and five years old when he began to reign, and reigned twenty and nine years in Jerusalem. And his mother's name was Jehoaddan of Jerusalem [2 Kings 14:2].**

Amaziah's mother was Jehoaddan. The mother of these kings will receive the credit if their sons are good kings and the blame if they are bad kings. Amaziah was a good king so he must have had a wonderful mother.

> **And he did that which was right in the sight of the LORD, yet not like David his father: he did according to all things as Joash his father did [2 Kings 14:3].**

Amaziah, the son of Joash, succeeded to the throne of Judah, and we are told that he did that which was right in the sight of the Lord although he failed to measure up to David's standard.

We also find that the civil war between the two kingdoms continued during this particular period.

> Now they made a conspiracy against him in Jerusalem: and he fled to Lachish; but they sent after him to Lachish, and slew him there.
>
> And they brought him on horses: and he was buried at Jerusalem with his fathers in the city of David.
>
> And all the people of Judah took Azariah, which was sixteen years old, and made him king instead of his father Amaziah.
>
> He built Elath, and restored it to Judah, after that the king slept with his fathers [2 Kings 14:19–22].

Amaziah fled to the city of Lachish, where there was a fortress which offered refuge, to avoid capture by conspirators.

JEROBOAM II REIGNS OVER ISRAEL

> In the fifteenth year of Amaziah the son of Joash king of Judah Jeroboam the son of Joash king of Israel began to reign in Samaria, and reigned forty and one years.
>
> And he did that which was evil in the sight of the LORD: he departed not from all the sins of Jeroboam the son of Nebat, who made Israel to sin.
>
> He restored the coast of Israel from the entering of Hamath unto the sea of the plain, according to the word of the LORD God of Israel, which he spake by the hand of his servant Jonah, the son of Amittai, the prophet, which was of Gath-hepher [2 Kings 14:23–25].

Jeroboam did evil in the sight of the Lord. He did, however, restore the border of Israel, according to Jonah, the son of Amittai, the prophet.

This is a historical reference to Jonah who wrote the Book of Jonah. This confirms the fact that Jonah was a real person and prophet in Israel. Finally Jeroboam II died and Zachariah came to the throne. We are moving toward the end of this nation.

AZARIAH (UZZIAH) REIGNS OVER JUDAH

In the twenty and seventh year of Jeroboam king of Israel began Azariah son of Amaziah king of Judah to reign.

Sixteen years old was he when he began to reign, and he reigned two and fifty years in Jerusalem. And his mother's name was Jecholiah of Jerusalem.

And he did that which was right in the sight of the LORD, according to all that his father Amaziah had done;

Save that the high places were not removed: the people sacrificed and burnt incense still on the high places [2 Kings 15:1–4].

In many ways Azariah (Uzziah) was a good king. However, he did something that he should not have done: he intruded into the priest's office. For this he was smitten with leprosy (2 Chron. 26:15–21). It broke Isaiah's heart when he died because Isaiah was afraid Azariah's successors would lead the nation back into idolatry. Azariah's fears were well-grounded, for his grandson did just that. We will spend more time on the reign of Uzziah when we come to Chronicles and Isaiah.

In Israel Zachariah, the last of the line of Jehu, was slain by Shallum after he had reigned for only six months. Shallum did not do very well, either. He reigned for only one month and was overthrown and slain by Menahem. Menahem reigned for ten years and did evil as had Jeroboam.

At this time Pul, king of Assyria, came against Israel, and Menahem paid one thousand talents of silver to preserve his kingdom. It

was a dark period for the nation. At his death, his son Pekahiah succeeded him to the throne but reigned only two years, when Pekah, his
captain, conspired and slew him.

During the reign of Pekah, Tiglath-pileser, king of Assyria, came
against Israel and took captive the tribe of Naphtali. Pekah was slain
by Hoshea. Jotham reigned in Judah, and was recognized as a good
king.

JOTHAM REIGNS OVER JUDAH

Now we return to the kings of Judah and the son of Azariah (Uzziah).

**Five and twenty years old was he when he began to
reign, and he reigned sixteen years in Jerusalem. And
his mother's name was Jerusha, the daughter of Zadok
[2 Kings 15:33].**

He is rated as a good king, and the Lord records the name of his
mother.

**And he did that which was right in the sight of the LORD:
he did according to all that his father Uzziah had done.**

**Howbeit the high places were not removed: the people
sacrificed and burned incense still in the high places.
He built the higher gate of the house of the LORD [2 Kings
15:34–35].**

He also tolerated the idolatry which would eventually send his people
into captivity.

As we begin chapter 16, let me say that if you enjoy history, you
will find this section intensely interesting. If you are looking for spiritual lessons, you will find some very practical things in this section.
Much of this part of God's Word is extremely helpful. Remember, all
of these things happened as examples for us.

AHAZ REIGNS OVER JUDAH

Twenty years old was Ahaz when he began to reign, and reigned sixteen years in Jerusalem, and did not that which was right in the sight of the LORD his God, like David his father.

But he walked in the way of the kings of Israel, yea, and made his son to pass through the fire, according to the abominations of the heathen, whom the LORD cast out from before the children of Israel [2 Kings 16:2–3].

Pekah reigned twenty years before he was murdered. In the seventeenth year of Pekah's reign in Israel, Ahaz began his reign as king of Judah. Ahaz was not a good king.

And he sacrificed and burnt incense in the high places, and on the hills, and under every green tree [2 Kings 16:4].

He walked in the wicked ways of the kings of Israel. He did the terrible thing of offering children as sacrifices to heathen gods—probably to Merodach (Marduk) or to Baal. This practice was about as low as a person could sink spiritually, and this is the thing Ahaz did. We are told that he "sacrificed and burnt incense in the high places, and on the hills, and under every green tree." In other words, Ahaz went the whole route into idolatry and pagan and heathen worship.

Then Rezin king of Syria and Pekah son of Remaliah king of Israel came up to Jerusalem to war: and they besieged Ahaz, but could not overcome him [2 Kings 16:5].

In the prophecy of Isaiah, chapter 7, there is an extended section on this. It is a very important section, because in it is the prophecy of the virgin birth of Jesus Christ. Isaiah is prophesying to this man Ahaz who will not listen to God. So Isaiah challenges him to trust God. Then Ahaz appeals to Assyria for help. This opens the door for Assyria to come down and ultimately take the northern kingdom into captivity.

> **At that time Rezin king of Syria recovered Elath to Syria, and drave the Jews from Elath: and the Syrians came to Elath, and dwelt there unto this day [2 Kings 16:6].**

"Unto this day" means, of course, up to the time that this record was written.

In this verse the word *Jew* is used for the first time in the Bible. There are those who hold that *Jew* applies only to those of the tribe of Judah. However, notice that here it refers to folk in the northern kingdom of Israel—in fact, up on the border of Syria. As we shall see, all twelve tribes were given that name.

> **So Ahaz sent messengers to Tiglath-pileser king of Assyria, saying, I am thy servant and thy son: come up, and save me out of the hand of the king of Syria, and out of the hand of the king of Israel, which rise up against me.**
>
> **And Ahaz took the silver and gold that was found in the house of the LORD, and in the treasures of the king's house, and sent it for a present to the king of Assyria [2 Kings 16:7–8].**

And so the Assyrians are bribed. They come to Ahaz' aid first by attacking Damascus in Syria and then by taking the city.

> **And king Ahaz went to Damascus to meet Tiglath-pileser king of Assyria, and saw an altar that was at Damascus: and king Ahaz sent to Urijah the priest the**

> fashion of the altar, and the pattern of it, according to all
> the workmanship thereof [2 Kings 16:10].

He wanted this altar copied and erected in the temple of God. All the while Isaiah was prophesying to him and against him for what he was doing.

> And king Ahaz cut off the borders of the bases, and re-
> moved the laver from off them; and took down the sea
> from off the brasen oxen that were under it, and put it
> upon a pavement of stones [2 Kings 16:17].

Ahaz is showing his utter disrespect for the temple of the true and living God.

> And the covert for the sabbath that they had built in the
> house, and the king's entry without, turned he from the
> house of the Lord for the king of Assyria.

> Now the rest of the acts of Ahaz which he did, are they
> not written in the book of the chronicles of the kings of
> Judah?

> And Ahaz slept with his fathers, and was buried with
> his fathers in the city of David: and Hezekiah his son
> reigned in his stead [2 Kings 16:18-20].

Ahaz mutilated the house of God and seems to have stripped it of its elaborate ornamentation.

The chapter concludes with the death of Ahaz and the record of the fact that his son Hezekiah reigned after him. It is an amazing thing that a godless man like Ahaz would have a son like Hezekiah, the story of whose reign we shall see in a following chapter.

CHAPTER 17

THEME: Israel goes into captivity

These are the reasons God permitted Israel to go into captivity:
1. *Disobeyed God* (v. 13)—"Yet the LORD testified against Israel, and against Judah, by all the prophets, and by all the seers, saying, Turn ye from your evil ways, and keep my commandments and my statutes, according to all the law which I commanded your fathers, and which I sent to you by my servants the prophets."

2. *Doubted God* (v. 14, see also 2 Chron. 36:15–16)—"Notwithstanding they would not hear, but hardened their necks, like to the neck of their fathers, that did not believe in the LORD their God."

3. *Defied God* (v. 15) in that they refused to observe the sabbatic year for 490 years—"To fulfil the word of the LORD by the mouth of Jeremiah, until the land had enjoyed her sabbaths: for as long as she lay desolate she kept sabbath, to fulfil threescore and ten years" (2 Chron. 36:21).

The story of this nation is the story of every individual.

HOSHEA'S REIGN

In chapter 17 we come to the end of the line as far as Israel is concerned. The ten northern tribes are carried into captivity by Assyria.

In the twelfth year of Ahaz king of Judah began Hoshea the son of Elah to reign in Samaria over Israel nine years.

And he did that which was evil in the sight of the LORD, but not as the kings of Israel that were before him [2 Kings 17:1–2].

He is not as bad as Ahab (and Jezebel), nor as bad as Ahaziah, but he is bad enough.

Against him came up Shalmaneser king of Assyria; and Hoshea became his servant, and gave him presents.

And the king of Assyria found conspiracy in Hoshea: for he had sent messengers to So king of Egypt, and brought no present to the king of Assyria, as he had done year by year: therefore the king of Assyria shut him up, and bound him in prison.

Then the king of Assyria came up throughout all the land, and went up to Samaria, and besieged it three years [2 Kings 17:3–5].

We are introduced to Shalmaneser, king of Assyria. He captured the northern kingdom and exacted tribute from them. When he discovered that king Hoshea had formed a conspiracy against him and was not paying his tribute, he besieged Samaria. Samaria was the city that Omri, the father of Ahab, had built. Ahab built a palace there. It was one of the most beautiful spots in the land. Now the king of Assyria besieged it.

ISRAEL'S CAPTIVITY

In the ninth year of Hoshea the king of Assyria took Samaria, and carried Israel away into Assyria, and placed them in Halah and in Habor by the river of Gozan, and in the cities of the Medes [2 Kings 17:6].

There are those who say that the ten tribes are lost; that is, the tribes have popped up in Great Britain from where they spread to the United States. This is a nice theory which ministers to the pride of many folk who would like to believe that they are members of the lost tribes, but this idea of ten lost tribes is entirely man-made. You will not find it in the Word of God. For example, in the New Testament James wrote in his epistle, "James, a servant of God and of the Lord Jesus Christ, to the twelve tribes which are scattered abroad, greeting" (James 1:1). Apparently James did not think the tribes were lost. The folk who hold this theory believe the ten tribes were lost when they went into Assyrian captivity. When the Jews returned to their land, you will find that some out of all the tribes came back. Actually, a small percentage of the people returned. Several million Jews went into captivity and only about 65,000 returned to Palestine.

SINS WHICH CAUSED ISRAEL'S CAPTIVITY

For so it was, that the children of Israel had sinned against the LORD their God, which had brought them up out of the land of Egypt, from under the hand of Pharaoh king of Egypt, and had feared other gods,

And walked in the statutes of the heathen, whom the LORD cast out from before the children of Israel, and of the kings of Israel, which they had made [2 Kings 17:7–8].

The Lord had been very patient with these people. Over a period of over two hundred years (after the division of the kingdom) the Lord had given them every opportunity and ample time to return to Him. But they did not. They continually went off into idolatry. The Word of God is very clear that he sent them into captivity because they insisted on worshiping other gods.

And the children of Israel did secretly those things that were not right against the LORD their God, and they built them high places in all their cities, from the tower of the watchman to the fenced city.

And they set them up images and groves in every high hill, and under every green tree [2 Kings 17:9–10].

On top of the hills and under the trees pagan worship was carried on. Israel indulged in this gross immorality and licentiousness.

And there they burnt incense in all the high places, as did the heathen whom the LORD carried away before them; and wrought wicked things to provoke the LORD to anger:

For they served idols, whereof the LORD had said unto them, Ye shall not do this thing [2 Kings 17:11–12].

God had put the heathen out of the land for their immorality and idolatry. Do you think that God would permit His own people to stay in the land and do the same things? Well, He would not. He allowed Assyria to come and carry them away into captivity.

Yet the LORD testified against Israel, and against Judah, by all the prophets, and by all the seers, saying, Turn ye from your evil ways, and keep my commandments and my statutes, according to all the law which I commanded your fathers, and which I sent to you by my servants the prophets [2 Kings 17:13].

God had sent the prophets Ahijah, Elijah, Micaiah, Elisha, Jonah, Amos, and Hosea to these people in the northern kingdom of Israel. To the southern kingdom of Judah he had sent the prophets Shemaiah, Joel, Isaiah, and Micah. Later on He will be sending Nahum, Habakkuk, Zephaniah, and Jeremiah. Every prophet warned the people of both kingdoms what would take place if they did not return to God and forsake their evil ways.

Notwithstanding they would not hear, but hardened their necks, like to the neck of their fathers, that did not believe in the LORD their God [2 Kings 17:14].

What was the basic sin? They were guilty of unbelief. The great sin of mankind is our refusal to believe God. You and I are living in a contemporary culture that has ruled God out. He has no place in our educational system. He is not appealed to by our government officials. Unfortunately, neither is He appealed to by many of our churches today. As a result, God will judge us as He judged His own people long ago.

> **And they rejected his statutes, and his covenant that he made with their fathers, and his testimonies which he testified against them; and they followed vanity, and became vain, and went after the heathen that were round about them, concerning whom the LORD had charged them, that they should not do like them [2 Kings 17:15].**

The northern kingdom was taken into captivity. What about the southern kingdom?

> **Also Judah kept not the commandments of the LORD their God, but walked in the statutes of Israel which they made [2 Kings 17:19].**

Judah will not profit from Israel's experience, as we shall see.

> **And the LORD rejected all the seed of Israel, and afflicted them, and delivered them into the hand of spoilers, until he had cast them out of his sight.**

> **For he rent Israel from the house of David; and they made Jeroboam the son of Nebat king: and Jeroboam drave Israel from following the LORD, and made them sin a great sin [2 Kings 17:20-21].**

You will recall that Jeroboam instituted calf worship in Israel.

For the children of Israel walked in all the sins of Jeroboam which he did; they departed not from them;

Until the LORD removed Israel out of his sight, as he had said by all his servants the prophets. So was Israel carried away out of their own land to Assyria unto this day [2 Kings 17:22–23].

"Unto this day" means, of course, the day 2 Kings was written.

ISRAEL'S CITIES REPOPULATED
WITH FOREIGNERS

When the king of Assyria took the northern kingdom captive, he brought in other people to inhabit the land. The area of the northern kingdom was called Samaria. The Samaritans of the New Testament are the descendants of the colonists brought in by the king of Assyria. This is their beginning.

Wherefore they spake to the king of Assyria, saying, The nations which thou hast removed, and placed in the cities of Samaria, know not the manner of the God of the land: therefore he hath sent lions among them, and, behold, they slay them, because they know not the manner of the God of the land.

Then the king of Assyria commanded, saying, Carry thither one of the priests whom ye brought from thence; and let them go and dwell there, and let him teach them the manner of the God of the land.

Then one of the priests whom they had carried away from Samaria came and dwelt in Beth-el, and taught them how they should fear the LORD.

Howbeit every nation made gods of their own, and put them in the houses of the high places which the Samari-

**tans had made, every nation in their cities wherein they
dwelt [2 Kings 17:26–29].**

This brings us to the end of the northern kingdom. The land has become a mixture of peoples, and there is a great deal of intermarriage.
The ten tribes will never again form the northern kingdom. They are
scattered now, but they are not lost.

CHAPTER 18

THEME: Revival and testing under Hezekiah

Now we come to King Hezekiah. This section is so remarkable that it is not only recorded here in 2 Kings, but also in 2 Chronicles, and in the historical section of the prophecy of Isaiah.

We have just seen that the northern kingdom of Israel was taken into captivity by Assyria. God gives three reasons why this happened: Israel disobeyed God, they doubted God, and they defied God. During the same period the southern kingdom of Judah had a very wonderful king. From this point on we shall be following only the history of the southern kingdom since the northern kingdom is out of the picture. The reason God did not send Judah into captivity at this time is because Judah did have a few good kings who were responsible for a time of revival.

Hezekiah was one of these. In fact, he was the best king who reigned in the land after David.

> **Now it came to pass in the third year of Hoshea son of Elah king of Israel, that Hezekiah the son of Ahaz king of Judah began to reign.**
>
> **Twenty and five years old was he when he began to reign; and he reigned twenty and nine years in Jerusalem. His mother's name also was Abi, the daughter of Zachariah.**
>
> **And he did that which was right in the sight of the Lord, according to all that David his father did [2 Kings 18:1–3].**

Ahaz, the father of Hezekiah, was a very wicked king; yet he had this wonderful son. This leads us to believe that the mother of Hezekiah was a very fine mother and a godly woman. We are told here that her name was Abi.

JUDAH'S REVIVAL UNDER HEZEKIAH

He removed the high places, and brake the images, and cut down the groves, and brake in pieces the brasen serpent that Moses had made: for unto those days the children of Israel did burn incense to it: and he called it Nehushtan [2 Kings 18:4].

Hezekiah was a remarkable man. He led his people in a revival and began by attempting to remove idolatry from the land.

This verse mentions the brazen serpent that Moses put up in the wilderness (see Num. 21:1–9). What happened to that serpent that Moses had made? Well, it had been kept. Naturally it would be a tremendous memento, and it was kept in the temple. Then the day came when the children of Israel began to worship it! Instead of looking at it in faith as their fathers had, when they had been bitten by poisonous serpents in the wilderness as a judgment from God for rebellion, they began to worship it. Now it was a stumbling block. They had forgotten the meaning of it. The serpent pointed to Christ according to John 3:14–15 which says, "And as Moses lifted up the serpent in the wilderness, even so must the Son of man be lifted up: that whosoever believeth in him should not perish, but have eternal life." The brazen serpent was a symbol that was fulfilled by Christ. These people had turned the thing all around and had begun to worship the serpent instead of God.

As I have studied the seven churches of Asia Minor, I have noted that in the city of Pergamos (more correctly, Pergamum), the serpent was worshiped. It seems the children of Israel were doing the same thing. They burned incense to the brazen serpent and called it Nehushtan. Now Hezekiah broke it in pieces. It was time to get rid of it.

There is a great spiritual lesson in this. There are certain organizations, certain movements, and certain methods that God has used in the past. Unfortunately, folk did not know when God was through with them, and they refused to disband them. I could name half a dozen organizations that I am confident God raised up and which served a great purpose, but which went to seed. They continued operating for no other reason than to perpetuate jobs for those they employed. They became Nehushtan. They became brazen serpents that at one time had served a purpose and were mightily used by God. Then the day came when God was through with them.

I have been in churches where people have been using the same methods for years and years. They say, "This is the way we have always done it." It may be that it is time to change some of those methods—there is no monotony with God. Do you realize that Paul never gave an invitation for people to come forward after a service? Apparently Dwight L. Moody began that practice. Now most evangelists think they have to give an invitation for people to come forward, and I have seen it actually become a stumbling block. God led Moody to do it, but He may not lead you to do it. Although I was pastor in a downtown Los Angeles church and there were many converts who responded to the invitation at the Sunday services, my most solid converts were those who were saved in the Bible study on Thursday night when no invitation was given. What God leads someone else to do, He may not lead you to do. You can certainly begin worshiping the equivalent of a brazen serpent and call it Nehushtan.

I have spent some time on this subject because I think it is important. Thank God that Hezekiah got rid of the serpent. I am of the opinion that many of the long-faced saints really criticized Hezekiah. They probably said, "He has gotten rid of our marvelous, wonderful, brazen serpent." Well, thank God he broke it to pieces, friend. If you have a few little idols lying around your church or in your life, I suggest you get rid of them. Maybe there is some method or some particular way you have of doing things that you ought to change.

He trusted in the Lord God of Israel; so that after him was none like him among all the kings of Judah, nor any that were before him.

For he clave to the LORD, and departed not from following him, but kept his commandments, which the LORD
commanded Moses [2 Kings 18:5-6].

If there was none after Hezekiah to compare to him, and none before
him, then we must conclude that he was outstanding. He is on a par
with David. He was a great king who was mightily used of God. That
is the reason that his life is given to us in three books of the Old Testament: 2 Kings, 2 Chronicles, and Isaiah.

THE FIRST INVASION OF JUDAH

And the LORD was with him; and he prospered whithersoever he went forth: and he rebelled against the king of
Assyria, and served him not.

He smote the Philistines, even unto Gaza, and the borders thereof, from the tower of the watchmen to the
fenced city.

And it came to pass in the fourth year of king Hezekiah,
which was the seventh year of Hoshea son of Elah king
of Israel, that Shalmaneser king of Assyria came up
against Samaria, and besieged it.

And at the end of three years they took it: even in the
sixth year of Hezekiah, that is the ninth year of Hoshea
king of Israel, Samaria was taken [2 Kings 18:7-10].

Hezekiah was a courageous king. Under his command Judah rebelled against Assyria and defeated the Philistines. During the sixth
year of Hezekiah's reign, Shalmaneser, king of Assyria, took Samaria.
The northern kingdom was defeated. Now there was nothing, not even
a barbed-wire fence, between Assyria and Judah. King Hezekiah was
in a bad spot.

And the king of Assyria did carry away Israel unto Assyria, and put them in Halah and in Habor by the river of Gozan, and in the cities of the Medes:

Because they obeyed not the voice of the LORD their God, but transgressed his covenant, and all that Moses the servant of the LORD commanded, and would not hear them, nor do them [2 Kings 18:11–12].

This is a review of Israel's captivity.

Now in the fourteenth year of king Hezekiah did Sennacherib king of Assyria come up against all the fenced cities of Judah, and took them.

And Hezekiah king of Judah sent to the king of Assyria to Lachish, saying, I have offended; return from me: that which thou puttest on me will I bear. And the king of Assyria appointed unto Hezekiah king of Judah three hundred talents of silver and thirty talents of gold [2 Kings 18:13–14].

Hezekiah tried to rebel against Assyria, but he was not successful. Because he did not succeed, he will have to pay.

At that time did Hezekiah cut off the gold from the doors of the temple of the LORD, and from the pillars which Hezekiah king of Judah had overlaid, and gave it to the king of Assyria [2 Kings 18:16].

THE SECOND INVASION OF JUDAH BY SENNACHERIB

And the king of Assyria sent Tartan and Rab-saris and Rab-shakeh from Lachish to king Hezekiah with a great host against Jerusalem. And they went up and came to

Jerusalem. And when they were come up, they came
and stood by the conduit of the upper pool, which is in
the highway of the fuller's field [2 Kings 18:17].

Sennacherib threatens Jerusalem with a great army.

And when they had called to the king, there came out to
them Eliakim the son of Hilkiah, which was over the
household, and Shebna the scribe, and Joah the son of
Asaph the recorder.

And Rab-shakeh said unto them, Speak ye now to Hezekiah, Thus saith the great king, the king of Assyria,
What confidence is this wherein thou trustest? [2 Kings
18:18–19].

Rab-shakeh attempts to frighten them by suggesting two things.

Thou sayest, (but they are but vain words.) I have counsel and strength for the war. Now on whom dost thou
trust, that thou rebellest against me?

Now, behold, thou trusted upon the staff of this bruised
reed, even upon Egypt, on which if a man lean, it will
go into his hand, and pierce it: so is Pharaoh king of
Egypt unto all that trust on him [2 Kings 18:20–21].

Knowing that Hezekiah is expecting aid from Egypt, Rab-shakeh ridicules Egypt as a bruised reed that would snap and pierce his hand the
moment he put any weight on it. He says, "You won't get any help
from Egypt!"
Now he attempts to knock out the second prop.

But if ye say unto me, We trust in the LORD our God: is
not that he, whose high places and whose altars Hezekiah hath taken away, and hath said to Judah and Jeru-

salem, Ye shall worship before this altar in Jerusalem?
[2 Kings 18:22].

When Hezekiah took away the high places, Sennacherib thought he
was taking down the altars to the living and true God. He did not
understand that Hezekiah was cleansing the land of pagan altars and
idols and that his action was obedience, not sacrilege. The Jews were
to worship God at the one altar in Jerusalem, and they approached
Him only through a bloody sacrifice. It looked to Sennacherib, however, as if Hezekiah had thrown over his God just when he needed
Him most.

> Now therefore, I pray thee, give pledges to my lord the
> king of Assyria, and I will deliver thee two thousand
> horses, if thou be able on thy part to set riders upon
> them [2 Kings 18:23].

This an insult and a strong expression of contempt for the military
power of Judah.

> Then said Eliakim the son of Hilkiah, and Shebna, and
> Joah, unto Rab-shakeh, Speak, I pray thee, to thy ser-
> vants in the Syrian language; for we understand it: and
> talk not with us in the Jews' language in the ears of the
> people that are on the wall [2 Kings 18:26].

The Jews were lined up on the wall of the city of Jerusalem hearing all
that was going on. The officials of Judah say; "Speak to us in the Syrian language; we can understand it." Old Rab-shakeh said, "Not on
your life—this is going on television!" He was really demoralizing the
troops.

> Then Rab-shakeh stood and cried with a loud voice in
> the Jews' language, and spake, saying, Hear the word of
> the great king, the king of Assyria:

> Thus saith the king, Let not Hezekiah deceive you: for
> he shall not be able to deliver you out of his hand
> [2 Kings 18:28–29].

He is getting through to the people, brainwashing them with propaganda.

> Neither let Hezekiah make you trust in the Lord, saying,
> the Lord will surely deliver us, and this city shall not be
> delivered into the hand of the king of Assyria.
>
> Hearken not to Hezekiah: for thus saith the king of Assyria, Make an agreement with me by a present, and
> come out to me, and eat ye every man of his own vine,
> and every one of his fig tree, and drink ye every one the
> waters of his cistern:
>
> Until I come and take you away to a land like your own
> land, a land of corn and wine, a land of bread and vineyards, a land of oil olive and of honey, that ye may live,
> and not die: and hearken not unto Hezekiah, when he
> persuadeth you, saying, The Lord will deliver us
> [2 Kings 18:30–32].

He is attempting to persuade the Jews to surrender. He repeats that neither Hezekiah nor God can help them. He promises that their lives will be spared only through surrender. He is saying, "Make terms with me and I'll leave you in peace to enjoy your own homes for a time." Then he adds, "Even if we transplant you, it will be to a beautiful land like your own."

> Hath any of the gods of the nations delivered at all his
> land out of the hand of the king of Assyria?
>
> Where are the gods of Hamath, and of Arpad? where are
> the gods of Sepharvaim, Hena, and Ivah? have they delivered Samaria out of mine hand?

> Who are they among all the gods of the countries, that
> have delivered their country out of mine hand, that the
> LORD should deliver Jerusalem out of mine hand?
> [2 Kings 18:33–35].

To Rab-shakeh this seemed a crushing and unanswerable argument. It was true that no god had ever delivered his people out of the king of Assyria's power. Of course he did not know that gods of the other countries were "no gods," while the living God was "the Lord of the whole earth."

> But the people held their peace, and answered him not a
> word: for the king's commandment was, saying, An-
> swer him not [2 Kings 18:36].

Whatever impression his arguments may have made in the hearts of those who heard, no one said a word.

CHAPTER 19

THEME: Hezekiah's recourse to God and Isaiah's prophecy

As we have seen, Hezekiah came to the throne at a troubled, disturbed, and uncertain time in the land. The northern kingdom had been taken into captivity by Assyria. Now the Assyrian army has come to the gates of Jerusalem. This is enough to frighten Hezekiah, but added to this, Rab-shakeh, who is the henchman of the king of Assyria, is outside the gate sending out taunts and insults. He is boasting about the great things Assyria is going to do to Jerusalem, and he ridicules the idea that God can deliver them. Poor Hezekiah wilts under all of this, which is natural because Hezekiah is just learning to turn to the Lord and trust him.

HEZEKIAH SEEKS HELP FROM GOD

And it came to pass, when king Hezekiah heard it, that he rent his clothes, and covered himself with sackcloth, and went into the house of the LORD [2 Kings 19:1].

Tearing his clothes and wearing sackcloth indicate Hezekiah's deep distress and heavy afflictions. Notice that he goes into the house of the Lord. That is a good place to go when you are in mental turmoil. It is time to turn to God.

And he sent Eliakim, which was over the household, and Shebna the scribe, and the elders of the priests, covered with sackcloth, to Isaiah the prophet the son of Amoz [2 Kings 19:2].

I wonder if you have noted the parallel to the days in which we are living. We think of our nation as being Christian and sophisticated and of Hezekiah's nation as being uncivilized and halfway pagan. Well, in our disturbed condition have you heard of any of our politicians, educators, leaders, or military men turning to God and appealing to Him for deliverance? No! Instead the nation looks to the "expert" and listens to the man who has a high I.Q. to give the best advice. We have listened to men like that, friend, since I was a young man, and that is a long span now. We get farther and farther into the night. Our problems are mounting. Our difficulties are overwhelming today. Nowhere, not even in the church, do you hear anyone appeal to God. Our only chance is to turn to God in this dark and late hour in the history of our nation. We are a young nation, but we are already old and on the way out. History tells us that the life of most nations is around two hundred years. Instead of turning to God, it is always, "Let's get together. Let's try a new approach. Let's get a new method. Let's work on this problem from a different angle. Let's get an authority in psychology, or medicine, or government, or education, and they will show us the way out." My friend, all of these experts have moved us farther into the night, and we are in trouble. We need God. No nation ever needed God as this nation needs God right now. Thank God Hezekiah had enough sense to call upon God in his hour of need! He sent a delegation to God's prophet, Isaiah.

And they said unto him, Thus saith Hezekiah, This day is a day of trouble, and of rebuke, and blasphemy: for the children are come to the birth, and there is not strength to bring forth.

It may be the LORD thy God will hear all the words of Rab-shakeh, whom the king of Assyria his master hath sent to reproach the living God; and will reprove the words which the LORD thy God hath heard: wherefore lift up thy prayer for the remnant that are left.

So the servants of king Hezekiah came to Isaiah [2 Kings 19:3–5].

Notice Hezekiah says, "It may be the LORD thy God will hear all the words of Rab-shakeh. . . ." He does not say "our God," he says "thy God." Poor Hezekiah—maybe he is not very well acquainted with God, but he has enough sense to appeal to Him at a time like this. As a matter of fact, he has no other place to go at this moment.

> **And Isaiah said unto them, Thus shall ye say to your master, Thus saith the LORD, Be not afraid of the words which thou hast heard, with which the servants of the king of Assyria have blasphemed me.**

> **Behold, I will send a blast upon him, and he shall hear a rumour, and shall return to his own land; and I will cause him to fall by the sword in his own land [2 Kings 19:6–7].**

This prophecy was fulfilled literally. Notice the encouragement that Isaiah gives to the king. He says, "Don't worry about this man. He is not going to come to your city. He is just a blowhard. He is boasting and blaspheming, but God has heard him and will deal with him. There is no need for you to worry."

Oh, if we would only learn to let God deal with our enemies. The trouble is that *we* deal with them, and when we do that, we move ourselves from the place of faith and trust in God so that God does not move in our behalf. The result is that we come out on the short end of the deal. The Lord can handle enemies much better than we can, just as He did in this case.

THE THREATENING LETTER

> **So Rab-shakeh returned, and found the king of Assyria warring against Libnah: for he had heard that he was departed from Lachish.**

> **And when he heard say of Tirhakah king of Ethiopia, Behold, he is come out to fight against thee: he sent messengers again unto Hezekiah, saying [2 Kings 19:8–9].**

Rab-shekah returned to his master and found him carrying on a war with Libnah. And a threatening move of the king of Ethiopia kept him from returning to attack Jerusalem immediately. So he sends this letter of warning to Hezekiah.

> Thus shall ye speak to Hezekiah king of Judah, saying, Let not thy God in whom thou trustest deceive thee, saying, Jerusalem shall not be delivered into the hand of the king of Assyria.

> Behold, thou hast heard what the kings of Assyria have done to all lands, by destroying them utterly: and shalt thou be delivered?

> Have the gods of the nations delivered them which my fathers have destroyed; as Gozan, and Haran, and Rezeph, and the children of Eden which were in Thelasar?

> Where is the king of Hamath, and the king of Arpad, and the king of the city of Sepharvaim, of Hena, and Ivah? [2 Kings 19:10–13].

It was a disturbing message. The king of Assyria had swept aside everything in his path. How did Hezekiah think he could escape?

> And Hezekiah received the letter of the hand of the messengers, and read it: and Hezekiah went up into the house of the Lord, and spread it before the Lord [2 Kings 19:14].

My friend, we need to spread our disturbing letters before the Lord just as Hezekiah did. Since my radio program has been on the air, I have received some wonderful letters, but I have received some of the other kind too. I learned a long time ago to turn them over to the Lord, and let Him work the problem out. He is a specialist at this sort of thing. Hezekiah did a wise thing when he spread the letter out before the Lord.

HEZEKIAH'S PRAYER

And Hezekiah prayed before the Lord, and said, O Lord God of Israel, which dwellest between the cherubims, thou art the God, even thou alone, of all the kingdoms of the earth; thou hast made heaven and earth.

Lord, bow down thine ear, and hear: open, Lord, thine eyes, and see: and hear the words of Sennacherib, which hath sent him to reproach the living God [2 Kings 19:15–16].

Notice how Hezekiah approaches God. Martin Luther prayed like that. My how these men could lay hold of God! Luther would cry out to God, "Lord, are you hearing me? Lord, hear me. Lord, let your ear be open to my prayer." Do you ever feel that God is not listening to you? This is the way Hezekiah felt.

Of a truth, Lord, the kings of Assyria have destroyed the nations and their lands,

And have cast their gods into the fire: for they were no gods, but the work of men's hands, wood and stone: therefore they have destroyed them [2 Kings 19:17–18].

What this man Rab-shakeh says is true. He is not boasting when he says that Assyria has swept everything before them and has cast each nation's gods into the fire.

Now therefore, O Lord our God, I beseech thee, save thou us out of his hand, that all the kingdoms of the earth may know that thou art the Lord God, even thou only [2 Kings 19:19].

GOD'S ANSWER

Now God will answer his prayer through Isaiah the prophet.

> Then Isaiah the son of Amoz sent to Hezekiah, saying, Thus saith the LORD God of Israel, That which thou hast prayed to me against Sennacherib king of Assyria I have heard [2 Kings 19:20].

God says, "I was listening when you were praying to Me."

> This is the word that the LORD hath spoken concerning him; The virgin the daughter of Zion hath despised thee, and laughed thee to scorn; the daughter of Jerusalem hath shaken her head at thee.

> Whom hast thou reproached and blasphemed? and against whom hast thou exalted thy voice, and lifted up thine eyes on high? even against the Holy One of Israel [2 Kings 19:21–22].

God intends to destroy the arm of Assyria.

> By thy messengers thou hast reproached the LORD, and hast said, With the multitude of my chariots I am come up to the height of the mountains, to the sides of Lebanon, and will cut down the tall cedar trees thereof, and the choice fir trees thereof: and I will enter into the lodgings of his borders, and into the forest of his Carmel.

> I have digged and drunk strange waters, and with the sole of my feet have I dried up all the rivers of besieged places [2 Kings 19:23–24].

God here repeats the boast of the king of Assyria that mountains do not stop him, deserts do not stop him—he digs wells for water. Rivers do not stop him—he will find ways of drying them up.

Now God addresses the proud Assyrian king. He says that the rise and fall of nations is *His* doing. As Isaiah had written earlier, God calls Assyria the "rod of mine anger" and the "staff . . . mine indignation" (see Isa. 10:5).

> Hast thou not heard long ago how I have done it, and of
> ancient times that I have formed it? now have I brought it
> to pass, that thou shouldest be to lay waste fenced cities
> into ruinous heaps.
>
> Therefore their inhabitants were of small power, they
> were dismayed and confounded; they were as the grass
> of the field, and as the green herb, as the grass on the
> house tops, and as corn blasted before it be grown up
> [2 Kings 19:25–26].

That is, Assyria's victims were unable to make an effectual resistance
because it was God who had put a fear in their hearts.

> But I know thy abode, and thy going out, and thy com-
> ing in, and thy rage against me.
>
> Because thy rage against me and thy tumult is come up
> into mine ears, therefore I will put my hook in thy nose,
> and my bridle in thy lips, and I will turn thee back by
> the way by which thou camest [2 Kings 19:27–28].

God says, "You have come into My land; you have made your boast.
Now I am going to put My hook in your nose, pull you right out of My
land, and send you home."

> And this shall be a sign unto thee, Ye shall eat this year
> such things as grow of themselves, and in the second
> year that which springeth of the same; and in the third
> year sow ye, and reap, and plant vineyards, and eat the
> fruits thereof [2 Kings 19:29].

The Lord now addresses Hezekiah. Apparently the presence of the
Assyrian army had prevented the farmers around Jerusalem from sow-
ing their land. God promised that there would be enough volunteer
growth to feed them, and even in the third year they would be able to

sow their crops and reap them in peace. Sennacherib and his army would not be around to destroy their crops.

And the remnant that is escaped of the house of Judah shall yet again take root downward, and bear fruit upward.

For out of Jerusalem shall go forth a remnant, and they that escape out of mount Zion: the zeal of the LORD of hosts shall do this.

Therefore thus saith the LORD concerning the king of Assyria, He shall not come into this city, nor shoot an arrow there, nor come before it with shield, nor cast a bank against it [2 Kings 19:30–32].

Isaiah is making a very bold statement, but it is the Word of the Lord. I am sure the people of Jerusalem are wondering if Isaiah is a true prophet. When Isaiah had made the prophecy that "a virgin shall conceive and bear a son," the people probably said, "My, that is a great prophecy. When will it take place?" Well, it wouldn't take place for seven hundred years, and none of them would be around to see its fulfillment. But now Isaiah is making a prophecy in a local situation, and they will see its fulfillment within days.

Here is the Assyrian army camped outside the gates of Jerusalem. This great army had swept everything before them. They were feared and dreaded in the ancient world. Now God says through Isaiah that they will not besiege the city of Jerusalem and that they will not even shoot an arrow into the city!

Now, you think that over for a moment. There are 185,000 soldiers around the walls of Jerusalem. Out of that number you would certainly find some trigger-happy soldier with a bow and arrow who would shoot at least one arrow over the wall. My friend, if he does that, Isaiah is not a true prophet of God. God says that not an arrow is going to fall in that city, and He says it by the mouth of Isaiah. That is the way the people of his day would know that he is a true prophet of God.

God says, "I'm going to save this city, and I will save it for two reasons."

For I will defend this city, to save it, for mine own sake, and for my servant David's sake [2 Kings 19:34].

He will do it for His name's sake—God does many things for His name's sake—and for David's sake. You see, God loved David. He did many things for David's sake.

And, my friend, David had a greater Son, a virgin-born Son, the Lord Jesus Christ. He will save sinners who trust Him—for Christ's sake. And when a believer prays to the Father in Jesus' name, the Father answers for Christ's sake.

And it came to pass that night, that the angel of the LORD went out, and smote in the camp of the Assyrians an hundred fourscore and five thousand: and when they arose early in the morning, behold, they were all dead corpses [2 Kings 19:35].

I love the way this translation reads, ". . . and when they arose early in the morning, behold, they were all dead corpses." Friend, the Assyrians did not wake in the morning. Why not? They were dead. Of course it means that when the folk inside the city awoke in the morning, they found about 185,000 dead bodies outside the city wall.

SENNACHERIB IS ASSASSINATED BY HIS SONS

So Sennacherib king of Assyria departed, and went and returned, and dwelt in Nineveh.

And it came to pass, as he was worshipping in the house of Nisroch his god, that Adrammelech and Sharezer his sons smote him with the sword: and they escaped into

the land of Armenia. And Esar-haddon his son reigned in his stead [2 Kings 19:36–37].

Sennacherib was slain by his sons. It is interesting that the prophecy concerning Assyria was literally fulfilled in that day.

CHAPTER 20

THEME: Hezekiah's illness and healing

This chapter is very meaningful to me because I have had an experience with illness and healing that is somewhat like Hezekiah's experience.

Keep in mind that Hezekiah was an outstanding king. There was none like him after David. "He did that which was right in the sight of the LORD, according to all that David his father did"—this is God's testimony concerning him.

HEZEKIAH'S ILLNESS

In those days was Hezekiah sick unto death. And the prophet Isaiah the son of Amoz came to him, and said unto him, Thus saith the LORD, Set thine house in order; for thou shalt die, and not live [2 Kings 20:1].

Hezekiah's illness is recorded three times in Scripture (2 Kings 20; 2 Chron. 32; and Isa. 38), and each account adds a little something to the total picture. It must have been a difficult task for Isaiah to deliver a death sentence to Hezekiah, the king. Very candidly, however, the sentence of death rests upon each one of us although we do not know the day or hour. The Scripture says, "And it is appointed unto men once to die, but after this the judgment" (Heb. 9:27). This is a divine date. If each one of us knew the exact time we would die, would it not change our way of living? Even many Christians say, "Death is way off yonder in the future. I won't worry about it now." Well, we may not worry about it, but we ought to live knowing that death will be the ultimate goal.

Many years ago when a fine young minister was told by his doctor that he had a recurrence of cancer and his days were limited, he sent out a letter to some of his friends. I was privileged to be included in that list and I was shaken when I read his letter. Let me give you an excerpt from it: "One thing I have discovered in the last few days. When a Christian is suddenly confronted with the sentence of death, he surely begins to give a proper evaluation of material things: my fishing gear, and books, and orchard are not nearly so valuable as they were a week ago." With that in mind, let us look at Hezekiah's experience.

Then he turned his face to the wall, and prayed unto the LORD, saying,

I beseech thee, O LORD, remember now how I have walked before thee in truth and with a perfect heart, and have done that which is good in thy sight. And Hezekiah wept sore [2 Kings 20:2–3].

Hezekiah turned his face to the wall and prayed to the Lord. I think I understand his position. Suppose you were told that you had cancer and neither you nor the doctor knew what the outcome would be. All of my life in the ministry I have visited people with cancer. I could understand how they could have cancer, but I never could understand how I could have it. It rocked me when the doctor told me I had cancer—I could not believe it. When I had to accept the fact, I was not given any assurance at all that I would live—nor have I any assurance today. I just know that I have cancer. May I say to you, it gives you a different set of values.

My life is a little different today. Many people have wondered about my conduct in certain areas. They ask, "Why did you resign as pastor of a church when you were still active?" I have no ambition in the ministry. God gave me the privilege of being pastor of a great church in its heyday and of conducting the largest midweek service in that day and generation. I considered that a privilege. But now my ambition is to live in such a way that I will please the Lord. It has caused me to change in many different ways. Someone said to me the other day, "You are trying to kill yourself in carrying on your radio ministry and holding conferences." You know, I am afraid if I don't, I am going to displease Him.

When I was taken to the hospital, I had no idea what the outcome of my illness would be. The nurse had to help me get into bed because I was so weak. I was not physically weak—I was frightened; I am a coward. She asked, "Are you sick?" I replied, "No. I am scared to death!" She was a Christian nurse, and she smiled at that. I asked her to leave me alone for awhile, and I turned my face to the wall, just as Hezekiah did, and I cried out to God. I told Him that I did not want to die—and I *didn't* want to die.

When we are ill, I believe we should go to God in prayer and ask others to pray for us. I believe in faith healing—not in faith healers—I know God can heal. Well, an acquaintance wrote me a letter in which she said, "I am not going to pray that you get well because I know that you are ready to go and be with the Lord. I am praying that He will take you home." I got an answer back to her in a hurry. I said, "Now look here. You let the Lord handle this. Don't try and tell Him how I feel. I don't want to die. I want to live. I want to live as long as I can."

When I turned my face to the wall there in the hospital, I promised Him, "Lord, if you will raise me up, I will teach your Word everywhere I can go." That is what I have been trying to do. I don't want to let Him down because I don't want Him to say, "Well, look here, preacher, I will have to call you home because you are not doing what you said you would do." Friend, we have a different outlook on life when we are in a position like this. The doctor, a wonderful Christian man, has told me that he cannot help me, but my recovery has come from the hand of God. Of course, I told him that I wanted to know why he sends me a bill if God is the One doing the work. It is wonderful, friend, to be in a position where you have to trust the Lord. I have no other alternative. Where in the world am I going to go if I don't go to the Lord? I am trusting the Lord and I am not being pious when I say that—it was forced on me.

Now Hezekiah was in that same position. Only God could help him. When he turned his head to the wall, he reminded the Lord that he had walked before Him in truth and with a perfect heart, and he had done that which was good in His sight.

And it came to pass, afore Isaiah was gone out into the middle court, that the word of the LORD came to him, saying,

Turn again, and tell Hezekiah the captain of my people, Thus saith the LORD, the God of David thy father, I have heard thy prayer, I have seen thy tears: behold, I will heal thee: on the third day thou shalt go up unto the house of the LORD [2 Kings 20:4–5].

The Lord had seen Hezekiah's tears. I am sure he has seen my tears, too, and yours.

And I will add unto thy days fifteen years; and I will deliver thee and this city out of the hand of the king of Assyria; and I will defend this city for mine own sake, and for my servant David's sake [2 Kings 20:6].

This is great news that the Lord will heal him and extend his life fifteen more years!

HEZEKIAH'S RECOVERY

And Isaiah said, Take a lump of figs. And they took and laid it on the boil, and he recovered [2 Kings 20:7].

God used natural means to raise up Hezekiah, but He also used supernatural means. This is wonderful. It is what James is saying, "Is any sick among you? let him call for the elders of the church; and let them pray over him, anointing him with oil in the name of the Lord" (James 5:14).

There are two ways a person can be anointed with oil. One is ceremonial, and the other is medicinal. A great many people seem to have missed it, but James is talking about a medicinal anointing. God is saying through James that we should be very practical. The doctor should be called, but the elders of the church should also be called to pray. And the prayer will raise up the one who is sick.

In Hezekiah's case they put figs on the "boil"—which may well have been cancer. God said, "I am going to add fifteen years to your life, but you had better put figs on that boil." Friend, my recommendation is not to be fanatical, but be sensible. If you have cancer, then face up to it. I wanted to know the facts and so did Hezekiah. Believe me, God laid it out before him, and God spared his life for fifteen more years.

And Hezekiah said unto Isaiah, What shall be the sign that the LORD will heal me, and that I shall go up into the house of the LORD the third day? [2 Kings 20:8].

Hezekiah asked for a sign to show that his life would be extended. The Lord has given me no sign whatsoever that my life will be lengthened. That, of course, is up to my heavenly Father, but I want Him to leave me here as long as He possibly can. If He has another plan, I will have to accept it.

It is not always God's will to extend our lives. I notice in the early church that James was a martyr—he was executed by Herod. Peter, on the other hand, was delivered from prison. I do not know why one man was delivered and the other man became a martyr. All of that is in the providence of God. It is His will that we want. Let's pray, "Oh God, bend me and reconcile me to your will—whatever it is." But I am going to let God know how I feel about it. I used to visit a dear lady who was in such pain that she knew she would not get well. She said, "Dr. McGee, don't pray for me to get well. Just pray that the Lord will take me." That is what the Lord did, by the way. But I do not pray that way unless the person wants me to do so.

And Isaiah said, This sign shalt thou have of the LORD, that the LORD will do the thing that he hath spoken: shall the shadow go forward ten degrees, or go back ten degrees?

And Hezekiah answered, It is a light thing for the shadow to go down ten degrees: nay, but let the shadow return backward ten degrees.

And Isaiah the prophet cried unto the LORD: and he brought the shadow ten degrees backward, by which it had gone down in the dial of Ahaz [2 Kings 20:9-11].

HEZEKIAH'S FOOLISHNESS

Now we come to a phase in Hezekiah's life that blanches my soul.

At that time Berodach-baladan, the son of Baladan, king of Babylon, sent letters and a present unto Hezekiah: for he had heard that Hezekiah had been sick [2 Kings 20:12].

He sends a get-well card and a gift.

And Hezekiah hearkened unto them, and shewed them all the house of his precious things, the silver, and the gold, and the spices, and the precious ointment, and all the house of his armour, and all that was found in his treasures: there was nothing in his house, nor in all his dominion, that Hezekiah shewed them not [2 Kings 20:13].

Hezekiah did a foolish thing. He let the ambassadors from Babylon see the treasure that Solomon had gathered. The wealth of the world was there, which was not general knowledge. Hezekiah was big-hearted— Babylon had sent him a get-well card, and so he gives these men from Babylon a guided tour of his kingdom.

Then came Isaiah the prophet unto king Hezekiah, and said unto him, What said these men? and from whence came they unto thee? And Hezekiah said, They are come from a far country, even from Babylon.

> And he said, What have they seen in thine house? And
> Hezekiah answered, All the things that are in mine
> house have they seen: there is nothing among my trea-
> sures that I have not shewed them [2 Kings 20:14–15].

He rolled out the red carpet and showed them everything.

> And Isaiah said unto Hezekiah, Hear the word of the
> LORD.
>
> Behold, the days come, that all that is in thine house,
> and that which thy fathers have laid up in store unto this
> day, shall be carried into Babylon: nothing shall be left,
> saith the LORD [2 Kings 20:16–17].

These ambassadors made an inventory of all the riches and took it
back to Babylon with them to wait for the proper time when they
needed gold. When they wanted to get the treasure, they knew where
to come.

> And of thy sons that shall issue from thee, which thou
> shalt beget, shall they take away; and they shall be eu-
> nuchs in the palace of the king of Babylon [2 Kings
> 20:18].

This is what is going to happen to Hezekiah's offspring.

> Then said Hezekiah unto Isaiah, Good is the word of the
> LORD which thou hast spoken. And he said, Is it not
> good, if peace and truth be in my days? [2 Kings 20:19].

I don't like Hezekiah's reply to Isaiah. It was not a confession of sin at
all. Rather, he wanted peace in his day and showed little concern for
his offspring upon whom the coming catastrophe would fall.

HEZEKIAH'S DEATH

And the rest of the acts of Hezekiah, and all his might, and how he made a pool, and a conduit, and brought water into the city, are they not written in the book of the chronicles of the kings of Judah?

And Hezekiah slept with his fathers: and Manasseh his son reigned in his stead [2 Kings 20:20–21].

This may seem like an awful thing for me to say, but Hezekiah should have died when the time came for him to die. Three things took place after God extended his life that were foolish acts: he showed his treasures to Babylon, which will cause great trouble in the future; he begat a son, Manasseh, who was the most wicked of any king; he revealed an arrogance, almost an impudence, in his later years. His heart became filled with pride. Second Chronicles 32:25 tells us, "But Hezekiah rendered not again according to the benefit done unto him; for his heart was lifted up: therefore there was wrath upon him, and upon Judah and Jerusalem." You see, it might have been better if Hezekiah had died at God's appointed time.

That is why I want to be very careful. The Lord has spared me and I do not want to do anything to disgrace Him. My friend, this is a wonderful chapter. We have a wonderful heavenly Father.

CHAPTER 21

THEME: Manasseh's evil reign

Chapter 21 is quite a let-down after chapter 20, and yet there is a tremendous message here for us. Hezekiah was the best king since David—there was none to compare with him. He was like David in another way: neither of these men were good fathers. Hezekiah fathered a son who was the worst king that ever reigned in the southern kingdom. It is a heartbreak when you read about Manasseh, Hezekiah's son, turning out the way he did. Now I cannot confirm the statement that I am about to make, but I believe that the shekinah glory—the visible presence of God—returned to heaven during the reign of Manasseh. As far as we can determine, the shekinah glory was present during the reign of Hezekiah, and I can't see any events that happened after the reign of Manasseh that would have caused the shekinah glory to leave. When God's presence left the temple, it was a desolate place, forsaken of God. As we look at the life of this man Manasseh, we will see his total abhorrence for the temple and all the things of God.

MANASSEH'S SINS

Manasseh was twelve years old when he began to reign, and reigned fifty and five years in Jerusalem. And his mother's name was Hephzibah [2 Kings 21:1].

Manasseh began his reign as a twelve-year-old boy. He was a rascal, but someone says, "He is young. He will outgrow it." Well, he did not outgrow it. He got worse and worse and worse. He reigned for fifty-five years. God gave him ample opportunity to change his ways. In 2 Chronicles we find that he did finally repent. God is always patient and long-suffering. He is not willing that any should perish.

Manasseh's mother's name is mentioned. Her name was Hephzibah. She will have to accept responsibility for her son. If there is any credit, she will receive that, too. She may have been a wonderful mother. I don't know how Hephzibah raised this boy, but Manasseh was as wicked as he could be, and the damage he did to his country was irreparable.

And he did that which was evil in the sight of the LORD, after the abominations of the heathen, whom the LORD cast out before the children of Israel [2 Kings 21:2].

Manasseh was as bad as any of the pagans that God put out of the land when he brought His people into the land.

For he built up again the high places which Hezekiah his father had destroyed; and he reared up altars for Baal, and made a grove, as did Ahab king of Israel; and worshipped all the host of heaven, and served them [2 Kings 21:3].

Hezekiah, you recall, had destroyed the pagan places of worship, and a partial revival took place under his influence. All of his work came to naught because Manasseh raised up altars for Baal, and he worshiped all the host of heaven and served them—which means he worshiped the sun, moon, and stars, and all the hosts of heaven that the Greeks named Apollo and Diana, etc. Manasseh was a wicked man.

Someone says, "My, but we have come a long way today." No, we haven't. We are seeing a strong resurgence of astrology, and multitudes of "civilized" folk live by the horoscope. Many people still worship the host of heaven today.

And he built altars in the house of the LORD, of which the LORD said, In Jerusalem will I put my name.

And he built altars for all the host of heaven in the two courts of the house of the LORD [2 Kings 21:4–5].

Manasseh defied Almighty God. He put up pagan altars in the house of the Lord where God had said, "Here is where I will set My name."

And he made his son pass through the fire, and observed times, and used enchantments, and dealt with familiar spirits and wizards: he wrought much wickedness in the sight of the LORD, to provoke him to anger [2 Kings 21:6].

He even made his own son pass through the fire or into the fire. This was actually a human sacrifice. An image was heated until it was red-hot and then a baby was placed in it as an offering! It was a horrible, sadistic, satanic form of idolatrous worship.

And he set a graven image of the grove that he had made in the house, of which the LORD said to David, and to Solomon his son, In this house, and in Jerusalem, which I have chosen out of all tribes of Israel, will I put my name for ever:

Neither will I make the feet of Israel move any more out of the land which I gave their fathers; only if they will observe to do according to all that I have commanded them, and according to all the law that my servant Moses commanded them [2 Kings 21:7-8].

These people did not know it at the time, but they were getting ready to travel. They were headed for Babylonian captivity, because the land was theirs on one condition: obedience.

But they hearkened not: and Manasseh seduced them to do more evil than did the nations whom the LORD destroyed before the children of Israel [2 Kings 21:9].

Not only was Manasseh as bad as the heathen, he was worse. I have news for him: God will not tolerate the Israelites' wickedness. He will put them out of the land.

And the LORD spake by his servants the prophets, saying,

Because Manasseh king of Judah hath done these abominations, and hath done wickedly above all that the Amorites did, which were before him, and hath made Judah also to sin with his idols:

Therefore thus saith the LORD God of Israel, Behold, I am bringing such evil upon Jerusalem and Judah, that whosoever heareth of it, both his ears shall tingle.

And I will stretch over Jerusalem the line of Samaria, and the plummet of the house of Ahab: and I will wipe Jerusalem as a man wipeth a dish, wiping it, and turning it upside down [2 Kings 21:10-13].

Just as God had judged Samaria and all Israel, God is now going to judge Jerusalem and all Judah. God said he will "wipe Jerusalem as a man wipes a dish"—God is going to do some dishwashing. Jerusalem is His land—His dish—the Israelites have made it filthy; so He is going to wipe them out of it.

You may be very clever and sophisticated and think you don't need God, but you are walking on His earth, breathing His air, using His sunshine, and drinking His water. He even gave you the body that you have. Every now and then He washes His dishes. Nations down through the centuries lie along the highway of time in rubble and ruin. Do you know why? They did the same thing that our nation is doing today: living without God, feeling no need of God. God said that He was going to wipe Jerusalem as a man wipes a dish, and He did just that.

And I will forsake the remnant of mine inheritance, and deliver them into the hand of their enemies; and they shall become a prey and a spoil to all their enemies [2 Kings 21:14].

God says that He is going to take His finger out of the dike and let the enemy come in like a flood.

> **Moreover Manasseh shed innocent blood very much, till he had filled Jerusalem from one end to another; beside his sin wherewith he made Judah to sin, in doing that which was evil in the sight of the LORD [2 Kings 21:16].**

When a man or a nation goes into sin, they don't sin in just one respect; they sin in many respects. Now we have not only forgotten God, we have become an immoral nation. Lawlessness and murder are the order of the day. Some companies have moved away from large cities, trying to get away from lawlessness. Well, we cannot get away from it until this nation returns to God. That is the first step.

> **Now the rest of the acts of Manasseh, and all that he did, and his sin that he sinned, are they not written in the book of the chronicles of the kings of Judah?**

> **And Manasseh slept with his fathers, and was buried in the garden of his own house, in the garden of Uzza: and Amon his son reigned in his stead [2 Kings 21:17–18].**

This is the story of Manasseh. There is not much to say except that he was evil and corrupt, and he died.

AMON'S BRIEF REIGN

> **Amon was twenty and two years old when he began to reign, and he reigned two years in Jerusalem. And his mother's name was Meshullemeth, the daughter of Haruz of Jotbah.**

> **And he did that which was evil in the sight of the LORD, as his father Manasseh did.**

And he walked in all the way that his father walked in,
and served the idols that his father served, and worshipped them:

And he forsook the LORD God of his fathers, and walked
not in the way of the LORD [2 Kings 21:19–22].

Amon is a bad one, too—he walked in his father's footsteps. He forsook the Lord. Therefore, the Lord forsook him.

And the servants of Amon conspired against him, and
slew the king in his own house [2 Kings 21:23].

Amon's wickedness led to revolution. Today we as a nation are on the
way to revolution. It is unfortunate that our leaders seem to be interested only in getting elected. It seems that they are actually willing to
sell their country in order to do that. We are living in dangerous days,
friend.

JOSIAH REIGNS OVER JUDAH

And the people of the land slew all them that had conspired against king Amon; and the people of the land
made Josiah his son king in his stead.

Now the rest of the acts of Amon which he did, are they
not written in the book of the chronicles of the kings of
Judah?

And he was buried in his sepulchre in the garden of
Uzza: and Josiah his son reigned in his stead [2 Kings
21:24–26].

This section brings us to the last of the great kings. Josiah was not
only a great king, but the greatest revival took place during the time of
his reign.

CHAPTERS 22 AND 23

THEME: Josiah's good reign

In chapters 22 and 23 we find that Josiah, who begins to reign when he is eight years old and reigns for thirty-one years, is one of the best kings who reigned after Solomon. During his reign a great and needed revival comes to the nation. Hilkiah, the high priest, is his counselor, assistant, and adviser.

JOSIAH'S GOOD LIFE

Josiah was eight years old when he began to reign, and he reigned thirty and one years in Jerusalem. And his mother's name was Jedidah, the daughter of Adaiah of Boscath [2 Kings 22:1].

Notice how young these kings are when they begin to reign. Why are they so young? Well, Papa got killed. God removed him.

And he did that which was right in the sight of the LORD, and walked in all the way of David his father, and turned not aside to the right hand or to the left [2 Kings 22:2].

The sun has come up again; the light is shining once more in the land. Josiah has come to the throne. He led a movement that resulted in the greatest revival these people ever had after David and Solomon.

It is my firm conviction today that the only thing that can save our nation is revival. It is either going to be revival or revolution. There is corruption in government on all levels. There is corruption in all organizations today. Immorality and lawlessness abound. Sex, liquor, drugs, filthy magazines, foul pictures, scandals, and riots reign. This nation is wallowing like a pig in a swine's sty. We are like the prodigal son in a far country in the pigpen with the pigs. Without revival, revolution stares us in the face. Socialism is creeping in today. Political parties are willing to sell the birthright of this nation in order to stay in power. The church today is under the blight of apostasy. Liberalism controls the organized church. There is a brazen denial of the Word of God even in so-called evangelical circles. The Word of God has been lost in the church, and there are atheists today in the pulpit.

The first thing Christians need to recognize is that revival is personal and individual. I don't think revival has ever begun as a mass movement. What we need today is not politicians calling other politicians crooks. We need politicians who will say, "I have been wrong. I am going to get right with God." It would be a strange thing, and I suppose it would frighten our nation, but it's what we need.

Josiah, the man at the top, did that which was right in the sight of the Lord. The revival began with him.

THE TEMPLE IS REPAIRED

And it came to pass in the eighteenth year of king Josiah, that the king sent Shaphan the son of Azaliah, the son of Meshullam, the scribe, to the house of the LORD, saying,

Go up to Hilkiah the high priest, that he may sum the silver which is brought into the house of the LORD, which the keepers of the door have gathered of the people [2 Kings 22:3–4].

The second thing that Josiah did was to repair the temple. Apparently, the temple was not in use when Josiah came to the throne. It had become sort of a warehouse, a storage area for odds and ends.

And let them deliver it into the hand of the doers of the work, that have the oversight of the house of the LORD: and let them give it to the doers of the work which is in the house of the LORD, to repair the breaches of the house.

> Unto carpenters, and builders, and masons, and to buy
> timber and hewn stone to repair the house [2 Kings
> 22:5-6].

He tells the people to get busy and repair the temple.

The church today is very much like the temple in Josiah's day. It is in great need of repair. I am not speaking of church buildings—there are many beautiful church buildings. I stayed in a motel back east some time ago, and there was a church right across the street from my room. I was told that it cost one-half million dollars to build. The week I was there I noticed on Sunday morning, as I was leaving for my speaking appointment, that there were about twenty-five cars parked by the church for the Sunday morning service. There weren't any more than twenty-five cars for the evening service, and the rest of the week the church was dark. That place needs repairing, let me tell you!

Our conservative churches today are torn asunder by strife and bickering. They are huge and attractive. But is the Spirit of God there? The church is not witnessing. True believers should be out telling people about the Lord. You frighten Christians when you talk about witnessing for Christ. We do not need any more pious platitudes, saccharin sweetness, back-slapping, and hand-pumping. Let's let these service clubs do that. They are better at it than we are anyway. What we need today is to get the church straightened out on the inside.

THE BOOK OF THE LAW IS DISCOVERED

> And Hilkiah the high priest said unto Shaphan the
> scribe, I have found the book of the law in the house of
> the Lord. And Hilkiah gave the book to Shaphan, and
> he read it [2 Kings 22:8].

The third thing that brought revival to the nation was a return to the Word of God. They had lost the Bible, and they had lost it in the church. But they found the Word of God and put it back into their lives. The Word of God is the only thing we have as a weapon, friend.

It is God's Word that is alive, and powerful, and sharper than any two-edged sword (Heb. 4:12). There is no short cut, no easy route, no new method to revival. We have a flood of books today on Christian experience. I have looked over quite a few of these books and find them as dead as a doornail. What is the problem? They present a method instead of presenting the Word of God. They are not saying, "Let's get back to the Word of God." We don't need So-and-So's book; we need the Bible. We don't need the book of the month; we need the Book of the ages.

How many churches today in this land really rest upon the Word of God and preach it? Although there are still many faithful pastors, there are many who have departed from the faith. They have lost the Bible in church. Remember when Jesus was a boy, Mary and Joseph lost Him in the temple. Believe me, Jesus, as well as the Bible, is lost in the church today. Hilkiah, the high priest, found the Word of God. Did he find it out on the dump heap? No! He found it in the temple. It had been lost. A return to the Bible has to be the beginning of a revival.

I was with a fine young preacher not long ago. He was questioning me about my method of study. I found out that he had read all the latest books. In fact, he rather embarrassed me when he asked, "Have you read So-and-So? Have you seen this book and the other book?" I said no to each one. He asked, "Have you quit reading books?" I said, "Well, I'm pretty much read up, and the new books coming out don't seem to interest me because they are presenting a method." He said, "What do you read then?" I told him that I read the Bible. Then I asked him the pointed question, "How much time do you spend each week in the Word of God?" His answer was amazing. He spent less than one hour a week studying God's Word! He had already told me about the problems he was having, and it was very easy to give him a remedy. He needed to get into the Word of God.

> **And Shaphan the scribe came to the king, and brought the king word again, and said, Thy servants have gathered the money that was found in the house, and have**

> **delivered it into the hand of them that do the work, that have the oversight of the house of the LORD.**

> **And Shaphan the scribe shewed the king, saying, Hilkiah the priest hath delivered me a book. And Shaphan read it before the king [2 Kings 22:9–10].**

Imagine this! Now Josiah is hearing the Word of God for the first time!

> **And it came to pass, when the king had heard the words of the book of the law, that he rent his clothes [2 Kings 22:11].**

The fourth step toward revival is repentance. The reading of the Word of God brought repentance. When the king heard the Word of God, he tore his clothes as an expression of deep emotion. Why? Because the Word of God revealed their sin. Without the Word of God they did not realize how far they had strayed from God's Law. A return to the Word of God brings revival. It wasn't like some of these nice little groups I often hear about today that are going to have a "revival" campaign. They have a banquet and call in all of the preachers. The object is to talk sweetly and optimistically and get everyone together. My friend, real revival does not come unless there is true repentance.

I heard of a man, a very fine Christian, who stood before a group of church officers and told them, "What this church needs is for this group of officers to get down on their faces before God and repent!" Do you know what they did? They got rid of him. They didn't want him around. Oh, if we would really come to the Word of God, it would bring conviction. There would be weeping and rending of clothes and a real revival.

> **Go ye, inquire of the LORD for me, and for the people, and for all Judah, concerning the words of this book that is found: for great is the wrath of the LORD that is kindled against us, because our fathers have not hearkened**

unto the words of this book, to do according unto all that which is written concerning us [2 Kings 22:13].

Josiah is frightened because he knows they deserve God's judgment. The message God returns to Josiah through Huldah the prophetess reveals both God's justice and His grace.

Thus saith the LORD, Behold, I will bring evil upon this place, and upon the inhabitants thereof, even all the words of the book which the king of Judah hath read:

Because they have forsaken me, and have burned incense unto other gods, that they might provoke me to anger with all the works of their hands; therefore my wrath shall be kindled against this place, and shall not be quenched [2 Kings 22:16–17].

Now notice God's grace to Josiah.

Because thine heart was tender, and thou hast humbled thyself before the LORD, when thou heardest what I spake against this place, and against the inhabitants thereof, that they should become a desolation and a curse, and has rent thy clothes, and wept before me; I also have heard thee, said the LORD.

Behold therefore, I will gather thee unto thy fathers, and thou shalt be gathered into thy grave in peace; and thine eyes shall not see all the evil which I will bring upon this place. And they brought the king word again [2 Kings 22:19–20].

JOSIAH'S FURTHER REFORMATIONS

And the king sent, and they gathered unto him all the elders of Judah and of Jerusalem.

And the king went up into the house of the LORD, and all the men of Judah and all the inhabitants of Jerusalem with him, and the priests, and the prophets, and all the people, both small and great: and he read in their ears all the words of the book of the covenant which was found in the house of the LORD.

And the king stood by a pillar, and made a covenant before the LORD, to walk after the LORD, and to keep his commandments and his testimonies and his statutes with all their heart and all their soul, to perform the words of this covenant that were written in this book. And all the people stood to the covenant [2 Kings 23:1–3].

The people said that not only would they read the Word of God, they would also walk it—they would live in the manner it prescribed.

We could have revival in many of our churches, but there must be a conviction of sin that only the Word of God can bring. When the Bible brings conviction to the heart, repentance must follow. To repent means to make things right, my friend. Repentance means to turn around and go in the opposite direction. If you are going the wrong way, you turn around and go the right way.

I heard of an evangelist who held meetings in upper New York State years ago. He preached for a week, and not one person made a move toward God. Then one night the leading deacon in the church came forward, shedding tears of repentance. That broke the meeting wide open because he was the one standing in the way of revival in that church. He apologized to someone he had wronged, and all during the night as he prayed, the Lord would convict him of something else—his life hadn't been right. He would go over and knock on the door of the person he had wronged, and say, "I'm here to make things right." That went on all night! Imagine getting folk out of bed in the middle of the night! By morning there was a revival going on in that town because one man repented.

Now Josiah as king has a tremendous influence. He will now put into operation a very bold plan. His repentance put him in first gear, and he started moving out.

First he put idolatry out of the temple of God.

> **And the king commanded Hilkiah the high priest, and the priests of the second order, and the keepers of the door, to bring forth out of the temple of the LORD all the vessels that were made for Baal, and for the grove, and for all the host of heaven: and he burned them without Jerusalem in the fields of Kidron, and carried the ashes of them unto Beth-el [22 Kings 23:4].**

All of the things that pertain to the worship of false gods were burned in the fields of Kidron, outside of the city of Jerusalem. The ashes were then taken out of town so that the people could not even look to the ashes.

Then Josiah put away immorality.

> **And he brake down the house of the sodomites, that were by the house of the LORD, where the women wove hangings for the grove [2 Kings 23:7].**

Today the church is looking upon homosexuality as permissible behavior. God says in Romans 1:26 and 27 that He gave up a people because of this unnatural thing. I'm of the opinion that God will give this nation up if we continue smiling upon the unnatural sex orgies that are taking place in our land.

Josiah had the courage to condemn the sodomites. He not only condemned their actions, he put them out of the kingdom. Unnatural sex is wrong even if the church today condones it. I know that there are groups that say, "We ought to accept this sort of thing among consenting adults and even among consenting teenagers. It is perfectly all right." Who told them it was all right? Somebody says, "Well, I think it is all right." Well, my friend, that judgment is no bigger than your little mind—and you may have a Ph.D. Your little mind and my little mind are not big enough to make judgments like that. God has said that sodomy will bring down His wrath. It has in the past, and He has not changed. We have changed, but God has not changed. Josiah was a brave man, and he got rid of the sodomites.

Josiah also stopped the offering of human sacrifices—children—to Molech.

And he defiled Topheth, which is in the valley of the children of Hinnom, that no man might make his son or his daughter to pass through the fire to Molech [2 Kings 23:10].

Josiah also broke down images, altars, high places, and groves that kings before him had brought into the land. He even went beyond the borders of Judah—as far north as Bethel. Second Chronicles 34:33 sums it up in one verse: "And Josiah took away all the abominations out of all the countries that pertained to the children of Israel, and made all that were present in Israel to serve, even to serve the LORD their God. And all his days they departed not from following the LORD, the God of their fathers."

It is interesting that at Bethel he came upon the grave of the prophet who had predicted he would do these things (1 Kings 13:2).

Then he said, What title is that that I see? And the men of the city told him, It is the sepulchre of the man of God, which came from Judah, and proclaimed these things that thou hast done against the altar of Beth-el.

And he said, Let him alone; let no man move his bones. So they let his bones alone, with the bones of the prophet that came out of Samaria [2 Kings 23:17–18].

Now Josiah makes a tremendous positive move. He reinstitutes the Passover.

THE PASSOVER IS REINSTITUTED

And the king commanded all the people, saying, Keep the passover unto the LORD your God, as it is written in the book of this covenant.

Surely there was not holden such a passover from the days of the judges that judged Israel, nor in all the days of the kings of Israel, nor of the kings of Judah;

But in the eighteenth year of king Josiah, wherein this passover was holden to the LORD in Jerusalem [2 Kings 23:21-23].

The holding of the Passover is a wonderful thing. Apparently it had not been kept for a long time; they had passed it by. What does it mean? The Passover speaks of Christ. The people had forgotten all about Him. Paul says, ". . . For even Christ our passover is sacrificed for us" (1 Cor. 5:7). Today we are trying to have religion without Christ. The deity of Christ is ridiculed in seminaries and in pulpits. The value of Christ's death is rejected and spurned. The efficacy of Christ's blood is hooted down as something evil—even by some men in the pulpit.

My friend, the only thing that can save our nation is revival. Somebody asks, "Can it come?" Yes, I believe it can come. There is a "sound of going in the tops of the mulberry trees" today. A flood tide came in the sixteenth century, which was led by the Reformers Luther, Calvin, and Zwingli. Wycliffe and John Knox in the fourteenth and fifteenth centuries were the Reformers before the Reformation. In the seventeenth century came another spiritual awakening known as the Puritan movement. In the eighteenth century, a time of darkness and deism, came another great spiritual awakening led by Wesley and Whitfield. In the nineteenth century there was a mighty turning to God in Oxford, and the missionary movement resulted. Toward the end of the century great revivals were led by Moody and Finney. In the twentieth century (hear me now very carefully) there has been no great world-sweeping, earth-shaking revival. There have been a few local revivals. The twentieth century is quickly drawing to an end. Look around you today. When we had a depression in this country, we did not turn to God as a nation. We were plunged into World War II and saw the spilling of American blood that had not been equaled. That experience apparently did not teach us a thing. There was no revival. Since then we have had the Korean and the Vietnam wars. Neither did they bring us back to God.

Many people seem to think that if they get out and protest, things will change. But what we need is some real deep conviction on the inside. We need to recognize our coldness and indifference. When was the last time you confessed your coldness and indifference to the Lord? Have you told Him today that you love Him? He is your Savior, my friend, and I am convinced that even in this dark hour, as has happened in the past, we can have a revival. The story of Josiah encourages me. It was in the darkest hour in the life of his nation that revival came.

JOSIAH'S DEATH

Now we come to a heartbreak in this story of Josiah. Great revival had come near the end of the kingdom of Judah. Soon his people will go into captivity. God moved in a mighty way to reveal the fact that He can send revival in the most difficult and dark days.

Now what ended the revival?

> **In his days Pharaoh-nechoh king of Egypt went up against the king of Assyria to the river Euphrates: and king Josiah went against him; and he slew him at Megiddo, when he had seen him [2 Kings 23:29].**

Josiah should have stayed home. He should have kept his nose out of it. This was not his fight, but he went out anyway. What happened? He was slain at Megiddo. (By the way, Megiddo in the great Valley of Esdraelon is the place where the War of Armageddon is to be fought in the last days.) Josiah was a great man of God, but he was foolish. He entered a battle that was none of his concern.

This story might be a message for another nation I know about. I am afraid that we have meddled enough throughout the world today. We need to recognize that the *only* message that America has for the world is not democracy but the Word of God. We were blessed when we were sending out God's Word. Today we are sending out propaganda and we have become an immoral nation. God is not in the things we do as a nation, and we are no longer being blessed.

And his servants carried him in a chariot dead from Megiddo, and brought him to Jerusalem, and buried him in his own sepulchre. And the people of the land took Jehoahaz the son of Josiah, and anointed him, and made him king in his father's stead [2 Kings 23:30].

JEHOAHAZ REIGNS AND IS DETHRONED

Jehoahaz was twenty and three years old when he began to reign; and he reigned three months in Jerusalem. And his mother's name was Hamutal, the daughter of Jeremiah of Libnah.

And he did that which was evil in the sight of the LORD, according to all that his fathers had done.

And Pharaoh-nechoh put him in bands at Riblah in the land of Hamath, that he might not reign in Jerusalem; and put the land to a tribute of an hundred talents of silver, and a talent of gold [2 Kings 23:31–33].

You would think that Jehoahaz would follow in the righteous steps of his father, but he did not. Jehoahaz was an evil king. As a matter of fact, he hardly got the throne warm sitting on it—he lasted for only three months. Pharaoh didn't like the way he was reigning. He removed him from the throne and took him down to the land of Egypt, where he died.

JEHOIAKIM IS MADE KING

And Pharaoh-nechoh made Eliakim the son of Josiah king in the room of Josiah his father, and turned his name to Jehoiakim, and took Jehoahaz away: and he came to Egypt, and died there.

And he did that which was evil in the sight of the Lord, according to all that his fathers had done [2 Kings 23:34, 37].

Jehoiakim was another son of Josiah, and he reigned for eleven years. He also was an evil king. We go from bad to worse. Jehoahaz was bad; Jehoiakim was worse.

At this time the great power of Babylon is rising in the east on the Euphrates River. Babylon is displacing Assyria. Babylon, in fact, overcame Assyria. Babylon will also overcome Egypt and become the first great world power, as we will see in the Book of Daniel. It is at this point that we ought to read the Book of Jeremiah, because Jeremiah was the great prophet during this era. He was the one calling Israel back to God and warning them that if they do not turn to God they will be taken captive and sent to Babylon. Jeremiah's words seemed unbelievable to the people of Israel, because at this time Nebuchadnezzar king of Babylon was not a formidable foe. The false prophets were telling the nation that God simply could not get along without them. Jerusalem was the city of God; His holy temple was there; they were His chosen people. He couldn't get along without them. Well, they will find that He could get along without them. Actually, He didn't need that temple; it would soon be destroyed.

CHAPTERS 24 AND 25

THEME: The kingdom of Judah goes into captivity

NEBUCHADNEZZAR COMES AGAINST JUDAH

In his days Nebuchadnezzar king of Babylon came up, and Jehoiakim became his servant three years: then he turned and rebelled against him [2 Kings 24:1].

Egypt's Pharaoh-nechoh had put Jehoiakim on the throne, but he lost all Egypt's Asiatic possessions to Babylon's Nebuchadnezzar. Now when Nebuchadnezzar comes against Judah, Jehoiakim knuckles under for three years, then rebels against him.

And the LORD sent against him bands of the Chaldees, and bands of the Syrians, and bands of the Moabites, and bands of the children of Ammon, and sent them against Judah to destroy it, according to the word of the LORD, which he spake by his servants the prophets.

Surely at the commandment of the LORD came this upon Judah, to remove them out of his sight, for the sins of Manasseh, according to all that he did [2 Kings 24:2–3].

As we have seen, Manasseh was an evil man. If the shekinah glory didn't depart during his reign, there was nothing worse afterward that would have caused it to depart. Because these people did not depart from the sins of Manasseh, they will be going into captivity.

And also for the innocent blood that he shed: for he filled Jerusalem with innocent blood; which the LORD would not pardon [2 Kings 24:4].

While it is true that God will pardon all sin, the sinner will have to come to Him in repentance. There are certain sins that are not pardonable. Although Christ died for all sins, they are not pardonable because men will not come to Christ in repentance. My friend, He is the only One in the world who can forgive your sin. He died for you and paid the penalty for your sins. Who else can forgive your sins? He alone is the way, the truth, and the life.

JEHOIAKIM DIES, AND JEHOIACHIN REIGNS

Now the rest of the acts of Jehoiakim, and all that he did, are they not written in the book of the chronicles of the kings of Judah?

So Jehoiakim slept with his fathers: and Jehoiachin his son reigned in his stead [2 Kings 24:5–6].

The names of father and son are so similar, it is easy to confuse them.

And the king of Egypt came not again any more out of his land: for the king of Babylon had taken from the river of Egypt unto the river Euphrates all that pertained to the king of Egypt [2 Kings 24:7].

This is the exact land that God had vouchsafed to Abraham and to those who came after him. Why was Babylon, instead of Israel, in control of this area now?

Jehoiachin was eighteen years old when he began to reign, and he reigned in Jerusalem three months. And his mother's name was Nehushta, the daughter of Elnathan of Jerusalem.

And he did that which was evil in the sight of the LORD, according to all that his father had done [2 Kings 24:8–9].

This is the reason. They have continued in sin and in their rebellion against God. Remember that God had given them the occupancy of the land on one condition: their obedience. Did they still own the land? Oh, yes. God had given them the land by an unconditional covenant. But their occupancy was conditional, and they failed to meet that condition.

JEHOIACHIN IS TAKEN CAPTIVE
(FIRST DEPORTATION)

At that time the servants of Nebuchadnezzar king of Babylon came up against Jerusalem, and the city was besieged.

And Nebuchadnezzar king of Babylon came against the city, and his servants did besiege it.

And Jehoiachin the king of Judah went out to the king of Babylon, he, and his mother, and his servants, and his princes, and his officers: and the king of Babylon took him in the eighth year of his reign [2 Kings 24:10–12].

The king and all the nobility were carried away in the first group that went into captivity. This took place about 605 B.C.

And he carried out thence all the treasures of the house of the LORD, and the treasures of the king's house, and cut in pieces all the vessels of gold which Solomon king of Israel had made in the temple of the LORD, as the LORD had said.

And he carried away all Jerusalem, and all the princes, and all the mighty men of valour, even ten thousand captives, and all the craftsmen and smiths: none remained, save the poorest sort of the people of the land.

And he carried away Jehoiachin to Babylon, and the king's mother, and the king's wives, and his officers, and the mighty of the land, those carried he into captivity from Jerusalem to Babylon [2 Kings 24:13–15].

This is a sad and sordid story.

ZEDEKIAH IS MADE KING BY NEBUCHADNEZZAR

And the king of Babylon made Mattaniah his father's brother king in his stead, and changed his name to Zedekiah.

Zedekiah was twenty and one years old when he began to reign, and he reigned eleven years in Jerusalem. And his mother's name was Hamutal, the daughter of Jeremiah of Libnah.

And he did that which was evil in the sight of the LORD, according to all that Jehoiakim had done [2 Kings 24:17–19].

Zedekiah was Jehoiachin's uncle. He did not improve the line of kings. You would think that the captivity would sober him. It did not at all. Trouble will do one of two things for an individual. It will either soften or harden you. It will either draw you to God or drive you away from God. You can never be the same after you experience trouble and suffering. The sun will soften wax, but the sun will harden clay. It is the same sun that softens one and hardens the other.

For through the anger of the LORD it came to pass in Jerusalem and Judah, until he had cast them out from his presence, that Zedekiah rebelled against the king of Babylon [2 Kings 24:20].

Once again the false prophets said, "Look, God is on our side." But God was not on Israel's side because Israel was not on God's side.

Presumption is something many people need to be careful about. I have heard people say, "I am doing this certain thing because I know it is God's will. He has revealed it to me." Then they go ahead and do whatever they had in mind, and they fail. God was not in it at all. I know missionaries who have gone to the field and come back to say, as one young man said to me, "I made a mistake in going out." "But," I said, "you told me you were in God's will. You were sure." He said, "I thought I was." Well, we had better not *think* so, we had better be sure when we begin to talk about God being on our side. Actually we should make sure not that God is on our side but that we are on His side.

This was Judah's problem. They were far from God, yet they felt that they were God's people and He would protect them.

In chapter 25 we see the final deportation of Judah. Nebuchadnezzar, king of Babylon, came three times against Jerusalem. He deported the royalty and the military and the skilled workmen, but he did not destroy the city until he came the third time.

We have seen that Nebuchadnezzar had made Zedekiah king of Judah, but after a few years Zedekiah rebelled, and now we see that Nebuchadnezzar comes the final time and makes an end of Judah.

THE SIEGE

And it came to pass in the ninth year of his reign, in the tenth month, in the tenth day of the month, that Nebuchadnezzar king of Babylon came, he, and all his host, against Jerusalem, and pitched against it: and they built forts against it round about.

And the city was besieged unto the eleventh year of king Zedekiah [2 Kings 25:1–2].

The exactness of the date indicates the extreme importance of this siege. It was the beginning of the end of Jerusalem.

And on the ninth day of the fourth month the famine prevailed in the city, and there was no bread for the people of the land [2 Kings 25:3].

The intensity of the suffering is described for us in Lamentations.

> And the city was broken up, and all the men of war fled
> by night by the way of the gate between two walls, which
> is by the king's garden: (now the Chaldees were against
> the city round about:) and the king went the way toward
> the plain.

> And the army of the Chaldees pursued after the king,
> and overtook him in the plains of Jericho: and all his
> army were scattered from him.

> So they took the king, and brought him up to the king of
> Babylon to Riblah; and they gave judgment upon him
> [2 Kings 25:4–6].

The enemy broke into the city, and the king with his troops tried to escape. But they were captured. The prophet Jeremiah had predicted the fall of Jerusalem, and he was considered a traitor because he told the people the truth.

> And they slew the sons of Zedekiah before his eyes, and
> put out the eyes of Zedekiah, and bound him with fet-
> ters of brass, and carried him to Babylon [2 Kings 25:7].

This man was deceived by false prophets but would not listen to God's prophet. Now he is carried away into captivity, blinded.

JERUSALEM IS BURNED

> And he burnt the house of the LORD, and the king's
> house, and all the houses of Jerusalem, and every great
> man's house burnt he with fire [2 Kings 25:9].

Because of the rebellion of Jerusalem, Nebuchadnezzar burned and leveled it to such an extent that when Nehemiah came to the city seventy years after the Captivity and looked upon that place, it almost seemed hopeless. But he rallied the people, and the biggest thing he had to overcome was discouragement. The armies of Nebuchadnezzar had devastated the city. The false prophets had insisted that God would not let the city be destroyed. They were indeed *false* prophets.

There are people today who are giving this country a false message. They are saying that Americans belong to the ten "lost" tribes of Israel. They are saying that God is on our side, and He won't let us down. My friend, God does not *need* us. Where did that notion come from? God sent His chosen people into captivity. It was a sad day for them. And it ought to be a lesson for us in this day.

> **And all the army of the Chaldees, that were with the captain of the guard, brake down the walls of Jerusalem round about.**
>
> **Now the rest of the people that were left in the city, and the fugitives that fell away to the king of Babylon, with the remnant of the multitude, did Nebuzar-adan the captain of the guard carry away.**
>
> **But the captain of the guard left of the poor of the land to be vinedressers and husbandmen [2 Kings 25:10-12].**

They left those who would be of no value to them. Also they wanted the land to continue to produce so they could exact tribute from it.

> **And the pillars of brass that were in the house of the LORD, and the bases, and the brasen sea that was in the house of the LORD, did the Chaldees break in pieces, and carried the brass of them to Babylon.**
>
> **And the pots, and the shovels, and the snuffers, and the spoons, and all the vessels of brass wherewith they ministered, took they away [2 Kings 25:13-14].**

The army of Nebuchadnezzar really cleaned house. The temple was cleaned out before it was destroyed with fire. All that wealth was carried away into Babylon. We will have occasion, when we get to the Book of Daniel, to find that those vessels from the temple had been stored away and were brought out when Belshazzar had his great banquet. Jerusalem was plundered, burned, and left a pile of rubble.

Jerusalem has been destroyed about twenty-seven times. Each time the city has been rebuilt upon the rubble. The hill that is Jerusalem today is largely built upon the rubble of past cities. Many people, especially tour agents, say, "Go to Jerusalem and walk where Jesus walked." Well, my friend, you will not be walking where Jesus walked. The city that Jesus lived and walked in is buried under tons of rubble. At some spots you have to look down twenty feet, twenty-five feet, sometimes forty-five feet to see the city where Jesus lived.

GEDALIAH APPOINTED GOVERNOR

And Gedaliah sware to them, and to their men, and said unto them, Fear not to be the servants of the Chaldees: dwell in the land, and serve the king of Babylon; and it shall be well with you [2 Kings 25:24].

Nebuchadnezzar appointed Gedaliah to govern the people who were left in the land. They should have listened to him—and to the prophet Jeremiah—who urged them to settle down and accept this form of government. Instead of that, they assassinate the governor Gedaliah!

But it came to pass in the seventh month, that Ishmael the son of Nethaniah, the son of Elishama, of the seed royal, came, and ten men with him, and smote Gedaliah, that he died, and the Jews and the Chaldees that were with him at Mizpah.

And all the people, both small and great, and the captains of the armies, arose, and came to Egypt: for they were afraid of the Chaldees [2 Kings 25:25–26].

A great company of them fled into Egypt and became colonists down there. By the way, Jeremiah went with this group—not willingly, but he was forced to go.

JEHOIACHIN RELEASED

And it came to pass in the seven and thirtieth year of the captivity of Jehoiachin king of Judah, in the twelfth month, on the seven and twentieth day of the month, that Evil-merodach king of Babylon in the year that he began to reign did lift up the head of Jehoiachin king of Judah out of prison;

And he spake kindly to him, and set his throne above the throne of the kings that were with him in Babylon;

And changed his prison garments: and he did eat bread continually before him all the days of his life.

And his allowance was a continual allowance given him of the king, a daily rate for every day, all the days of his life [2 Kings 25:27-30].

Evil-merodach extends amnesty as he comes to the throne of Babylon. Although other captured kings are in his court, Jehoiachin is given a position of honor among them. It is interesting that the period of the kings should conclude with kindness being shown to this last descendant of David who had grown old in a Babylonian prison.

BIBLIOGRAPHY
(Recommended for Further Study)

Crockett, William Day. *A Harmony of the Books of Samuel, Kings and Chronicles.* Grand Rapids, Michigan: Baker Book House, 1951.

Darby, J. N. *Synopsis of the Books of the Bible.* Addison, Illinois: Bible Truth Publishers, n.d.

Davis, John J. and Whitcomb, John C., Jr. *A History of Israel.* Grand Rapids, Michigan: Baker Book House, 1970. (Excellent.)

Epp, Theodore H. *David.* Lincoln, Nebraska: Back to the Bible Broadcast, 1965.

Epp, Theodore H. *Elijah—A Man of Like Nature.* Lincoln, Nebraska: Back to the Bible Broadcast, 1969.

Gaebelein, Arno C. *The Annotated Bible.* Neptune, New Jersey: Loizeaux Brothers, 1912–22.

Gray, James M. *Synthetic Bible Studies.* Old Tappan, New Jersey: Fleming H. Revell Co., 1906.

Jensen, Irving L. *I Kings and Chronicles.* Chicago, Illinois: Moody Press, 1968. (A self-study guide.)

Jensen, Irving L. *II Kings with Chronicles.* Chicago, Illinois: Moody Press, 1968. (A self-study guide.)

Kelly, William. *Lectures on the Earlier Historical Books of the Old Testament.* Addison, Illinois: Bible Truth Publishers, 1874.

Knapp, Christopher. *The Kings of Israel and Judah.* Neptune, New Jersey: Loizeaux Brothers, 1908. (Very fine.)

Krummacher, F. W. *Elijah the Tishbite.* Grand Rapids, Michigan: Baker Book House, n.d.

Krummacher, F. W. *Elisha*. Grand Rapids, Michigan: Baker Book House, n.d.

Mackintosh, C. H. *Miscellaneous Writings*. Neptune, New Jersey: Loizeaux Brothers, n.d.

McNeely, Richard J. *First and Second Kings*. Chicago, Illinois: Moody Press, 1978.

Meyer, F. B. *David: Shepherd, Psalmist, King*. Fort Washington, Pennsylvania: Christian Literature Crusade, n.d.

Meyer, F. B. *Elijah and the Secret of His Power*. Fort Washington, Pennsylvania: Christian Literature Crusade, n.d. (A rich devotional study.)

Pink, Arthur W. *Gleanings from Elisha*. Chicago, Illinois: Moody Press, 1972.

Sauer, Erich. *The Dawn of World Redemption*. Grand Rapids, Michigan: Wm. B. Eerdmans Publishing Co., 1951. (An excellent Old Testament survey.)

Scroggie, W. Graham. *The Unfolding Drama of Redemption*. Grand Rapids, Michigan: Zondervan Publishing House, 1970. (An excellent survey and outline of the Old Testament.)

Unger, Merrill F. *Unger's Commentary on the Old Testament*. Vol. 1. Chicago, Illinois: Moody Press, 1981. (A fine summary of each paragraph. Highly recommended.)

Wood, Leon J. *Israel's United Monarchy*. Grand Rapids, Michigan: Baker Book House, 1979. (Excellent.)

Wood, Leon J. *The Prophets of Israel*. Grand Rapids, Michigan: Baker Book House, 1977. (Excellent.)

Note: The dates listed are those of the first printings.